AN ASHIN
OPINIO

1934-1974

By Mike Kirkup

Hirst North Schoolgirls, 1949. Doorway in rear on left leads to 'Doonies' corridor, door on right leads to 'Uppies' stairs. Girls in left group include Ruth Eastlake, Ellen Sling, Sheila Kinghorn, Mary Hudson and Evelyn Davison. Group on right includes Ann Brotherton, Dorothy Hall, Margaret Barrass, ?Redpath., Jean Cadman, Margaret Gray, Jenny Bamborough, Jean Stubbs, Wendy Copeland, Pat Paulin, Patsy Sword, Jean Cummings, Andrea Dixon, Linda Slee, Isobel Wren and Olive Tait.

Previous page: *Top of North Seaton Road leading to Grand Corner with Portland Park top left, c1930.*

Front cover: *Harmonic Clock in the 1930s; Central Hall in the 1970s.*
Back cover: *Mike Kirkup aged eighteen; Ashington Colliery in the 1970s.*

First Published in 2006 by
Woodhorn Press for
A Creeful of Coals
5 Aqua Terrace
Newbiggin by the Sea
NE64 6PB

ISBN 1 – 902832 – 07 - 8

CONTENTS

Portland Park favourites of 1948. Lanky chap on left was former Newcastle United player, Jimmy Denmark, the Colliers first player/manager. A future boss (then trainer) is seen on right, Jackie Dryden. Team includes Ron Brown, Jackie Gallon, goalie Reg Charlton, Norman West, Gordon Dent, Ronnie Harrison and Sammy Scott.

VIP OPINIONS OF ASHINGTON

"The main street on a Saturday evening is crowded: the men in smart blue suits, hanging somewhat loosely around the hips, owing to their triangular physique; the women of a smartness comparable with Regent Street and beautifully permed - there are seventeen women's hairdressers in Ashington." *The Times*, July 1942

"The Metro Centre at Gateshead was built on the premise of a 1950's Ashington main street with a roof on. It was where everything happened." Sir John Hall

"By the time I arrived in Ashington in 1956 there was something of a boom in mining and the workingmen's clubs were turning posh." David Bean – *The Guardian*

"With the population down by 1,000 in ten years, unless drastic action is taken, Ashington may become a 'dead town' because the district pits have an estimated life of only 20 years." *Ashington Post* November 1963

"I suppose me and our kid are as much to blame as anyone for Ashington's cloth-cap image." Jack Charlton 1972

"It was obvious there was *not* a great deal of money in Ashington – most of the shops were of the Pricebuster/Superdrug/Wotta Loada Crap variety." Bill Bryson – *Notes from a Small Island, 1993*

The Main Street in 1952: 'The Metro Centre with a roof on' or shops of 'Wotta Loada Crap' variety? You decide.

INTRODUCTION 1934 – 1974

First of all, why these two particular dates? The year of 1934 is an obvious starting point for me because that was the year I was born, on Wednesday 21st February. The year of 1974 proved a life-changing period for me when I stumbled into the teaching profession which itself was about to embark on a change of direction into the comprehensive era. And that year, in my opinion, was an arbitrary date forced on the mining community when Ashington was officially subsumed into a previously non-existent territory called Wansbeck, and, in the political process, surrendered ninety-nine-and-a-half per cent of its own identity. And now, as I compile this book in the Year of Our Lord 2006, I feel the town is more fragmented than ever.

Don't get me wrong; Ashington wasn't doing all that well in 1934 either. The Thirties saw the community ankle-deep in the clarts of depression like so many other northern coal towns. The all-powerful Ashington Coal Company closed coal seams – and sometimes whole collieries – on the flimsiest of excuses: 'We cannot afford to keep the Duke Pit open until the Coal Trade picks up.' Not a thought about the hardship that drastic decision would bring. Men were laid off at will, yet only found out that their livelihood was being threatened by reading a notice board affixed to Ashington's railway bridge. No letters of apology or reasons for closures in 1934. The humble collier was last in the line of communication in those days.

Living conditions in the town then had changed little since the majority of colliery houses had sprung up in the late 19th and early 20th century. In the 1930s, indoor sanitation was still light-years away, but at least Ashington residents no longer drank water that came straight out of the pit Bathing in a tin bath in front of a coal fire using hot water boiled in a set-pot was a regular sight. It was a demeaning ritual, enacted every weekday for dusty-faced miners, and on Friday nights for the rest of the family. And Heaven help the unfortunate sprog destined to take the last dip and swill around in the ever-blackening bath water.

By 1974 the colliery houses had been modernized with the addition of a bathroom and toilet, some streets even had a few garages in which to park their cars. Whole swathes of colliery rows at the top-end of Ashington had been demolished, some to make way for the new

Northumberland Close Estate, others to accommodate a new ring-road on the north and west side of town. Bits and pieces of some First Avenue rows at the Hirst were later tinkered with to provide more green breathing space, but that too was gradually swallowed up by that present-day evil, the parked car.

And even the phrase used above, '*the Hirst*', was destined to disappear, not only from the vocabulary, but also the very face of the town map itself once the meaningless term 'East Ashington' was coined, concocted for political expediency. But, hey, that didn't happen till the new Millennium was upon us and the remit for this book is 1934 to 1974. So read on and, hopefully, some of the events, incidents and characters mentioned within may jog a memory or two. I apologise in advance for the ruffling of any feathers but, who knows, perhaps one or two readers will agree with what is, after all, only ... an Ashington Opinion.

Mike Kirkup
December 2006

Not many Ashington characters are still around like 'Cowboy' Fred Curry (see later article) whose horse is being watered outside Portland Arms by mine host owld Bill Kell, c1950.

ACKNOWLEDGEMENTS

Thanks to the numerous folk who provided memories and photos and to Vince Gledhill of the Evening Chronicle, Ross Weeks of the News Post Leader, John Mordue former local journalist and the late Tom Chape for saving invaluable newspaper cuttings from the past.

SOME ASHINGTON PERSPECTIVES

'Ashington had far more than smoke and dust to offer' by Ray Wear

"Having been born in hard-up street in 1927 and living there till I joined the Army in 1945, I learned a lot about poverty and 'mekkin ends meet'. But at that time, all the folks in Ashington were doing the same; some of the bairns at Hirst East School were even worse off than me.

"But all that changed when I was demobbed in 1948. I had travelled half-way round the world as a soldier on 28 bob a week, and got my old job back at a fiver a week. I was rich, and life in dear old Ashington looked a lot brighter. Of course my marras at the pit were even better off, but most of them would be paid in full long before they were due to retire ... bless them.

"With petrol at three shillings a gallon, I could afford to buy a 250 cc motor bike on Hire Purchase to fly away from the smoke and the dust and the pit heaps. The 1950s and '60s were great years when I could park my BSA at the Haymarket in Newcastle and watch all the famous stars at the Empire for about five shillings. There was Nina and Frederick, Micky and Griff, Joseph Lock and Guy Mitchell – remember them?

"But Ashington had far more than smoke and dust to offer. We had the Colliers at Portland Park; and the less famous football teams at Hirst Welfare, such as the Ashington Wednesday Tradesmen; my marra Raffy Coupland played for them – they were never famous at all.

"For the more Musical folk, we had the beautiful Central Hall where quality artistes appeared such as the Dagenham Girl Pipers, the Kirkintilloch Boys Choir and many more I can't remember, but I can never forget the swirl of the pipes in that lovely building.

"I recall my feeble attempts to learn to dance at the Walton Assembly Rooms and failing miserably. But I spent a lot of time at the Arcade Hall, listening to the Arcadians; another marra of mine, Joe Tomlinson, used to play for them; and Eric Nichol sang there – he was a show all by himself.

"In the 1960s, I swapped my BSA for a Norton Big Four with sidecar to take my mam and dad around the countryside. It was a beautiful outfit, in fact, the bonnie lass across the back lane fell in love with it ... she even married me for it. Unfortunately, I had to sell the bike to put down a deposit for a house for us to live in.

"Nevertheless, we had forty-eight wonderful years together, raised a couple of bairns who have bairns of their own who, I hope, will never know the taste of poverty. But will the highlights of their growing years ever shine as brightly as mine? I doubt it.

"For my memories are built on the need to survive on jam and bread, tops and whips, and the joy of walking down the Narrow Path to a magical place called Newbiggin, and then back to good old Ashington ... back home."

'What is it about this bloody town, eh?' by Alan Richardson
"What is it about this bloody town, eh? Since leaving Ashington I've worked my way across America, twice (thinking I was Ariel Street's answer to Jack Kerouac); round the world once; made a living in a dozen different and often bizarre ways, had numerous books published on a variety of weird topics, and can name-drop like no-one I've ever met.

"And yet, despite my exile, I am still an Ashington lad with all that that implies. My real and enduring heroes are still the old miners and their stock. Everything I experience is measured against a template of its Ashington equivalent. *'Lunch at the Café Royal?'* Bah! Give me Crawford's Café with a sticky bun and the Sporting Pink. *'A drink with Van Morrison'*, Yeah, well, but a pint of Fed Special with Kipper Herron in the owld 'Varsal was more fun.

"I now live in Wiltshire in an area designated as having 'Outstanding Natural Beauty', and yet I still find myself pining for what I know is the dog-shit awfulness of Second Avenue. And when I take my little daughters to their school and look through their work, in some parallel experience I am actually back at the old Hirst North School, seeing the things I used to do, though not so well. I know this is all a common enough middle-aged sort of thing to do, but you'll forgive me for this piece of indulgence ... I hope!"

'No Money to Spare in 1930s' by John Foster
"I loved the Hirst South School and can honestly say that the time spent there were the happiest days of my life. I remember the teachers with gratitude and respect, especially Mr Armstrong, my teacher for the last two years. I was so pleased that many years later when I had a son of my own, I was able to visit Mr Armstrong and felt honoured that he remembered me.

"I obtained what was called a Scholarship Standard allowing me to attend Bedlington Secondary (later Grammar) School in September 1934. I did not like my time there, apart from the sport, but I received an excellent education which has stood me in good stead many times since. During these formative years, we played many games: top and whip; hoop and stick; skipping; dodge-ball; kitty-kat; to name but a few. Football and cricket were my favourites; Tom Bowman the butcher gave us a pig's bladder because the genuine article was hard to come by, but it lasted a long time and never looked like bursting.

"My brother Lawrie was a practical boy, taking up fretwork and various artistic hobbies. We used to go round the shops asking for tea chests (3d each) for the plywood, and out of the corners he made cars and buses. He then bought a white paper window blind on which he painted a village scene; he made bridges etc with plywood, laying it on the blind with his painted vehicles. My mother called in a neighbour's little boy to see it, and when he expressed delight, Lawrie promptly gave him the lot.

"We were regular visitors to the rubbish tip, looking for old bikes which we took home and painted. Some of us went for a bike ride to Bothal, and, as I was the youngest, I had the dodgiest bike. In Bothal village the front tyre split and the inner tube swelled like a balloon. We found a piece of old rag and bound it round the tube, creating a lump which made the bike jump every time the wheel went round. Not long after that my pedal broke clean off and my foot had to be tied to the crank to enable me to pedal home. Not a very successful venture into bicycle manufacture.

"Financially, times were bad, with Dad lucky to work three or four shifts a week. If there were three consecutive days off then the miners were entitled to dole. At six shillings and nine pence per day it is obvious that there was no money to spare in the 1930s, so we lived without luxuries.

"When he was fourteen, my brother Lawrie started work at Woodhorn Colliery, a job he hated. At sixteen, he joined the Royal Navy, leaving Dad as the sole breadwinner. I began to think it was time I did something to help the family finances, especially as sport at Bedlington Grammar School demanded two shillings each game, which was not easy to find. In Ashington at that time (1936) the league table for desirable jobs went like this:

School teacher (attainable to a few)
Employee of local Co-op Society
Other shop work
Apprenticeship
Coalmining

"This was not, as I found out later, a wide or even accurate choice. However, when I saw the Co-op advert for a Temporary Errand Boy in the Hardware Department, I decided to apply. I turned up at the Head Office, in the Arcade, all washed and scrubbed, to find about fifty other boys with the same goal in mind. We were ushered into a large room with tables and chairs, and given an arithmetic and a general knowledge written test. A few of us who had most marks were held back and the rest allowed to go home. I was then taken into the Board Room where about sixteen committee members asked me questions. You would have thought I was being interviewed for the position of Prime Minister not a temporary errand boy. I was given the job and started work at the Ashington Branch under Mr Harry Scott, another man who had a good influence on me, and who taught me several skills."

'The Green Lonnen was a Child's Paradise' by Harry Speight

"In the pre-war days of the 1930s, I was one of a number of children living in the then new housing estate known as Garden City Villas in the Hirst part of Ashington. Friends I remember included: Bob and Peggy Humble; Albert, Joyce and Stan Griffiths; Mona and Eddie Perkins; Sid and Ronnie Wake; Ray Purvis; Bill Robinson; Jack Williamson; Jackie Musgrove; Alice Cochrane; Ken Hogg; Tom Bateman; John Watson; Sid Steele (who was killed when his ship was sunk); Fenwick Bradley and many others.

“Money was scarce, so most of the children’s entertainment was homespun. Once you tired of the tops and whips and mount-the-cuddy it was the most natural thing in the world to make for the countryside. Garden City Villas in those days was nearly new with many of its houses standing empty. You had to prove you could pay the rent before they would give you a council house. Jack Harrison was the rent collector and his word was law.

“One winter’s day it was bitterly cold and there was a commotion in the middle lane: a family was being evicted. They stood around the street lamp – a mother, father and four sons of varying ages - with nothing in their pockets and less in their bellies. My mother made them a meal of broth and bread and butter, and it was my job to fetch the youngsters into our house. They were sat in front of a roaring coal fire until the four had eaten. When they left we never saw them again.

“The Villas were built on a tip with allotments to the south and west. You had to cross a narrow road (called the Aad Road) to reach the Green Lonnen. The Aad Road, or North Seaton Road to give it its Sunday name, was a narrow ribbon of tarmac lying between hawthorn hedges where wooden bungalows sat beyond the stream that flowed behind the hedge. Higgledy-piggledy cottages seemed to have taken root between the hedge and the busy railway line, which took coals from the collieries of Ashington, Woodhorn, Linton, Ellington and Lynemouth, bound for the Port of Blyth and other far away places.

“Each cottage was approached over a small make-shift bridge across the stream; some had old sweet scented roses festooned on a rough wooden trellis. An old man I met there once insisted that that stream had once held trout, and he seemed to know what he was talking about.

“The Green Lonnen (Green Lane) was a child’s paradise: nobody told you to ‘shut up and be quiet’ down there. You could make as much noise as you liked. Mind you . . . courting couples who wandered the length and breadth of the Lonnen didn’t make much noise either – they were too busy doing other things. Far too busy to take notice of young John Humble serenading his latest young lass as they went past our poke tent late in the evening. Aye, John was a canny singer.

“The high hedges along the Lonnen were punctuated at intervals by allotments. After you left those gardens behind, you came to the open fields. To the left, a rutted track that led to Black Close Dene; to the right the St Aidan’s Scout Hut which was burnt to the ground. What a disaster that was.

“Beyond that was land that was unfenced, lying outside Bobby Gray’s field – land about 50 feet wide was ours to camp on, play on in poke tents made from old sacks. It was there we ate potatoes blackened in the hot ashes of a camp fire. And then went to sleep on a bed of hard earth, covered by an old blanket.

“To the right of the Lonnen lay the hay field owned by Douglas of Home Farm which is now covered forever with houses and concrete. Then it was the most beautiful field of wild flowers and grasses cut by teams of men and women, to be gathered later and made into large stacks, ready to be hauled off by horse drawn hay bogies. That was the signal for half a dozen of us to leap on the back of the bogie.

"Then the government took the hay field and made it into 'dole' gardens. Alec Aisbett got one of the first of them and we went with him the first time he fed the hens. It was good for the men and their families, but bad for us young'uns for we had lost our field."

"Folks might think I was a deprived child living amongst the pit heaps. Fools!" by Evelyn Dickinson (nee Davison)

"The words leaped off the page as I sat and read my copy of your book *'Hirst Ashington – The Larkey playing field'*. What memories! I am back in the past and it's the mid 1940s-1950s. I have climbed the fence at the bottom of Aln Street and Blyth Terrace straight into the Larkey, our playing field. Magic!

"Woodhorn Pit dominates the skyline, smoke belching from its tall chimneys mingling with sooty clouds from countless household chimneys. Machinery clanks and the huge wheels whirls, and the wind blows in from the north sea. Steam trains hoot as they are shunted to sidings, waiting to be filled with coal, with the pit heaps glinting in the sun.

"The sun always shone on the Larkey in the summer. In winter it was thick with snow. Rose-coloured spectacles? Probably, but never mind. I'm here with 'our gang'. We've got sandwiches and a bottle of pop for a picnic.

"The grass has been allowed to grow long in the Larkey so we roll around and flatten a patch to make our camp. Soon the grass will be cut short and left in piles, and that's even better. Pile the grass high and make walls, but we must be on guard, our sworn enemies: the 'Villas' kids might steal it. There were some mighty big lads in Woodhorn Villas at the time; the names of some of them could strike terror into many a young kid in Ashington.

"Shivers of fear and excitement. Enemies from the Villas have been lurking near the swings and are now stalking our camp. A fierce battle follows, with both sides grabbing armfuls of grass and claiming it as their own. On to the next game. Over the fence and through the hedge to the 'dirty lonnen'. There's some gypsies there in caravans. What are they doing? Nothing much ... so it's off along the lonnen towards Nellis's Farm to climb trees.

"Far superior camps could be made in the Larkey in winter. Build a wall and pack the snow tight. Make an arsenal of snowballs to hurl at the Villas kids when they come looking for a fight. Back home to thaw out frozen fingers. When our mittens were steaming in the hearth, dash out to make a slide. Awesome slides were made the whole length of Aln Street by a dozen kids trudging in a line to pack the snow down hard. Then the glee and exhilaration of flying down the glossy length of Aln Street. Pure Magic!

"I believe many people reading or listening to my recollection of a childhood growing up amongst the pit heaps would consider I was a deprived child. Fools! Growing up in Ashington was special and memories now come back thick and fast: a certain day in summer when the congregation of St John's and St Andrew's suddenly swelled to encompass the whole population of Ashington. Hundreds (thousands?) congregated at the railway station to board the steam train for the annual church trip to Whitley Bay ... but I'll leave that for another time."

"In winter it was always thick with snow." Well, it was in 1963 when games in the Welfare League were cancelled for six weeks because of the drifts. Eventually, Ashington Athletic got a game on the Larkeys fielding this team. Back left Fred Atkins, Bill Locke, Alan Robson, Gordon Thompson, Eric 'Spike' Newman. Front Derek Redman, Vic Adams, Alvin Drysdale, Billy Ross, Eric Moore and Michael Gale.

Arcade Dancehall decked out for King George VI Coronation celebrations, 1937.

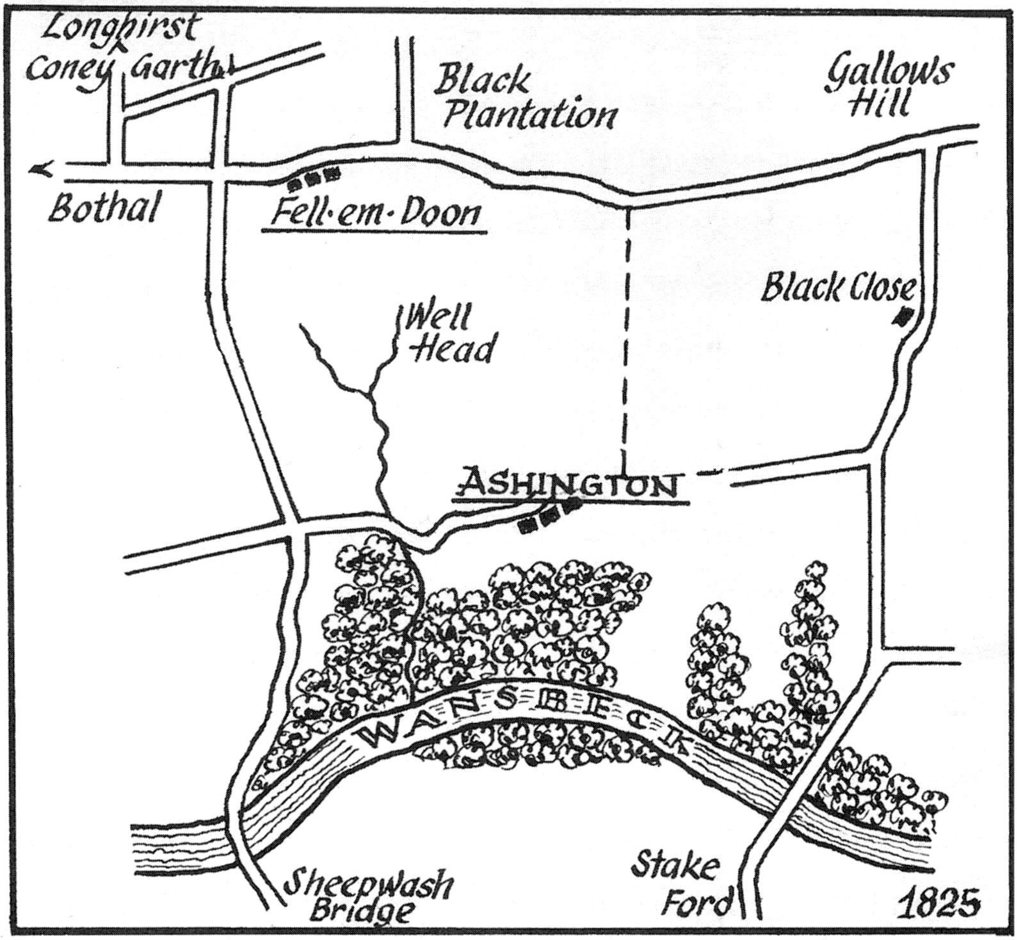

IN THE BEGINNING

To get a perspective of what was happening to Ashington in the Thirties, we need to look back at the origins of what began as a small rural village (map from c1825). First of all, in order to find out how the name 'Ashington' was derived, let's examine the research of Mr J K Hamilton who became headmaster of Hirst North 'A' School in 1933, a position he held until retiring in 1950. During his stay in Ashington he became interested in local dialect and place names. This is what he wrote in the Ashington Colliery Magazine of March 1937:

"Frequently I hear that Fell-em-Doon is the old name for Ashington. I know of no evidence in support of this. In the study of names of places it is essential to have very old records to which to refer and to be sure the geographical and topographical conditions harmonise with the suggested derivation. Fell-em-Doon seems to be a comparatively recent word.

"There is no mention of Fell-em-Doon in an 1826 Northumberland Gazetteer, which includes the tiniest hamlets. Ashington has a place, though. But this is little argument. In place-name books that I have consulted. nowhere is there any mention whatever of Fell-em-Doon. On the other hand, Ashington (as Essende) appears in a document of nearly 800 years ago and has been Ashington for 300 years.

"From the table below it is plain to see how our Ashington has developed from the Anglo-Saxon word for 'dene'. In addition, the local conditions fit. All Ashingtons are not similarly derived. The Ashington in Somerset is from Essentone, Estinton, Estington, and is identical with Eastington, meaning a place in the east of the village. The Sussex Ashington was originally Essingetona, meaning the tun (enclosed place) of Aesc's people. It is as well then not to jump to conclusions in place-name study."

EVOLUTION OF A NAME

Ashington

1170	Essende	1428	Esshenden
1199	Esinden	1487	Eshenden
1205	Essenden	1637	Assinton
1255	Essenden	1663	Ashington

1. Old English, aescen-denu, valley of the ash tree or
2. valley of Aesc or of his sons

The discovery of coal in the mid-19th century changed the lifestyle of a population that soared from a few dozen farm labourers into an urban town sprawl of around 30,000, a third of whom were employed by the Ashington Coal Company in any one of its five collieries operating locally in the 1930s: Ashington, Woodhorn, Linton, Ellington and Lynemouth.

The Coal Company's main directors – the Priestmans – were Quakers who owned coalmines scattered around Tyneside and Northumberland. Jonathan Priestman brought his Quaker values to Ashington, one of which was Temperance - an abstinence from alcoholic drink. This idea of making Ashington a 'dry' town was abhorrent to the thirsty miners who circumnavigated the Quaker ideology by opening their own drinking establishments, sometimes in ordinary houses or grocery shops, such as those in Woodhorn Road which eventually boasted five workingmen's clubs within yards of each other: the Hirst East End, the Northern, Linton and Woodhorn, Premier and Hirst Industrial. The first two clubs to open in town around 1900 were the Ashington and District (West End Club) at the top end, and the New Hirst (Mortimer) at the juncture of North Seaton Road and Milburn Road. They were soon followed by others until no fewer than twenty clubs existed in a town that was to be castigated as 'Satan's Citadel' in 1952 by a group of Methodist Missionaries who held open-air meetings in Ashington, and where, at one meeting, a zealous missionary observed 'A woman who was obviously drunk'.

The clubs were affiliated with Federation Breweries at Dunstan, and no other beer but 'Fed' was allowed to be sold over the bar for many years. But they were not simply drinking dens – each had its own identity, such as the Ashington and Ellington on Station Road which catered for miners from those two collieries, as did the Linton and Woodhorn; the RAOB had its origins with the Royal Ancient Order of Buffaloes; the Conchi was initially a haven for true-blue Conservatives; the Fell 'em Doon took the name of Ashington's first colliery, sunk in the 1840s. Many clubs had their own library and reading room as well as a games room for billiards, dominoes, darts, cards etc. Sporting leagues sprang up, giving club members a sense of comradeship and affiliation to their own particular club. Many clubs formed a football team that competed in the Ashington and District Welfare League, based at Hirst Welfare and Ashington Recreation ground.

There was fierce rivalry too among the schools in the 1930s. Two relatively new schools had opened: Hirst Park in 1928 and Wansbeck Junior School in 1932. These two additions to the education system in Ashington had been brought about by a rising school population, especially in Hirst Ashington which by then had outstripped 'High' Ashington by more than three to one. Both the schools were innovative in their own way. Wansbeck School was the first to cater specifically for five to eleven year-olds, while Hirst Park School was the forerunner of a purely Secondary education for its pupils. Ashington's oldest school was the Bothal (named after the first school in the district in the 18th century which was based at Bothal Village); schools in Hirst were named geographically in order of being built: Hirst North, South, East and Central (the original name chosen for Hirst Park).

Corporal punishment played a significant part in enforcing school discipline. By all accounts, schools in the 1930s were ruled by an iron fist or maybe it was just strap and cane. It was related by a Bothal School pupil that a young girl called Lena Ward gave a new teacher, Miss Elizabeth Joisce, a parcel one day, saying that it was 'a present'. Inside was a leather taws with the schoolmistress's initials EJ cut into the top. The girl's father was a saddler at the colliery. This was his way of saying: '*Use it with my blessing.*' It was a parental attitude far removed from the line in a 1979 song: *'Hey. Teacher, leave that kid alone.'*

It is also recalled by a former pupil at the Bothal School that a certain teacher, Miss Farrell, had a bell which was intended to bring the mixed class of between forty and fifty pupils to order. Some teachers worked a 'rota system' where the best-behaved children and most able, known as 'good', sat at the back of the classroom in a graduated order which brought the 'worst' pupils to the front. Any slip, either academic or behavioral brought a 'back' pupil forward whilst the most promising 'front' child moved back.

Bothal School 1947 team, back left Alan Gebbie, Pat Lawson, Gordon Campbell. 2nd back Dick Hankinson, Bruce Mather, Larry Marshall. Seated Emerson Williams, Malcolm Taylor, Jimmy Whitworth. Front Derek Wanless and Steve Mavin.

THE 1930s

For anyone to give an 'Ashington Opinion' (drawing from 1949 *Ashington Advertiser*) first of all you need to establish how easy or difficult, it was to get into the town itself? Back in the '30s, Newcastle was just over 18 miles away by road; today, in 2006, because of the 'Spine Road', that distance has been cut to 15 miles. Back then it took the United bus the best part of an hour to get to the Haymarket, via Bedlington, Hartford and Wideopen – it is now a twenty-minute run by car ... if you keep to the speed limit.

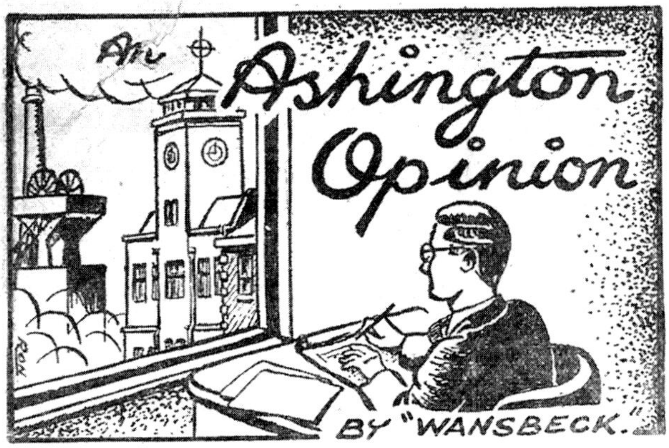

Driving (or walking, as most folks did) into Ashington in 1934, from the Bedlington side, across the Stakeford Bridge (erected 1909), there was only the one stone-built house on the left going down Stakeford Bank – Leeches Estate was not built until the 1950s. That particular bridge has been replaced and re-located twice since then to accommodate more traffic. Looking out of a double-decker upstairs' window on a clear day you could catch a panoramic view of Sheepwash Wood on the left, a single well-trodden dirt pathway snaking through its jungle of trees and tangled bushes.

To the right, spanning the River Wansbeck, was (and still is) the Black Bridge, built originally of wood in the mid-19th century to carry the tons of black diamonds hewed out of the ground at Ashington Colliery. Coming up the bank, nearing the top, again there were no houses, left nor right, as neither Jubilee Estate nor Black Close had been erected. No Trading Estate either, but North Seaton railway station was there: a manned crossing catering for the many wagonloads of coal, plus a generous portion of passenger trains carrying canny folk from Ashington and Newbiggin, perhaps on a Christmas shopping trip to Newcastle. Venturing further afield than the Toon in 1934 was rarely an option.

Over the crossing, there was a left turn that took you up the Old Road (now North Seaton Road) or if you ventured straight on you came to the North Seaton Hotel on the left with the Hippodrome Theatre opposite. To get to Ashington this way, you turned left up the New Road (now Milburn Road). Now your view of the town would be very much as it is today with long grids of colliery houses on the right, but only a few private houses on the left as the Norham/Bywell Road council estate was not built until a decade later. But Milburn Road then was much narrower then it is today as the house gardens took up much of the space. At the top of the road on the right was the spacious Pavilion Theatre (now Gala Bingo) and beyond that the red-brick Hirst North School complex, perched on the Second Avenue corner since 1896. (closed 1996).

For those travellers who had turned left after North Seaton rail crossing and taken the Aad Road, there would be the railway line on the left and, beyond the west side of the line - and also the east side of the road - were hundreds of ramshackle allotments. There was no avenue of mature trees then – saplings were planted by council Parks Superintendent John Stewart and colleagues a few years later. After passing the wooden United Servicemen's Club (now the Comrades) on the left, the Aad and New roads merged at the New Hirst and District Club (the Mortimer), first club to be built in Hirst. Further up on the right was the Priestman's Institute (built 1890s – demolished 1970s) with its glass canopy sheltering the men who were not inside playing billiards on one of its six immaculate tables. Opposite the 'Tute' was the dental practice of Stanley Bird (sons Eric and Ivor), working from one of the private houses in North Seaton Road that also accommodated the Constitutional and the Hirst Progressive clubs, and later the British Legion and further up the road the premises of WJ Nichol & Sons, coal merchants and Ferrell's hairdressers.

Approaching the Grand Corner in 1934, two more social clubs to pass on the left - the Central and Grand Street - after Stanley Cook's 'Grocery & Corn Store'; while his cousin Russell Cook's department store, was one of the most prestigious retailers in town, destined to become Shephard's then Jopling's and today (2006) Ethel Austin. And there, on the right, in all its majestic glory, stood the Grand Hotel itself. Who would have thought that in less than forty years (1973) the building that many believed was the throbbing heart of Ashington, would be torn out and replaced with a stomach ulcer which still festers there today?

If you entered Ashington from the 'top end', you were either coming from Bothal or from Longhirst (the Pegswood Road, although begun in 1939, because of war restrictions, was not completed until the late 1950s). The road from Bothal terminated at Cooper's Shop where you turned left to eventually join up with the road from Longhirst. The United buses (two an hour) went both ways, and there was a standing joke that, if you are going to Morpeth by bus. "the Longhirst (pronounced Laang'est) way was the shortest way."

Apart from Bothal Terrace, not many houses on the left, but set back was the Coal Company Granary where food (choppy) was prepared for the hundreds of pit ponies that spent the best part of twenty-years underground – if they managed to live that long. Two of the oldest colliery streets – Cross Row and Long Row – were in this area, both built in the 1860s to a high standard with long gardens. These two rows are no longer standing, but Portland Terrace still remains. Ellington Road Ends, again on the left, provided a junction between the road and the railway line running out of the colliery. We shall see later how dangerous this coming together of two modes of transport proved to be.

And now we reach High Market, called Market Place in the mid-19th century when the first shops in town were built here. But by the 1930s the main shopping area had moved further down Station Road, towards and beyond the railway station. On the left, the houses belonging to the pit officials – the First Row – were the first to get electricity in town, long before the ordinary miners in the colliery houses of Second to the Sixth Row, the latter sitting practically in the pit yard itself. As a youngster, Jackie Milburn lived here with his granny for a while. He said: "I used to lie awake at night listening to the tankeys puff, puff, puffing away, but ye got used to it."

And that was the thing about Ashington in those days ... you got used to it. This was the life you were born into and, not knowing any other, it was accepted that you lived in a house without an indoor toilet and bath; it was accepted that every time the wind was in the north, you were showered with pieces of grit, blown in from the ugly pit heaps that circled that part of town; it was accepted that nine lads out of ten would follow their fathers underground; and it was accepted by the women of Ashington that, almost from the moment they were born, they were destined to a life of toil, bordering on drudgery.

Shakespeare once asked: 'What's in a Name?' and it would appear that in the late 19th century, an unimaginative official at the Ashington Coal Company attached some feeble labels on to streets, such as the '*Six Houses'*. Folks living in any of the rows from 2nd to 11th might have been a little embarrassed when giving such an address. The Duke of Portland (residence Bothal Castle) owned the land on which the then village stood, and his connection was carried on by street names such as Duke Street, Portland Terrace and Cavendish Gardens (Bentinck/Cavendish was a family name); Welbeck Road was named after two other countryside residences owned by the wealthy Duke; Bertram Terrace was named after Robert Bertram who was the first of his family living at Bothal Castle to be called 'Baron of Bothal', given this title by King Richard I, c1199; two streets were named after Coal Company mining engineers: Henry Richardson and William J Charlton; and Milburn Road was so named because of ACC director and entrepreneur William Milburn.

But by the mid-20th century, Ashington's newly-built council housing estates derived their titles from other towns and villages in the county. The names were meant to suggest a pleasing atmosphere, such as Hartford Crescent, Haydon Road or Bywell. It is a fact that Hirst Ashington's colliery rows between Milburn and Hawthorn Road were once named after famous rivers, the tongue-in-cheek theory being that, given the lack of proper roads and drainage, they were almost like rivers: vast expanses of clarts that required residents to walk a plank of wood in order to leave or enter their homes.

Changes from river names to those of trees in the Hirst area happened around 1910 when Ashington Council wanted to 'rationalise' the system, making it easier for postal deliveries. But this had to be done in such a way that the residents themselves would not be confused. So, in all cases, the initial letter remained. For example Mersey Terrace changed to

Milburn Road; Severn Street to Sycamore; Medway Street became Maple; Clyde Street changed to Chestnut; and Humber Terrace became Hawthorn Road. For some reason, Pont Street still retained its name, although the street corresponding to it, north of the Hirst North School, is called Poplar Street. The GPO at the time had to keep the name Humber Terrace for the sub-post office in Hawthorn Road.

Many of the street names at the Hirst are worthy of attention for, after you leave the tree-named group, culture creeps in so that four streets derive names from heroines in Shakespeare plays. Rosalind, for whom her lover wrote:

'From east to western land
No jewel is like Rosalind'

is the heroine of *As You like It.*

Beatrice Street conjures up a vision of the witty Beatrice of *Much Ado About Nothing,* who was something of a man-hater; Katherine Street was named after the tamed shrew of *The Taming of the Shrew,* and Juliet Street would almost need balconies to live up to its origin; Portia Street can claim to be named after the most intellectual of Shakespeare's heroines, as portrayed in *The Merchant of Venice.* Chasing the four heroines, as it were, is the elusive and mischievous sprite, Ariel, a character in *The Tempest.*

But perhaps the most intriguing set of street names was that given to houses near People's Park, erected by the Ashington Coal Company in 1923 for their own employees, at a selling price of £450 - now on the market for well over £150,000. In an almost De Vinci Code-like plot, it seems that young Will Cookson, an ACC surveyor, came up with these names in the shape an acrostic, forming the words, Park Road.

Park Road East
Arundel Square
Ridsdale Square
Kenilworth Road

Rutland Street
Oakland terrace
Ashbourne Terrace
Darnley Road.

Clever, wasn't it. The estate became known as the ACC Housing Scheme, and the houses still standing between the Park and the railway line, are some of the most sought after in Ashington.

To get a feel of what locals thought about their own town in the Thirties, here is a tongue-in-cheek piece from the Ashington Colliery Magazine, penned by Will Cain who worked in the Time Office at Linton Colliery. Like most of Will's stuff, it was written in Pitmatic (Ashington's very own language) and entitled:

'Ashin'ton's Not See Bad'

"When ye taak aboot Ashin'ton ye want ti think o' waat it used to be, and then be varry thankful ye weren't born twenty or thorty yeors syunner. Nee shops, nee pictor haals, nowt atween the Grand and the Portland. Whey, chaps had nowt ti dee but get drunk, an' thi dee tell me, though A'ave nivvor seed it, that on New Yeor's Eve they carried men hyem in coal bogies.

"Aye, that's Aad Ashin'ton, but just luk at it thi day (1930). Waat di ye think o' the railin's alaang the Sivinth Raa front, eh? Waat di ye think o' the skyscrapers Blacklock's and McDonald's? Daresay they wud mek any Yankees feel duzzy. Then there's Woolworth's ... if a toon hes a Woolworth's it is kind o' classy, ye knaa.

"Then there's the Fire Brigade. Waat odds if there's nee wetter when thi get tiv the fire, they always luk bonnie in those uniforms. An' the football team! Aa divvent want nee arguments so Aa'll say nowt aboot it, but it's a gud ground thi hev. (MK says in 2006 'or did hev').

"An' then there's the pictor haals! The Wallaw for the folks wi brains, ye knaa, a quarter o' chocolates for thi wife and a pipe o' baccy for the owld chep, an' there they sit. The Buff for t'other kind – in at the fowerpenny end, and oranges an' monkey nuts for the wife and a packet o' Woodbines for the chep. Then the Miners (before it was called the Regal) that's where ye gan when yor wife wants aal thi officials' wives to see hor new hat that's as gud as theirs ony day, or so shi says. Nee toon can beat Ashin'ton for pictor haals. Aa've missed the Piv oot, but ye knaa waat kind o' folks gan there!

"Ashin'ton has nee Boxing Pavilion, not proper like, but thi built thi Cooncil Chambers insteed, an' Aa think it's ivory other Thorsday neet thi meet.

"An' so Aa cud gan on, showin' ye that Ashin'ton not haaf see bad as people mek oot. Nee other toon's like it. So fetch yor sooth-country folk an' Aa'll taak tiv them. An' if thi divvent like it, Aa'll just hev ti tell them waat a great bus service wi hev and hoo easy it is to get oot of it.

Petty Crime in the Thirties – taken from Morpeth Herald

Convictions for Petty Offences at Ashington Magistrates Court in 1935

Regarding what we would now call trivial offences, the heavy hand of the Law was much more in evidence in the 1930s than it is today. Here are some of the cases that came before the Magistrates in Ashington in 1935.

A charge of Loitering for the purpose of bookmaking was preferred against Herbert Smith (38), miner, of 68 Myrtle Street, Ashington. William M Wealleans (37), miner, of 34 Myrtle Street was charged with the same offence.

PC McKenzie said that from previous observations he got the assistance of two other constables and along with them entered a 'place of concealment' (somebody's back yard). He saw nine men, seven women and one child hand papers and what appeared to be money to Wealleans, and, on another occasion, 17 men, 15 women and four children went into the yard followed by either Wealleans or Smith. The Chairman of Magistrates ordered that Wealleans would be fined £4 and Smith £2.

Frederick L Curry (29), unemployed, of The Bungalow, Cresswell, was summoned for using a motor cycle without a Road Fund licence and for failing to have a policy of Insurance in respect of third party risks. Frank Gilroy of Cresswell said that he and Curry got off a bus at Cresswell. Curry then asked him along to see a motor cycle and when there asked him to go for a ride to Druridge Farm. Coming back they struck a kerb and were both thrown off. PC Hume said that he went to Cresswell Village after receiving a report of an accident. He found on the motor cycle that the Road Fund Licence had expired on December 31st 1934. Defendant said that the motor cycle was his only means of finding work. He was fined £3 and had his licence suspended for 12 months.

Insecure Load

John W Turner (24) motor driver, of 11a King Georges Road, Newbiggin, was summoned for using a motor lorry, the packing and adjustment of the load being in such condition as to cause danger to other persons on the highway. Adam Elliott of Pegswood said he saw a lorry going towards Pegswood laden with boxes. As the lorry went round the corner, the load seemed to move and some of the boxes came off. Bottles were broken. Defendant said there was a weak spring on the lorry which caused the load to slip. He was fined £2 and costs.

No Seat on Motor Cycle

Unlawfully carrying a passenger on a motor cycle which was 'not equipped with a fixed and secure seat' was the charge against Philip Sydney 'Sid' Kirkup (19), miner, of 91 Katherine Street, Ashington. It was stated the defendant only had a leather cushion on, which had slipped down the mudguard. A fine of 5 shillings was imposed. (Editor says: 'Sid Kirkup was my uncle and the 'unlawful passenger' was my 33-year-old father, Jack Kirkup').

No Entry in Log Book

Henry P Hill (19) motor driver, 19 West View, Ashington, was summoned for being the driver of a motor van and failing to make a current entry in the log book. Hill said that he thought he did not need to fill the log book in till his day's work was finished. He was fined 5 shillings.

No Dog Licences

The following were summoned for having kept dogs without a licence: William Lock of 31 Pont Street, and George Wedgewood of 81 Castle Terrace. Both fined 7/6d.

Cycling in Park

Adam Matthews (28) miner of 10 Tosson Place, Ashington, was fined 2/6d for riding a cycle in Hirst Park.

Clothes Line Danger

Elizabeth McDowell (50), married woman, of 77 Maple Street, was summoned for placing a rope across the highway (back street) so as to cause danger to other passers-by without giving adequate warning. Janet Wheeler of Richardson Street said she was cycling in Back Maple Street and going slowly. She was caught in the neck by a clothes-line and thrown from her cycle. Two people were taking the line down and 'carrying-on' at the time. PC Turner spoke to the defendant later and she admitted having put the clothes-line over the street. McDowell said she had put the line up but the props fell down. Fined 5 shillings.

Ashington Operatic Society Perform at the Miners' Theatre (March, 1935)
From Monday to Saturday, between 11th March and 16th March, the Ashington Operatic Society presented the musical play 'Rio Rita' in aid of local charities. The previous year their choice had been 'Rose Marie'. For the present production some of the leading parts were taken by Donald Strong, Harry Pyle, Lewis Mather, Mary Stannard, Jack Bell, Harry Habberjam, Matt Gibson, Bob Boutland, Mona Moncaster, William Riley, Kitty McHugh, Jim Shaw, Matt Ledgerwood, Jean Pyle and Edie Stubbs. Some of those featured in the male chorus were Tom Allison, Leslie Ashman, Tim Brown, Billy Dent, John Greener, Frank Grenfell, George Horn and Ernie Jameson. Lady dancers included Hilda Allison, Ivy Anderson, Allie Bell, Gladys Boutland, Ena Conway, Nancy Crichton, Jean Davison, Anna Gray, Ruby Hall, Jean Hart, Joan Ledgerwood, Laura Newman, Nelly Potts, Hannah Robson, Mabel Satterly and Dorothy Sowerby.

Retailers advertising in the programme included: Miller's Station Café, 21 Station Road, Ashington; 'Nanette', Ladies and Children's Hairdresser, 18 Station Road, Ashington (above Benny Creigh's music shop), who specialised in *Kerka* permanent waving, with prices 'to suit all purses', 7/6 – 21/-; J W Gibson of the West End Garage, Ashington, advertised the new *Morris '8'* for £142 10s. Also in the programme the society acknowledged the help given to them by Mr Walter Lawson, Managing Director of Wallaw Pictures Limited and the manager and staff of the Miners' Theatre. The souvenir programme was printed at High Market, Ashington, by Wilkinson's Printers, as was this one from 1923 Miners Theatre production by Ashington Thespians of 'The Mikado'.

THE 1930's SHOPS

So what was happening 'up the street' in the 1930s? Will Cain has already mentioned Blacklock's which in turn became Doggart's then Mackay's. The phrase 'up the street' is still in use today, carried on by countless grandmothers and mothers who have passed it on to their female offspring; It was coined initially mainly by womenfolk living in Hirst Ashington to signify a shopping spree to one of a score of quality retailers on Station Road ... up the street. Even today you will find young mothers (bairns having bairns) dressed in flimsy tops exposing pierced navels and skimpy thongs, pushing space-age buggies, reaching for mobile phones to enquire: 'Are ye comin' up the street, Chelsea? There's a closin' doon sale at the sports shop.'

How times change. In the 1930s, what an array of classic shops existed up the street, more than enough to whet any shopaholic's appetite: huge department stores such as Doggart's, Shephard's and Arrowsmith's, not forgetting the all-embracing Co-op Arcade on Woodhorn Road, probably the forerunner of the present-day shopping mall with everything you might wish to purchase under one roof, plus your dividend. Children were 'rigged out' at least once a year. My own personal outfit (white shirt, socks and sandshoes) was bought every Easter by my mother who invariably 'had a Club out'. This was a means of purchasing goods on credit; a modified system is still in use today by money-lending firms. In those days, mother used a woman who lived in Woodhorn Road, I can't remember her name. Money borrowed in this way was repaid weekly, plus interest, of course.

Sir John Hall talked of the time he was growing up in North Seaton Colliery Village when Ashington was the place to go, especially on a Saturday. He said that his mother took him 'up the street' and while she went shopping, young John went along to Portland Park to watch the local lads play against one of the First Division's reserves sides, such as Sunderland or Middlesbrough, glittering with star names. And after coming out of the match he would join the queue to get into the Wallaw Cinema. Sir John had Ashington's Station Road in mind when he built the Metro Centre at Gateshead. 'The Metro Centre', he said, 'was where you could go to meet your friends, go shopping and socialise. In other words, the Metro Centre is Station Road with a roof on!'

And there were grocery shops, too, on the 'Main Street' (another phrase used to denote Station Road) each with its own individual style, immaculate shop frontage and loyal clientele. Who can forget the aromas drifting out on to the dusty Station Road pavement from Lipton's, Brough's or the Meadow Dairy (and much later the Value Stores) where staff in crisp white coats were only too pleased to rummage around in the back shop for any item that might not be on display on the shelves behind the counter. No self service yet in evidence in the Thirties. Butter and cheese were sliced to order from massive slabs; sugar and flour scooped from a sack into paper bags; and a whirring bacon slicer cut up a ham into pieces that could fill any large frying pan.

The Grand Corner was the epicentre of the town. Not only a convenient meeting place whether you lived at the 'top end' (a phrase used to denote any houses to the west of Station Bridge) or in the *Horst*. The Grand Hotel itself, built in the 1890s, was a magnificent building by any standards with its own stables and courtyard. At the turn of the 20th century the Grand catered mainly for the well-to-do gent who had business to transact in the town or perhaps was just passing through. Maids such as my father's sister, my Aunt Dot, dressed in white caps and black dresses, were employed to either wait on table or keep the dozen or so bedrooms neat and tidy. Each bedroom had a stained-glass window depicting the coat of arms of one of Northumberland's famous families, such as the Percys and Ogles.

Two other hotels were built around the same time: the Portland Arms, opposite the Seventh Row and the North Seaton Hotel. Each of them built to the specifications of north-east breweries. It was Deuchar of Sunderland who chose the site for what became known as the White Elephant, a derisory title adopted by local folk who thought that North Seaton was too far away from any regular drinkers to allow a profit to be made. But when Robert Deuchar began to build his hotel in the late 1890s, it was mooted that a tram service would run from North Seaton Railway Station directly to Newbiggin, putting the hostelry in an ideal position to service the many travellers that, it was thought, would use this mode of transport. In effect, the tramway was never built, scuppered in no small part by the then vicar of Seaton Hirst who refused to allow the tram company wayleave (permission to cross) over church land.

1930's EDUCATION

Jackie Milburn, of Newcastle United fame, attended the Hirst North School as an infant. He said: 'I remember the day I started the Hirst North School, and this is the gospel truth. My mother took me on the first day, and she had knitted me a special outfit. You know what it was like before the war – I'm talking about 1930 here. Anyway, she had knitted a thing with a knitted top, and I cried my bloody eyes out because I hadn't a pair of pants like the other lads. You felt as if you were a Jessie with your knitted stuff on.'

Are Ye an Uppie or a Doonie? by Miss Audrey Stimpson
"I attended Hirst North Girls School between 1934 – 38 when the school was divided into four schools – a boys' school and a girls' school on the ground floor, and the same on the first floor. The inevitable question on hearing that one attended the 'North' was: 'Are ye an Uppie or a Doonie?' The intake depended on the catchment area – west of Hawthorn Road to the railway line, bounded by Third Avenue, became 'Doonies'; and east of Hawthorn Road with the same southern boundary became Uppies with the excellent Miss Isobel Smith as Headmistress."

Jackie Milburn's cousin, Cissie Charlton, had difficulty preserving female modesty in her 1930's schooldays. She said: 'I went to the Hirst South School where they segregated lads from lasses, and I used to have to play netball. You had to wear this short gymslip and showed all your knickers when you jumped up to catch the ball. My four brothers would sit on the wall and watch us lasses playing in the schoolyard, and the whistles and jeers that came out of them whenever you jumped up made me blush.'

If you were a Catholic living in Ashington then the school you attended was St Aidan's at the top of Park Road. However, many Catholic children, me included, were often sent to the nearest school to where they happened to be living at the time. In 1938, when I was approaching school age, the Kirkup family lived in Monkseaton Terrace. The Hirst South School was only yards away so, for a few months, I went there. It was only when we moved to second block Poplar Street that I was sent to St Aidan's, often accompanied by 13-year-old Ellen Taylor who was in the 'Big School' there at the time. It was Ellen who was elected by my mother to chaperone me in my early days at St Aidan's Infants where the teachers in the late 1930s were Hannah and Dolly Bell (not related) and Miss Kathleen Newton.

A St Aidan scholar's favourite 'dare' was enacted on the way home. It happened on Station Bridge. If we spotted a train on the platform, just about to set off for Newbiggin, the children would hang their heads over the parapet, waiting for the blast of steam on the face as the train chimney puffed its way under the bridge. Not content with one dose of sooty smoke and the accompanying foul smell, they raced across to the other side of the bridge for a second helping. That unique way of youngsters 'letting off steam' ended when the station closed to passenger trains in 1964.

Another risk the Catholic lads took was when they did battle with the boys from the nearby Bothal School. The venue this time was People's Park. On leaving school, as if by some magic prior arrangement, two opposing armies met to slug it out near the battered old bandstand that stood rather forlornly below the plantation running along Wansbeck Road.

The weapons used in the conflict were stones. Not massive boulders that might do some serious damage, but teeny ones which were more easily come by, lying on the ground beneath the trees. On reflection, they could still have put many an eye out if delivered on target. But it was more of a slanging than a slinging match. And after about half an hour, when the stones and the rhetoric had dried up, a young lad's hunger pangs overcame his need for sectarian appeasement, and the battle ended with each set of warriors trooping home for tea, both armies claiming the victory.

North Seaton Railway Bridge afforded yet more excitement. Nicknamed the Black Bridge, for obvious reasons, it was here that the "Horsty Doggers' fought out many a bloody battle with the 'Stakie' lads from 'ower the waater'. This thinly-veiled animosity between the two separate communities of Ashington and Bedlington, I believe, still exists today, but more in a political sense than the eyeball-to-eyeball, stone-throwing days of sixty or seventy years ago.

Getting over the River Wansbeck presented another challenge. It was too easy to walk over Stakeford Road Bridge. To get the adrenalin really going you had to cross the Black Bridge ... when a train was coming! How was that achieved? Well, a few feet below the rail track is an inspection platform that runs from one side of the bridge to the other. Your mission, should you choose to accept it, was to traverse this narrow walkway, underneath a moving train, while at the same time dodging stones being flung at you by the enemy. Sadly, deaths were recorded here as common sense gave way to impetuosity and boyish bravado.

1930's FOOTBALL SCENE

Ashington Welfare League had begun in 1920 when Welfare schemes were set up at Hirst Welfare and Ashington Rec, plus institutes and sports fields adjoining the pit villages of Linton and Lynemouth. Three football leagues catered for Midgets of under-15, Juniors up to eighteen, and Seniors. Many teams were an amalgamation of fellow workers from the pit, such as Woodhorn Bank, Loco United or Carl Pit; church teams entered the league from the Wesleyan Central Hall and St Aidan's; mini districts got together and formed a side, like Maple Street and Hirst Villa; even patrons from two picture halls pulled on their leather-studded boots to turn out as Hippodrome White Star and Wallaw United. Initially, the schemes were funded by the Miners Welfare Fund. But when nationalization came in 1947 the responsibility fell upon the Colliery Institute Social Welfare Organisation (CISWO).

Ashington Football Club by 1930 had spent almost ten years in the newly-formed Third Division North of the Football League before being relegated back to the North Eastern League in 1929. They still had a formidable squad of professional players on the books, such as big Frankie Kenyon and former football league player Jimmy Randall who were both paid top whack of 35/- per game. An ex-Newcastle United player, Jackie Dryden, was only offered 25/-, but the Board raised their offer to 30/- to which Jackie agreed. He eventually went on to become first team coach.

The Colliers also ran a Reserve team then in the Northern Alliance, fielding some familiar local lads such as goalie Tommy Rigg of Linton who eventually was transferred to Middlesbrough; Bobby Farrington also of Linton played in the Reserves in the late 30's before leaving for the 'big time'. In 1939, amateur forms were signed by J R Richardson, Tom Shears, Tommy Proctor, George Donnison and Tommy Cowan. Ashington's prolific goal-scorer in the 1930s, Arthur Bolton, was transferred to Sunderland for £700, a massive fee then which helped the Board to pay off some of their debts.

In 1936, to help the Colliers stay afloat, it was agreed to allow a Greyhound Racing Company to share the ground. It was an uneasy alliance with constant squabbles between the Company owner, Mr W Ulliott, and Ashington FC's board of directors. Some of the rules laid down by the footballers included:

- To put the ground behind the goals in good condition by turfing it before the new season began;
- To erect a handrail at the foot of the stand;
- To pay a sum of £25 if four meetings are held over and above the number allowed (104).

1930's THEATRE-LAND

Will Cain has already mentioned that Ashington boasted four cinemas in the early 1930s, a total boosted to five when Walter Lawson took control of the Hippodrome on Newbiggin Road. Walter had begun his working life as an electrician at Ashington Colliery, but his first love was silent movies, so he bought a motor bike and sidecar and began touting the films around Northumberland until he acquired his first home-based venue for showing films. This had been above the post office beside the Station Bridge, while another early venue was in the Linton & Woodhorn Miners Hall. His first purpose-built cinema was the WALLAW (using the first three letters of each name), which went up in 1914 beside what later became the town's first bus terminus on Woodhorn Road. Each cinema was capable of holding an audience of up to and beyond one thousand people.

In the Thirties, the Miners' Theatre played host to travelling troupes of actors, as did the Pavilion Theatre. These two large auditoriums were also ideal venues for the Ashington Operatic Society which, from its inception in the early 1920s, had specialized in Gilbert and Sullivan operettas. An offshoot of the Society, the Thespians, tended to perform more mainstream theatre. Each group had its own loyal followers and, consequently, shows were often sold out for a full week, costing as little as sixpence or one shilling (5p) for entry.

The Coal Position by Ridley Warham; Managing Director, Ashington Coal Company – June 1938
There is little change since last month. Buyers are still holding off and prospects for the next month or two are not encouraging. We are afraid that idle time at the pits is inevitable, we are trying to arrange it in such a way as to cause as little inconvenience to our workmen as possible. We are glad to find that our men can work so well when work is available. We are getting record outputs when the pit does work. But it would be a great help to everybody if they worked like this, and produced these great quantities of coal, when we can sell the stuff, and not only at a time when it can be disposed of.

Ashington Welfare League awards for 1937/38 season were won by YMCA Juniors represented by Bill Thompson captain, Ed Thain, Bill Robinson, J Turnbull, C Gittens, Les Redpath, Tom Coombs, Cyril Butters, Jack Anderson, Norman Campbell, J Gibson and A Gittens.
Booth Cup winners Hirst Ex-Juniors with George Wilkinson captain, T Foster, Sammy Pringle, Norman Johnson, J Nichol, M Cummings, R Anderson, J Scott, J Sawkill, John Dodd, Bill McLean and John Mordue.

Ashington On The Air – Ashington Colliery Magazine, November 1938
This is the title which the BBC has given to the variety programme which will be broadcast on Friday night, 18th November, 1938, from 9-9.45 pm. It will be the second of a new series of Town Variety Hours which have been planned to give the North East a greater measure of representation on radio programmes. The artistes for this broadcast programme were chosen from fifty acts which were presented at a private audition held in the Princess Ballroom, Ashington, at the beginning of last month, and in making their selections the BBC representatives chose a substantial number of Ashington Coal Company employees.

The dance band chosen for the programme was that of the Princess Ballroom, directed by Dryden Phillipson and of its eleven members, two are employees of the ACC. Leslie Easton, who plays the piano, bass and accordion, works on an engine in the pit at Woodhorn. He is of an old musical family, his father having played in northern theatre orchestras for over 36 years. Leslie is 27 years of age and his hobby, apart from music, is sketching in black and white. William Edward Ord, trumpeter, pianist and accordionist, works on a conveyor at Linton Colliery. He has fourteen gold and silver medals for performance with the cornet in local brass bands. In addition to his musical interests he experiments with television.

The solo accordionist chosen is the long-limbed William 'Buck' Milburn, who is a shift worker at Lynemouth. Born in Ashington, he is twenty years of age. When nine years old he had a couple of years' tuition on the piano, but in a short time he turned to the accordion and acquired an instrument when he was fourteen. Today Buck Milburn is one of the most popular of local concert artistes. Apart from the occasional game of billiards, all his spare time is occupied to perfecting his technique as an accordionist.

Johnnie 'Taffy' Williams, a Lancashire lad who is now a fully naturalised Ashingtonian who works on the coal cutters at Woodhorn, is another of the successful candidates for radio fame; his song and patter act having been chosen for inclusion in the broadcast programme.

During the broadcast there will be a few minutes of vocal harmony by the Wansbeck Gleemen, a quartet of singers, all of whom work for the ACC and graduated from the Ashington Parish Church choir. George Turnbull, first bass, is an ACC draughtsman, and is leader of the church choir. This quartet was formed in 1924 and George was one of the founder members. First tenor, Ernie Hamilton, is taking the tenor lead in the Linton Operatic Society's forthcoming production of HMS Pinafore. He was a member of the Ashington Welfare Rugby first XV. He is a coal cutter at Linton Colliery. Second tenor, William Henry 'Hennor' Wanless, is a coal filler at Ashington. He has been in the church choir since his boyhood days and is to be the next Toc H Secretary and is an Assistant Scoutmaster. Second bass, Jack Summers, is Assistant Foreman Blacksmith at Ashington Colliery. Never ventures upon a solo, but confines himself to the quartet and church choir work.

All the artistes are now bound by contract to appear in the programme and are anticipating mixed feeling the day of the broadcast, when they will have to put in five hours rehearsal at the studio for acts, none of which occupy more than five minutes.

1930s NEWS IN BRIEF

1930 – Ellington Pit baths open, the first in Northumberland; Ashington Colliery 'buzzer-time' ends; Ashington Institute opened by Manny Shinwell.; Ashington Welfare Men's hockey team beat Bede College 4 – 1 with goals from Robertson and Tapson.

1931 – Seven-and-a-half hour Coal Mines Act passed; death of Arthur J Cook, secretary of Miners Federation; death of George Arrowsmith whose shop dominated the Grand Corner for over 50 years; Ashington cricket team successes with bat and ball included Tim Brown, Bart Conn, Len Finlay and Joe Ward.

1932 – First Ashington & District Advertiser printed; electric wiring installed at 118 Ashington colliery houses at a cost of £2-18-0d each; former Hirst East schoolboy J R Richardson plays leading part in Newcastle United's controversial FA Cup win over Arsenal; pit pony races held at People's Park; Mr Fred Booth handed over the 'Booth' Cup to be contested annually in Welfare League.

1933 – On 1st December, the Cubs, Scouts and Rovers of the 4th Hirst (St John's) held a combined family night in their headquarters; troop flags were dedicated by the Rev J S Turnbull; Ashington pit canteen celebrates their 10th anniversary with record sales of milk; Mining School student successes included Dave Armatage, Len Morris, William Gustard and Eric Wade.

1934 – Running water connected to houses in 7th Row; Duke Street Depot opens with Jimmy Little as manager; in April, Florrie Ford stars at Miners' Theatre; report on Nutrition states that miners, because of their strenuous work, should have an intake of 4,600 calories a day; after several years delay, Lynemouth Colliery at last to be 'fully equipped'; Scouters who judged this year's sports included George Tomlinson, Joe Tomlinson, Wilf Kirkup, Robert Guy, Jack Dorgan, Richard Miles, Ferguson, Pears, Finnegan, Waite and Wanless. Ross Miles acted as secretary.

1935 – Bob Taylor elected MP for Morpeth (Ashington was then included in that constituency), he held seat until death in 1954; first safety helmets worn at Ashington Pit; Nichol, Trobe and Fitzpatrick buy Harmonic Hall for £1,400 with lease on Billiard Room of £1 per week; in a Badminton tournament, it was stated in the ACC magazine that 'Mary Scott played remarkably well'; Evening Class results held at Hirst South School saw successes for George Dodd Bell, David Kinnaird, John Robertson Williams, George Norman Chicken and John Thomas Steele.

1936 – Greyhound Racing begins at Portland Park; Northumberland "Worst county in England for overcrowding" of 60,000 working-class families; Long-service awards to Mining were given out to John Crawford of Woodhorn Road, George Hunter, Patrick Arnott and Bob Wilkinson all of Chestnut Street, Thomas Grieves 10th Row, Joe Ord of Bolsover Street, and Tom Dixon of the 8th Row.

1937 – A reunion of former scouts was arranged by 1st Hirst Scout Group to be held in their headquarters at St George's Hall, Old Lane, Ashington; Physical Training Display at Portland Park in July during Ashington Youth Festival; the movie 'Dimples' starring Shirley Temple shown at Miners' Theatre; massive bonfire lit in Peoples Park celebrating Coronation of King George VI and Queen Elizabeth.

1938 – Agreement reached on Miners' Holidays with Pay; 2,125 pits now operating in UK, a drop of over one-third in 25 years; Coal Industry only attracts £18 million investment compared with four times that amount for Retailing; survey shows that 51 MPs hold directorships in Coal and allied industries; First Aid awards given out to Jean Cairns, Mary Summers, Mary Bell, Florence Parry, Ray Graham, Alice Kirsopp, Ina Jackson, Jean Duddridge, Jean Henderson, Ethel Douglas, Ella Hedley, Margaret Goldsbury and Nellie Redpath.

1939 – Second World War starts; schools affected and some pupils are taught privately; first Air Raid alert in Ashington in December lasts for one and a half hours; Miners' Theatre revamped to become Regal Cinema; North Seaton Colliery Band notch up a hat-trick of victories at Miners' Picnic held in Morpeth; It was reported that there were 50 Co-op Stores trading in Ashington and District; in Ashington Welfare Midget League, 15-year-old Jackie Milburn turned out for Hirst East Old Boys together with Dickie Freeman, Jackie Donkin and Nichol Dalkin to beat Linton Juniors 10-0; Air Raid Certificates presented to Margaret Abbott, Margaret Craigs, Ethel and Maud Pattison, Doris Robinson and Linda Summers. (Note – Linda went on to write *'The Pit Village and the Store'* and other books).

The Ashington Cricket team that played in 1930s and beyond.

Ashington Rugby Club had a healthy squad of players at the 'Rec' in late 1940s.

THE 1940s

Woodhorn Colliery (above) had two direct hits on the afternoon of Saturday 20th December, 1941. One demolished the fan-house and a second damaged the boiler house and screens. Being a Saturday, few men were at work and no one was seriously hurt.

With the onset of the Second World War, King Coal was suddenly in its supremacy and the Ashington Group of Collieries could not get enough men and boys. Coalmining was deemed a deferred industry, meaning miners were not required to enlist in the Armed Forces. Some men who had actually joined up in the first month of the conflict in September 1939 were released from duties to return to their collieries. Isn't it strange how successive governments only turned to the miners in times of crisis? But it was full steam ahead for the country, and the black diamonds were needed to fuel train and ship engines, to feed furnaces in manufacturing, and to keep the home fires burning in colliery rows from Myrtle to Maple Street and from the Cross Row to the Long Row.

Although many of them didn't know it at the time, the children of Ashington were among the first to be affected by the War. Initially, many schools were closed so that effective sand-bagging and taping of windows could be carried out. Education was haphazard as children attended school for a half a day; some children even going to private houses to be taught. Priority was given to pupils who were about to sit the 'scholarship', an early version of the eleven plus.

As the War dragged on to the early 1940s, shortages of foodstuff and household commodities meant only one thing: large queues. Folk often joined a queue without even knowing what it was that was available. When some luxury item arrived, word spread like wildfire: It only took the words: *'Hey, Jinny, there's tabs at the Store'*, for dozens of pinny-clad housewives to leave the dishes draining in the scullery sink to hurry up the street to stand in a long queue and, if they were lucky, to come away smiling, clutching a packet of Woodbines for the 'owld chep'.

The very young children were deprived without being aware of it. Never having had the choice of grapes or bananas, peaches or nectarines, I thought that the gooseberries and strawberries grown on our allotment beside the old Ashington Hospital were the only fruit that existed – apart from an orange and an apple that mysteriously appeared in my father's pit stocking, hung at the bottom of the bed on a Christmas morning. Chocolates and sweets were strictly rationed on a points system. An 'E' coupon enabled you to guzzle a quarter pound of Maynard's Wine Gums, while a 'D' only got you two ounces or a small bar of Five Boys chocolate. With materials also scarce, children's toys were usually made of wood: forts, tops and whips. There were no footballs, so us lads had to make do with kicking pieces of material, like felt, stitched into a round shape and stuffed with clippings left over from a proggy mat. But there was always a tin can lying around in the gutter to kick and chase on the way to school.

Fish and chip suppers were a luxury even for the well-off, and many shops vied for customers – at one time no fewer than 27 fish-fryers opened nightly in the streets and avenues of Ashington. Most folk proved loyal to one shop whether to be in the Hirst with Renzo Cosimini's, opposite the Mortimer Club, Meg Dawson's in First Avenue or Baileys in Hawthorn Road. At the top end of Ashington, Cuthbertson's was a good place to visit after coming out of the Regal Cinema or even rolling drunk from the Portland Arms.

Air-raid warnings during the war often came in the middle of the night and when the sound of the siren blasted out from on top of the Police Station, my mother would lift me out of bed and carry me downstairs to the flat below – we then lived around 100 Poplar Street – where our neighbours, the Lynch's, had converted some space below the stairs where we huddled until the All-clear went. For some reason, folk thought that this was the safest place in the house. Many people crouched under Morrison shelters (a steel table) while others, my father among them, said that if they had to die they would prefer it to be in their own beds.

Many Wartime concerts took place in Workingmen's Clubs, such as a 'Weekly Concert for Soldiers' every Monday evening at the Middle Market with pianist Raffy Reay; the Hirst Progressive Social Club ran concerts: 'To provide Xmas gifts for members and members' sons serving in His

Majesty's Forces'. Artistes engaged included Madam Poxton, Peter Rigg, and O'Keefe the Comedian, with concert chairman Temp Atkinson and Mrs G Thompson on piano. The Comrades and Fell 'em Doon ran a Sunday Night Go-As-You-Please with a two-pound first prize, featuring Tommy Camsell and Raffy Reay, respectively, on piano.

Ashington at Work and Play (The Times, July 1942)
Ashington is a one class and one industry town. 30,000 people live here, and all their activity centres round the colliery, noted for many years of prosperous and liberal management. The town is alive with the virile energy of the mining community. There is more uniform prosperity than in many places where the earning of the few may be higher.
The main street on a Saturday evening is crowded: the men in smart blue suits, hanging somewhat loosely around the hips, owing to their triangular physique; the women of a smartness comparable with Regent Street and beautifully 'permed' (there are seventeen women's hairdressers in Ashington).

Before going further into how miners enjoy themselves on Saturday night, one must recall the toughness of the job they have to do. On a weekday, going to and from their shifts, they are constantly moving along the street in small groups, dressed in loose, dirty clothes. There is never a real rush at particular times, as with factory workers.

Arrived at the bottom of the pit, they have a long walk to the face, at least a mile, sometimes two miles. The phrase goes that 'a man works a hard shift when he walks in-bye' – in Northumberland 'work' and 'walk' are pronounced the same. Stooping down, bending sideways, and watching the roof so as not to bump ones head. Stone dust on the floor, laid to prevent possible coal dust explosion, rises in your face and muffles your footsteps.

It is pitch dark where you do not shine your lamp; it is, of course, very quiet. You do not meet many people, it seems deserted. Sweating, you arrive at the face. This is a narrow seam (the narrowest in Ashington) – it is 24 inches high, with five more inches cut out of the stone. This means that the entrance looks like the opening of a dog kennel, 29 inches high. The fillers crouch, shovelling the coal on the conveyor.

"Divven't gan up and tell them it's an easy life," the fillers told me with a laugh, hearing I was a newspaper man. That miners do not want to send their sons down the pit, that they resent being on lower rates of pay than other skilled workers, that they stay away on Saturday and Monday – this is more easily understood when you have just re-ascended to the pit-head, with the tremendous din of discharging tubs and smell of acetylene where the men opened their lamps. The pit is worse and better than you thought; less noisy, less smelly and stuffy, lonelier, darker, far more unlike the surface than you had imagined.

Production for the Ashington group of collieries was four million tons a year before the War began. Present figures are not available, but everybody agreed that output had gone down since the War, and nearly all gave different reasons. Probably the biggest is call-up.

The four cinemas in Ashington include the large, splendid Regal, which used to be the Miners' Theatre, built by the miners until it was bought up by the cinema company. The cinemas are nearly always full. On Saturday evening one was showing a full house card for the second time that night. With a bi-weekly change of programme it is possible to go every night of the week and many of the boys do so.

At the dog track, which has races every Saturday, I found about 4,000 men, mostly dressed in their blue suits. On three races, the bets registered by the Tote were 1,052, 949 and 1,375. Here the betting units are of two shillings, but I saw men pulling out their pound notes to bet with the bookies. A young man, asked why he came to the dogs, said *"There's nowt else to spend me money on."*

At one of the two dance halls, I found over 1,000 dancers on Saturday night. The Princess Ballroom is open all the week, four nights for dancing, two for roller skating; entrance 6d on weekdays, 1s on Saturdays. Since the war, they come earlier and stay to the end. Alf Shepherd, the manager, said: *"Like the butterflies, they like to be where the bright lights are."* On Monday night, I found nearly as many people again, mainly young men, coal fillers, soldiers, young girls dressed beautifully. This was the Jitterbugs' night. More than 100 couples 'jittered' with tremendous energy and skill. Whirling, bouncing and executing a fantastic, rapid, mark-time with their feet.

All the cottages have gardens, mostly well kept. Just now, people are beginning to nurture their leeks, in preparation for the great leek shows in the late autumn, which are carried on in the Working Men's Clubs for over a month, with people touring the clubs to see the shows. A week before a leek is shown, it is visited and stamped as it grows, so that there can be no showing of leeks grown in other gardens. Miners do not stick to vegetables alone; there are plenty of flowers.

The remarkable Ashington Art Group (whose paintings were seen in London and made a deep impression) is the undoubted fine flower of Ashingtonian culture. It is still going strong with fourteen members, each with an individual and striking talent.

From an Ashington Window (Morpeth Herald – 26th April, 1940)
Record of 'failure'. Various records are held by public men and County Councillor Will Cookson holds more than a few, but as a member of the Ashington Council he holds a record the like of which has never happened and probably will never happen again. Indeed, while figures are not available, it is safe to say that the record extends far beyond the confines of Northumberland County. Where is there a local councillor who has been *unsuccessfully* nominated for Chairmanship of his local authority more often than Mr Cookson?

This may appear a derogatory sort of record, but it is due to the overwhelming majority of the Labour Party on the Ashington Council, together with a persistence of certain Independent members in putting forward his claims despite the fact that they have never had, in recent years, a voting strength of more than five out of twenty to back their nomination. Annual appeals to the Labour majority to break away from the Party line and elect to the chair an able administrator with a long record of service, a man who tops the poll in each election, fall on deaf ears. Labour had a long spell in the minority some years ago, and now that they have secured power they are not likely to relinquish it until they are out-voted.

Any Other Business (Morpeth Herald – 26 April, 1940)
The new Chairman of the Ashington Council got an early opportunity to exert his authority last week, when he found it necessary to rule a member out of order when he tried to raise a new subject of discussion on 'any other business'. There were isolated protests when the Chairman, supported by the Clerk, ruled that 'any other business' did not mean what it said – that is, any other business – but any business on the agenda which had been inadvertently passed over without being presented to the meeting. Obviously there existed in the minds of one or two members the idea that this loose phrase, loosely employed in more free and easy organisations, should be interpreted literally in Council affairs. It is certainly the practice in many organisations, and often provides most of the excitement and controversy, for 'any other business', in some quarters is a signal for all-in scrapping, during which all and sundry mount their particular hobby horses.

The war affected the printing trade more than most and the Ashington Advertiser ceased publication at the back end of 1941 for the duration. Edwin Norman Davison, the boss, was called up as a sapper in the Royal Engineers and another partner, Billy Davison, went into the Navy, while Charlie Marshal, was conscripted into the Royal Artillery. This left Bridget Davison and her three sons, Norman, Tony and Terry to carry on as best they could, still printing lottery and dance tickets as well as greyhound programmes which were done at the Morpeth Herald printers.

In June 1941, a journalist for the *Blyth News* reported: 'A small poorly dressed woman approached me as I was waiting for a bus to Ashington. She asked if I would go into a shop and buy her a packet of cigarettes for her husband. I had to refuse as I knew very few women are served with cigarettes nowadays, and certainly never in a shop where they are unknown.'

A week later, it was reported that a lady butcher had been fined for selling rabbits at a price above the going rate of 10d a pound. She was charging one shilling and tuppence for skinned rabbit, and was fined £4 plus costs.

Many Ashington housewives cheered when they heard that the Northumberland Miners Association had decided to make Thursday a payday rather than Friday. One miner's lady remarked: 'With shops closing early and limited stocks going so quickly, a Thursday payday will give us a chance to do our weekend shopping before the last minute.'

Ashington Youth Group Debate (Morpeth Herald – 27th June, 1941)
At a mock Parliamentary debate staged by the Ashington branch of the British Federation of Co-operative Youth, the 'Government' facing a vote of censure tabled by the 'Opposition' had a rough passage and escaped

defeat by a narrow margin of one vote.

The Ashington Co-operative Youth Group, who meet weekly, have interesting programmes, which include social evenings, parlour games, general knowledge tests, spelling bees, talks and debates, have already staged a mock Council meeting and plans are being made to enact mock police court sittings and a breach of promise trial. The mock Parliamentary debate was considered to be a natural step forward after the successful experiment with the Council meeting and the event provided the members with an amusing and instructive evening. Taking part in the Parliamentary debate were: The Right Hon. Billy Gibson, member for Maple Street North; Jack Southcott, member for Maple Street Centre; Prime Minister Colin McNiven; Captain Frank McGuckin, Secretary for War; Miss Margaret Swann, Minister for Home Security; Miss Peggy White, Minister for Food; and vote tellers Terry Bowman and Miss Milly Raye.

The Ashington Group of Painters received a timely pat on the back from Lady Ridley when she opened an exhibition of their work in the Laing Art Gallery in Newcastle, in June 1941. She invited the artists to visit her at Blagdon Hall. James Brownrigg accepted on behalf of the Group.

The vexed problem of Sport on Sunday was solved by Ashington Council passing, by fourteen votes to six, that: 'Sunday games be allowed in the Veterans' Hut at Hirst Flower Park. Prior to this, the man in charge of the Park had been struck by an old man while trying to take away his dominoes.

In December 1943, when I was nine years old, my mother announced one Friday morning just before Christmas: '*Howay, Michael, put yor coat on, we're gannin to get a cream cake at Donkin's.*' Now cream cakes were in extremely short supply during wartime, and those that were made available in shops like Donkin's meant long, long queues. Anyway, we gets to the baker's shop beside the Wallaw Cinema and, sure enough, a straggly line of women stretched almost as far as the bus station. Without any hesitation, mother marched up to the front of the queue, into the small shop, and said: '*One jam sponge cream cake, please.*' I was amazed that no one complained, though one or two ladies gave my mother a suspicious look. It transpired that pregnant women were allowed to go to the front of the queue at Donkin's the Bakers on a Friday morning. My brother John was born a week or so later.

The 1st January 1944 arrived in Ashington on a wash-day-blues Monday. Folks didn't know it, but the end of the War was still eighteen months away, and even if they had been told, few would have believed it. Pessimism and optimism had merged into one, as reflected in the speech given by Alderman Will Cookson at a safety awards ceremony to LNER motor drivers at the Grand Hotel:

"I envisage a time when the ordinary man, enjoying holidays with pay, will own a cheap car in which he can take his family into the country. I wonder whether Ashington's antiquated system of arterial roads can carry with safety the increased volume of traffic which will ensue after the exceptional developments which can be expected in the motor industry after the war."

Sport, like most things in Ashington, was still rationed in January 1944; Ashington football club still kept their promise of the previous year *not* to play in the North Eastern League until the cessation of hostilities. Not so patriotic, the Ashington Greyhound Racing Company held a dog meeting at Portland Park every Saturday afternoon. Winner of the first race of the year was the evergreen KTM with Dashing Corporal coming in a close second. At the famous New Year's Day Powderhall meeting in Edinburgh, local lads Ossie Sword and RJ Hale both won heats; and Tom O'Keefe, the Lynemouth-born boxer, defeated Seaman Davis of Chatham on points over ten rounds.

Attention was drawn to the problem of pit heaps on 10th March 1944. It was already recognized that they presented a serious health problem to the town. Further reinforcement was provided by the Northumberland Association of Urban Councils which reported: 'The new process of delivering refuse on to Ashington heaps increases the height thereof, with the result that light and breathing space is being depleated. This, coupled with the smoke and fumes, is bound to have a detrimental effect on the health of the community.'

With regard to the above, Ashington Colliery had just introduced an aerial ropeway system to carry its waste from the heapstead in the colliery yard to the sprawling tip. Gangs of small boys gathered to watch, fascinated, as cable-car buckets transported their unwanted cargo to the top of the festering black slope. The pit heap often flared into life as the contents were strewn from above. It became a leisure activity for the children as the giant mountain turned into an escalating Everest on their doorstep. Winnie Oxnard's father and brothers ran a building firm from their house in Council Road, only a couple of hundred yards from the pit heap. She said: 'It was my job to get up at six o'clock to polish the brass plate we had fixed near our front door. In less than an hour, it had been all discoloured by the fumes from the heap ... and, oh, the smell.'

The Porter Award Minimum Pay for Miners came into force in February 1944, meaning that underground workers were guaranteed a minimum of £5 a week. But the scheme was closely linked to stop absenteeism (always a bug-bear in the industry). Anyone who lost a shift risked being fined and sacked. It was looked upon as a serious dereliction of duty, akin to cowardice in the face of the enemy. Fining one man ten shillings, Ashington magistrate William Reavley, asked witheringly: 'Do you want our men to fight with their bare hands?'

In 1944, after I had spent a year in the 'Big School' at St Aidan's with schoolteacher Stephen Shippen, who would have made an excellent Captain Bligh, it was a great relief to head for the relatively safe harbour of Standard IV and Maisie White, later to become Mrs Mazzolini. She taught the scholarship class, equivalent to the 11-plus. It was mainly through her skill and endeavour that seven of us – six lads and Bernadette McDonald – all obtained Grammar School places in Newcastle: boys to St Cuthbert's; Bernie to the Convent of the Sacred Heart in Fenham.

When the exam results arrived at St Aidan's one Monday morning in May 1945 the headmaster Mr McGough entered our room. This wasn't strange as he came in every Monday morning, asking who had been to church the previous day. And it was no use telling fibs because he attended all three masses. We had a standing joke in school, a verse which went: *"Mr McGough has a bad cough, he goes to church on Sundays. He prays to God to give him strength to whack the kids on Mondays."* But there was no whacking from McGough that day. He waltzed in, smiling, as though he'd just entered the Pearly Gates, and whispered something to Maisie who returned his grin. And then he announced the seven names of those who had been successful, in what, to be honest, was simply a basic IQ test based on multiple choice questions, on arithmetic, grammar and common sense.

To have *seven* passes was a great occasion for the little school because, up until then, if even one pupil managed to scrape through the exam then that was a major event. But here we were, this magnificent seven, destined for greatness, or so we thought. Children are heartless, self-centred creatures, and it never once crossed my mind to feel sorry for some of my other classmates, who must have been on the borderline between passing and being passed over. If they were disappointed I never noticed; if they shed silent tears, I smiled at the thought of a new bike that had been dangled in front of me as a bribe by my mother all those months before.

We successful pupils were allowed to go home to tell our mothers – the fathers would all be at the pit – by then it was almost 11 am. I raced along Station Road, pedestrian as well as traffic free, turned down into North Seaton Road, past the old men sitting outside the Priestman's Institute, round Renzo Cossimini's fish shop into Milburn Road, then home to number 67 Pont Street. Mother was obviously delighted, but I had no idea of the expense that going to Grammar School would entail. On top of my new bike, black and shiny, purchased at Main's the Cycle Shop, there was the cost of being rigged out at Isaac Walton's, a shop in Newcastle, catering exclusively for the city schools.

Up until then I had gone to school in my everyday clothes. Now a new red blazer was obligatory, together with grey shorts – I never wore long trousers until I was almost 15 – a pullover, red cap, tie and scarf in the school's colours of red and mauve. Then there was a football strip, yellow for my house of Wickwar, shorts, stockings, satchel, fountain pen; the list was endless. But I was a thoughtless arrogant boy, taking for granted that there was money in the family coffers available to buy everything. To cap it all, within two short years, after having my head stuffed with facts on Algebra, Trigonometry, History, Chemistry, French and Latin, I was back at St Aidan's, taken out of the Grammar because of a stupid boyish misdemeanour. Yet that prank proved almost disastrous, knocking me off a life-course that took me over twenty years to correct. But that was far from my mind one day in 1944 as I waited outside the back gate of the huge Co-op building in Woodhorn Road. I was there to try to cadge a lift on one of the horse-drawn wagons that left the Co-op each Friday afternoon laden with groceries that had been ordered by customers who lived too far away to collect their own. Once I was in luck and was taken on by Jack Gaffney, one of the horse drivers. I felt like a million bucks sat up there next to Jack, like a guy riding shotgun in a Wells Fargo western. We must have travelled miles to outlying districts such as Lynemouth, Ellington, Stobswood and Red Row. A much-loved and respected character, Jack later became a chauffeur and then worked for the Co-op funeral department.

As an adolescent, I began to notice girls. One of lasses I took a fancy to lived in the even numbers of Pont Street just after the War. Her name was Maureen Poole and she had the most wonderful auburn/bronze hair. I recall that once I went to an all-night dance at North Seaton Welfare because I knew she would be there. But I sat from midnight right through till five o'clock in the morning, too shy and gauche to dare ask her up for a dance. She later married one of my pals from Pont Street, Bobby Lisle. Maureen, who sadly died a couple of years ago, is seen in this 1946 school photo.

Hirst Park Modern Girls 'Tyne' Class, 1946. Back row left Mary Hall, Joan Taylor, Maureen Poole, Rita Merryweather, Maybeth Yates, Ann Crooks, Ann Robson, Shirley Crosby, Clorinda Arthur, Freda Wilkinson, Shirley Patterson, Glenda Morse, Freda Wyley, Joan Harrison. Middle row Headteacher Miss Winnie Auty, Margaret Younger, Joan Lawson, Joan Shields, Minnie Burrell, Audrey Birnie, Sylvia Stephenson, Marjorie Cuthbert, Joan Baker, Mina Morse, Jean Taylor, Margaret Auld, teacher Miss Youngs. Front row Angela Brannigan, Dorothy Corbett, Audrey Jobson, Jenny Swan, Mary Langen, Margaret Aisbett, Vera Lyndsell, Joan Bartholomew, Mildred Steele, Lillian Downie, Jessie Robinson, Nora Laws and Betty Taylor.

Bevin Boys at Ashington
In Britain near the end of World War II a new term entered the vocabulary. Bevin Boys were young men selected by ballot to work in a coal mine instead of doing conventional military service. They were named after Ernest Bevin, Minister of Labour from 1940-45, who originated the scheme. Contrary to what some people believe, these young men did not volunteer to go down the pit in order to avoid military service. They had no choice.

Tommy Hughes of Liverpool wrote: "I was called up in February 1944 and went to Cramlington to do my training; there I lodged with a family in Jesmond, called Cunningham. I was soon moved to Ashington and lived with Mr and Mrs Hall in Pont Street.

"My first job was hanging empty tubs onto the endless-rope haulage system after they came out of the cage. After that I went on putting, where the ponies were great. I had some good marras too, such as Aubrey Keech. Billy Bolam, Big Geordie Pye and many others.

"Being very interested in football, I played for Ashington Reserves, Fell 'em Doon and Barrington United. My first club was Ashington YMCA with Mr Pearson as Secretary. Bobby Gibson played, Bobby Sweet and the Weddell twins. I was then working in the Duke Pit on filling alongside Bobby York, the Thompsons – father and sons – and Alec Milburn (Wor Jackie's father). Some days we used to go to Newbiggin and train on the beach after doing foreshift. Stan Miburn and Dickie Slaughter were another couple of lads who went with us. I returned to my home town of Liverpool in 1949 after marrying a local lass. We celebrated our Golden Anniversary in Australia."

On 6th March 1944, Cllr John Brotherton likened Ashington's allotment holders to: 'Everybody's Cinderellas.' This was because two more sites of gardens were being lost; the first because of a new extension to the Darnley Road Mining school and the second to make way for 120 houses at the end of Woodhorn Road, destined to become Woodhorn Villas.

At an exhibition of Children's Art on 9th March 1944, HM Spink, Director of Education, said: 'Ashington is one of the liveliest communities in the county, in the widest sense of the word.' The school children's display was combined with the work of the Ashington Art Group, its excellence prompting Cllr Hugh Reilly to comment: 'Although Ashington could never be made into a health resort, much good is done by providing local people with the opportunity to view such wonderful works of Art. What the town needs now is a good public library.'

One fine Saturday afternoon in the summer of '44, ten thousand people crammed into Peoples' Park to see the many delightful exhibits at the Ashington and District Agricultural Show. The only unhappy people that day were a group of ladies representing the Temperance Society who were objecting to the granting of a liquor licence allowing beer to be served from inside a tent.

Ashington Youth Clarion, by Miss Valerie Tully, County Youth Organiser

Ashington was one of the first Youth Councils to be formed in the country and the first in Northumberland. It was John Mordue of St Andrew's Youth Club who proposed the first County Youth Council Conference and, later, the first and only National Youth Council Conference run by young people.

St George's Presbyterian Church FOY (Fellowship of Youth) and Ashington YMCA provided the main support from young people for the first Remscheid visit. (later 'twinned' with Ashington). Alan Robson, a local reporter and great friend of Youth, was advisor to the Youth Clarion editorial group. (*Extracts follow from 1945 Youth Clarion):*

Bouquets for Boys and Girls

Almost every youth group in the area contributed to the success of Youth Week (9th – 15th June 1945). Four hundred young people took part in the games, dancing, Scouts' Model camp, and Young Farmers' Display on Saturday.

On Monday, Boxing in the Arcade Hall, and PT and Keep Fit in the Mining School, were well supported. St Aidan's boxing club and the Sea Cadets were largely responsible for these two attractions. The Girls Life Brigade, the Co-op Youth Club and Sea Cadet Hedley provided the programme for Wednesday's Youth Theatre.

On Friday, over 200 people attended the Swimming Gala where only two girls competed, but boys from the YMCA, the Mining school, the Sea Cadets, the Scouts and the Young Farmers competed. The treasurer Mr R Garbutt reports the week was a financial success.

Larry Bell's Boys

Should anyone ask you where the Ashington Athletic Boys' Club is held you should direct them to Park View, the home of Larry Bell. It was he who built the club up to what it is today (1945) with about 100 members, from the age of 14 up to young men in their late twenties.

The Club is open every day of the week where restricted accommodation is the only drawback – they have two wooden huts at their disposal, one of which is used as a workshop in which machines are set up such as a metal lathe, wood lathe, electric drill, circular saw and welding machine. Also in this room is a store-room, office and club-leader's room. The other hut is used as a canteen and entertainments' room, holding a piano and half-size billiard table.

In their boxing honours list is one Alan Robson, undefeated Schoolboy Boxing Champion of the North of England, but unfortunately a few months ago he had an accident at work at the colliery which resulted in the amputation of his left leg. However, he remains cheerful and is a keen Club member.

Ashington Mining Students

When school was resumed for the winter session in September 1944, it was decided to form an organization which would safeguard the students' interests. The principal, Mr Charles Pulford, suggested supplying mid-morning refreshments which had to be organized by students, so a students' association was formed.

In April, new committee members were elected and a constitution was drawn up. A Sports Committee was formed to organize inter-class and inter-school games. In Youth Week a swimming team was selected. At the end of the term, social events for the students were arranged.

Venture – Adventure
In 1941, an Air Training Corps Squadron was set up in the Mining school to act as a feeding ground for the RAF to whom they have given 80 members. The main pioneer of the Squadron was Mr Robert L Hay, then principal of the Ashington Mining School where the ATC had its first headquarters.

Training there consists of squad drill, physical training, arms drill, rifle shooting, mathematics, Morse, navigation, aero engines, machine guns and workshop practice. At one time the ATC had 120 members, now that figure is down to 60, all those keen on pre-service training having joined HM Services.

They also had many flights in aircraft when visiting aerodromes. Their sideline is Sport, and through the ability of their trainer, Mr Morton, they have done well. Several of the boys gained honours in county football teams, one gaining international honours.
(Note – one ATC member in those days was the legendary Jackie Milburn)

St Andrew's Youth Club
The Club has done a good deal of country dancing, full use having been made of Miss Vida Sample's class held in the Park School, while Miss Perry also provided coaching in Netball. Recently, club members helped to present two plays – *More than Conquerors* and *Choose Ye* – the restoration of the Church Hall *(on Third Avenue)* is welcomed as giving scope of further development of Youth Club activities.

The Church Youth Club meets regularly each week on a Tuesday evening, but now that the ARP services have vacated the Parish Hall, more frequent meetings are anticipated. The Club is linked with the Church Youth Fellowship which meets on Sunday mornings for instruction and discussion on matters of the Christian Faith.

Ashington folk were well used to queuing as the War dragged on into its sixth year, but it was waiting of a different sort that was queried by Ashington councillors following complaints that the cinema queues at the Regal were getting out of hand. It was suggested that the cinema management bring back the system of booking seats in advance which had worked so well in the past. A councillor remarked: 'No Ashington housewife wants to spend all day working in the kitchen, then, just when she should be putting her feet up, be asked to spend up to an hour in this time-wasting exercise.' But queuing for the Regal pictures was made more tolerable if you had a Pieroni's ice cream to lick to help you pass the time away in the queue which often meandered around St Aidan's School as far as Larry Bell's Boys Club headquarters in Park View.

The Italian connection, with regard to opening up ice cream and fish 'n' chip shops in Ashington, can probably be traced back to one Alfredo Marchetti who began selling fruit at 41 Station Road, next to the Buffalo Picture Hall, in 1911. Below the shop, in the basement, Alfredo, using ice-packed hand-filled freezers, made his first helping of delicious ice cream. His brother, Guiseppe, opened up a confectioner's at 10 Station Road, but left after a couple of years. Alfredo was married in 1918 to a sweet Italian girl called Amelia Rossi.

Together they changed the name of the shop to the Station Temperance Bar. By then many of the town's workingmen's clubs had opened, selling Federation Ale from their own brewery. But the shrewd, business-minded Italian knew that there was still a need for a place where the *women* of the town could congregate. He brought in an American Soda Fountain which he had seen working while on a brief working visit to the States. The shop proved extremely successful so Alfredo was able to employ three more Italians who came from the same part of Tuscany: Giovanni Rossi, Renato (Sammy) Badiali and Christopher Arrighi. In the course of time, all three left to start up on their own. Other Italians followed: Lorenzo Cosimini had a fish shop over the road from the Mortimer Club; his brother Harry owned a similar business on Seventh Avenue; Peter Mazzolini opened another Temperance Bar on Station Road, near the Miners' Theatre; the Pieronis also set up on Station Road where Bobby and his sister Norma occupied various premises before eventually settling in the shop opposite the council chambers. Bimbi had a fish shop next to the Arcade on Woodhorn Road.

Other Italians who came to Ashington but didn't settle included Gallone and Notarianni, both from the Naples area, as was Fella who ran a bus service in the early 1930s from Ashington to remote parts of Northumberland. One who did stay was Bertorelli, but he settled in Newbiggin; a daughter Giaconda, played piano with great expertise at many concert halls all over England before retiring to the fishing village as a teacher of pianoforte.

When the Second World War broke out, because Italians were thought to be a 'security risk', some of the older men were interned as prisoners of war on the Isle of Man. One such man was Jimmy Padretti, then living at Cresswell, who had been appointed as a part-time coastguard before Italy entered the War. This ludicrous situation was quickly resolved and the Italian prisoners, who also included Rossi and Badiali, were allowed to return to Ashington.

Ashington was Always a Rough, Tough Mining Town where men were men and women were . . . yes, they were content to take a back seat in the very early days, to bear and rear sons to take their places down the pit and to bring up girls to be servile and well-equipped with culinary skills. But the second war changed all that. Women found themselves needed for other tasks beyond child-bearing, and the era of emancipation began.

Ashington Business and Professional Women's Club was founded in 1945. It was soon attracting attention from all sides of the community. One of the most outspoken members was Mrs Eva Stimpson, whose husband Vic owned a bakery in Woodhorn Road. As the club's secretary in 1948, she wrote the following open letter to the people of Ashington:

"There are quite a number of keen-minded, spirited women in our town, but up to the present time they have usually been content to labour in the background, and to carry out those tasks allotted to the female, such as voluntary work in the social and public health service. There are those amongst us who will suggest that a woman's place is in the home with her family, but it should be stressed that a woman's concern for her family necessitates her interest in local government and national affairs as much as her interest in home-making. She must be prepared to accept outside responsibilities and women's organisations should aim to train individuals to accept public office as readily as men.

"Marriage does not mean the sinking of one personality in another, but should tend to develop own personalities to mutual advantage. Man generally is still a little jealous of women's intrusion into public life and of repeated proofs of her ability. A woman herself is her own severest critic, she needs to dispel that feeling of inferiority which is so apparent when she is asked to compete with men on equal footing."

During the club's AGM in September, 1949, Mrs Stimpson was elected Honorary President, following on from Mrs Jean Richardson. The latter had stung would-be male councillors by winning the seat as a Rent and Ratepayer candidate at an earlier council election. Other women on the committee included: Miss J Morris, Miss T Clarkson, Mrs E W Graham, Mrs E Harrison, Mrs Sarah Cook, Mrs Cookson, Miss Haggerty, Miss B McFarlane, Mrs Ina Deitz, Miss Audrey Stimpson, Miss Rogerson, and Mrs T W Furness.

The B & P ladies were not the only active female group in Ashington. Various women's guilds sprouted up all around the town depending on their location. The Co-operative Society's Women's Guild met regularly, as did the *Tuesday Afternoon Club,* who adopted the Great Ormond Street Children's Hospital, sending many donations of cash to help sick youngsters. More and more women of Ashington were *coming out,* and now it wasn't just the vociferous Women's Temperance League that was making its voice heard.

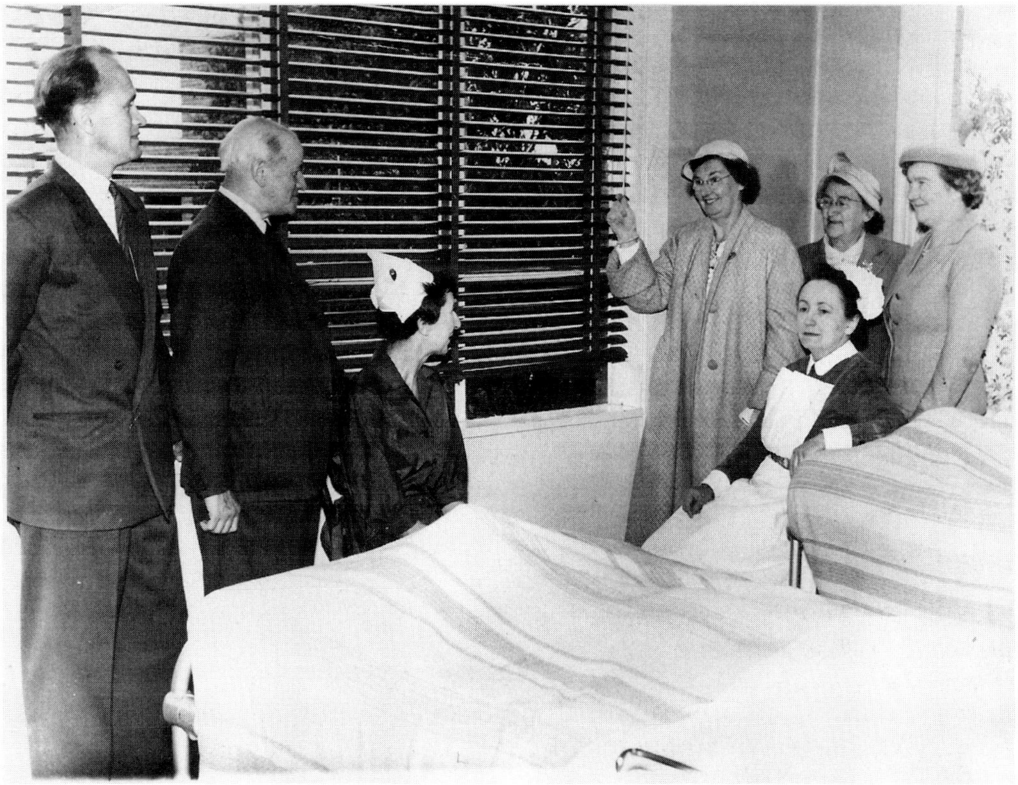

The League of Friends of Ashington Hospital hand over a blind costing £41-12-7d to one of the wards. From left Mr Wright (sec), Mr Scott (pres), Matron Olive Tanner, and founder members Mrs Eva Stimpson, Mrs Scott and Mrs Winifred Barron.

New Ashington Rotary Chief (Morpeth Herald – July, 1946)
Youth will be at the helm of Ashington Rotary Club during the next twelve months. In choosing as Club President, Mr W Proudlock, Managing Director of Messrs Proudlocks Ltd., Wholesale Bakers, the Rotarians have deviated from custom by conferring the high honour upon a member of the junior group within the club.

The Proudlock family have been in the business, in and around Ashington, for thirty six years, and the present modern mass-production bakery, with its sixty employees, at North Seaton Station had its origin in the small family bakery established in Morpeth by 'Granny' Proudlock. The new Rotary Chief is Vice President of the Mid-Northumberland Master Bakers' Association, and was, throughout the war, unpaid Area Liaison Officer for the Ministry of Food on the emergency bread supply scheme.

When able to lay aside the masses of official forms government departments require him to complete concerning his extensive training operations, Mr Proudlock takes an interest in the Ashington Cricket Club, Newbiggin Bowling Club, North Seaton Veterans' Institute, amateur theatricals, does a spot of woodwork, and is something of a specialist with cucumbers and tomatoes – although the last accomplishment is vehemently denied by his many rivals in this intensely competitive field.

The Eventful Year of 1947
Vesting Day for Ashington Colliery, 1st January (North Mail)
Impressive Ashington Pit Ceremony.
The gaudy red, blue and gold battle standard of the Ashington miners, an elaborately designed forty-year-old banner, embodying in bold text on vivid tableaux a demand for nationalisation, made its last public appearance on New Year's Day, when, with the Lynemouth Band in attendance, the men marched to the pit head for the ceremony to mark the transfer of the mines to public ownership.

At the colliery, to the accompaniment of enthusiastic cheering and a thirty second blast on the pit buzzer, the brand new blue and white flag of the National Coal Board and a commemorative plaque were unfurled and unveiled. The Ashington Council was well represented in the parade and at the subsequent meeting, and a welcome addition to the programme was the formal announcement that Mr Thomas Cowan of 28 Third Row, Ashington, a seventy-six-year-old coal filler, who had worked in the pit for fifty-five years, had received notification of the award of the BEM for services to the industry.

Mr John Elliott, President of the Ashington Miner's Federation, was in the chair, and speeches were made by Alderman William McLean, Divisional Deputy Director of Labour for the Coal Board, Mr Donald Hindson and Mr William Gibson (for the management), County Councillor Fred Bennett (Ashington UDC), and Mr Bill Allan (County Miners' Agent). The arrangements were in the hands of Councillor Frank Millican.

Fourteen-year-old William Ferguson of 127 Alexandra Road, and seventy-year-old Thomas Nicholson of 121 Hawthorn Road were the chosen representatives of youth and age in the coal industry in connection with the formal transference of the collieries from private to public ownership. In fifty-eight years of continuous service underground, Mr Nicholson has worked in every pit in the Ashington group and has tackled most jobs. He went into the pits at the age of twelve, following not only in the footsteps of his father, but also those of his grandfather. Today he has one son and two grandsons in the pits. He began at Longhirst Colliery as a trapper boy and remembers trudging through the snow from Longhirst to Ashington to attend mining classes.

The Winter of 1947 was one of the worst in living memory with snow and ice bringing industry to a halt and snowdrifts up to ten feet thick cutting off small villages like Newbiggin and Lynemouth, Widdrington and West Sleekburn from the main shopping centre at Ashington. Much use was made of the tankey from Linton to get folks into Ashington. Sport was hard hit with football matches postponed way into the following March. A report in the *Ashington Advertiser* for 22nd February 1947 stated 'There is a fifty-fifty chance of play at Portland Park on Saturday for the Northumberland Senior Cup 'derby' tie between

Ashington and Blyth Spartans. The Hirst end of the pitch is clear of snow but the west side is covered by a depth of snow of four inches. The bulk of the snow is expected to be cleared away by Saturday, although enough will be left to cover the hard turf underneath. The Colliers team will be chosen from Pattison, Grundy, Brown, Guthrie, Richardson, Jackie Clough, John 'Pop' Dodd, James, Billy Fenwick, Ray Poxon, Cyril Brown and John Homer.'

The Boiler Road to North Seaton was closed in 1947 and men had to come out of that pit to clear the way.

At the end of 1947 it was reported that a Jazz Jamboree had taken place at the Arcade Hall on Friday 5th December, in aid of the Musicians' Benevolent Fund, which had attracted over 500 dancers. A list of affiliated Musicians' Union bands which operated in the area was given: Harry Hogarth and his band; Joe Dalkin's Rhythm Boys; Steve Howard and his band; George Mason and his band; R Barron and his Boys; Arcadian Dance Orchestra; Jack Summers and his band; Gilbert Grieves and his band; Tommy Allison and his band; Dave Grieves and his band.

Earlier in the year, two local musicians had been well received at the Newcastle City Hall: 'Tommy Camsell, deputy at Woodhorn, was an outstanding artiste in the big Miners' Broadcast Show. He walked on to the platform to play before a vast audience and gave a magnificent interpretation of his own pianoforte composition "Happy Fingers".

'Another local entertainer who did well was Billy 'Buck' Milburn, accordionist. The concert was the first to be held under the auspices of the National Coal Board.'

Another concert covered in that 1947 edition of the *Ashington Advertiser* was headed 'Hospital Show by Ashington Entertainers: 'An excellent non-stop variety entertainment was given for patients of Wooley Sanitorium by members of the Ashington Thespian Operatic Society last week. Artistes were: Tommy Allison and his band (Jim Hunt, Alan

Armstrong, Hector Imrie, Harry Gordon), Edna Hudspeth, Olive Weddell, Stan Pearson, Billy Robinson, Dave Parker, JW Straker, Archie Summers and John Hodgson.

Ashington School Wins First Prizes in North Tourney (North Mail – May, 1947)

Ninety marks were gained out of a possible hundred by one of the teams from Hirst North Junior Girls School, Ashington, in winning first place in the Country Dances Competition for boys and girls aged 8-11 in the North of England Musical Tournament in Newcastle.

A team of four girls, tutored by Miss Vida Sample, entered for the team reading, which took place in the Central Methodist Hall, Newcastle. They won first place with 166 marks out of a possible 200. The under-eleven winning team was Jean Erskine, Shirley Williams, Patricia Barrass and Lorna Mavin. Another team of over-eleven girls won first prize, too. They were Patricia Keegan, Dorothy Wilkinson, Shirley Richardson and Patricia Regan. The first team won the Dickens Banner and the second team won the Drinkwater Banner.

The Communist Party was very active in Ashington after the War, and had made several attempts to gain seats in local elections. There was much concern shown by Tom Holliday, secretary of the Woodhorn Miners, at a meeting of Ashington Labour Party in February 1948, when he was reported as saying: 'In my opinion it is not the intention of the Communists in the Urban District Elections to become councillors, but their object is to prevent Labour candidates from being councillors. At a national level, the Communist aim seems to be to bring down the Labour Government. It is they who have split our local union over the question of longer hours to help the country in a time of crisis.'

Ashington Wives find College a Pleasure (Evening Chronicle – 8th March, 1948)

Three hundred Ashington housewives believe a woman is never too old to learn – even if she is fifty or sixty-five with house and family to look after, so they go to college. It is these energetic and apparently tireless housewives who complicate the acute overcrowding problem at the Ashington County College (Mining School), where a highly-qualified staff wrestles with the necessity of forcing a quart of students of all ages and both sexes into a pint pot of accommodation.

House-work is a full time job, yet some of Ashington's housewife collegians spend eight hours a week in the college producing, with naturally skilled hands, clothing, embroidery, soft toys and furnishings and fine needlework. Most of their productions find their way into the homes in the form of screens, lamp shades, furniture coverings and decorative gadgets. They all show an appreciation of colour and line which will one day exclude from the working class home many of the shoddy, inartistic features once accepted as pleasing and appropriate.

High standards are set for the work of the women students, some of whom have produced ecclesiastical embroidery of a high quality, suitable for church, altar adornments. One student with special talents is now busy with work for Whitfield Church, near Hexham. One star student, a seventy-year-old woman, who cycled to the college in fair weather and foul, entered a big local exhibition and walked off with ten first prizes and a trophy. Indicative of the determined spirit of the women is the example of one student who continued her classwork when recovering from a serious illness. One day, with the support of her husband, she reached the college for new instruction and materials, and went back to bed.

Housewives, of course, have a keen eye for a bargain. They get as many as a hundred hours of tuition for half-a-crown. What woman could resist the chance of producing a nine-guinea sports jacket for the master of the house for 27s 6d without coupons.

School Dinners for Ashington pupils began soon after the war ended. They were cooked at Pegswood Central Kitchens and brought by motor wagon to the various schools. According to an entry in the Hirst North School Log for 10th November 1948: "At 11.40 am this morning the East Strap of the Main Gate was dislodged by the Pegswood food-motor, driver Mr Harry Popely of Morpeth. There is now an element of danger to the children."

These Wansbeck schoolchildren in the late 40s certainly enjoyed their school dinners. Back left Roderick Dewar, Lloyd Thain, Gordon Appleby, Brian Laws, Allan Gilbey, Peter Stewart, Alan Morpeth, Joe Thompson, Mike Hall, Tom Elliott, Jimmy McPhail, MissYoung. 2nd back row Frank Ward, Tom Hall, Norris Otterwell, Ruby Hall, Sheila Summers, Irene Rouse, Jean Bell, Sally Forrester, Heather Wilkinson, Irene Wheatley, Doreen Hall, Isabel Godsmark, Ian Cummings, Tom Proctor, Bobby Grey. Front row Margaret Tapson, Pat Todd, Eileen Lyle, Betty Spicer, Ann Chambers, Ann Kennedy, Joan Peart, Joan Young, Jane Tippler, Hazel Blythe and Mary Young.

Readers' letters – Ashington Advertiser, December 1948

Houses take the place of allotments

In approximately one month's time the allotments on the left of Alexandra Road, near the Hirst Welfare Sports Ground, must be vacated by their present tenants. The land has been requisitioned for building purposes, (*Woodhorn Villas*) and while one realises that houses are an urgent necessity in the locality, we must also remember that the taking over of this plot of land is leaving some of the allotment holders with problems of their own. Many have acquired livestock, and finding alternative accommodation is no easy matter in terms of pigs, poultry, pigeons and even racing greyhounds.

Bananas

On the assumption that when an allocation of bananas is made to the district there are enough to honour all the relevant ration books, why is it that over the past twelve months I have only been able to obtain supplies four times, and these were due entirely to chance when I was passing shops where limited supplies were being sold?

Town Bus Service

Some weeks ago I boarded the town service bus at Bothal Schools and unfortunately had no change smaller than half-a-crown. It was perhaps also unfortunate that it was at a busy time and the conductor was somewhat pushed. I tendered my half-crown with apologies and was informed, not very politely, that on that particular run this amount could not be accepted. I pointed out that one could not always be expected to have the correct change at any given time, but this argument did not appear to carry much weight and I was faced with the problem of whether I should get off at the next stop or just sit tight and not pay at all. At this point a gentleman sitting opposite gave me a penny for my fare and saved the situation. But I should still like to know whether there is any specified amount which cannot be tendered on the town service bus.

Fish (and Chips)

I read with interest the recent complaint on the amount of fish sold for 8d in our local fish shops, and would like to point out that individuals can purchase fresh fish in the shops or streets at retail prices that make it go much further than by buying it at the fish shop ready cooked. But it must be borne in mind that the fish fryer has his labour too – and his fuel - and it is probably this factor that brings the price of our 'one of each' up into the region of one shilling. But if anyone is dissatisfied about not receiving value for money when buying fried fish when the remedy is in their own hands – they need not buy it.

Expensive Trains

Will some reader or employer of British Railways put forward the reason why trains are allowed to run to and from Newcastle with a handful of passengers on board whilst one has to wait sometimes more than half an hour for a bus. Surely with the demand for travel facilities to and from Newcastle being on hand, British Railways could slash their fares to 1/- or 1/6, and instead of a handful of passengers they could increase their carrying capacity a hundred fold.

Greyhound Winners
I think your hints on how to find winners should be very acceptable to punters at Ashington Stadium. The trouble is that most people don't realise that what are running are dogs – not machines. For a greyhound to do its time, one must realise that it has to trap in a split second and, without putting a foot wrong, negotiate two bends (with other dogs) at something in the region of 30 miles per hour. There is usually an obvious reason when a dog doesn't do its time. Whilst Ashington Stadium hasn't the best of track dogs (which makes 'weighing up' more difficult) the form of the dogs is as good as will be found anywhere.

Cigarettes
I think Sir Stafford Cripps (*Chancellor of Exchequer*) must realise by now that whatever prices he places on cigarettes and tobacco, he will never be able to stop people from smoking. When cigarettes went up to 3/6 a packet there was at that time a marked decline of sales, but this did not last very long and we are back in a position where the supply is exceeded by the demand. Were the same thing to happen again and another stiff increase occur at the next budget, the results would be just the same, as confirmed smokers will go to great lengths to satisfy their craving for tobacco. So it would appear that Sir Stafford may take a lot of our money back in taxes – a more or less compulsory way of making us spend less – but he will never make us give up the solace afforded by Madame Nicotine.

Situations Vacant
Linton and Woodhorn Social Club. Lady Waiter wanted, Friday, Saturday and Sunday nights. 2/6 per hour. Apply by letter to George D Bell, Secretary.

Obituary – December 1948
'Tanner' Milburn, uncle of Jackie Milburn, England International and Newcastle United centre forward, died at his home 18 Laburnum Terrace, Ashington, last week. The funeral took place at Seaton Hirst Church Yard on Friday afternoon. His four footballer sons, George, Jack, James and Stan, acted as under bearers.

Tanner Milburn was a well-known sportsman, but his first and foremost love was football. His death at the age of 62 years was therefore a great loss to the sport. In his younger days he was well known on the sports field as a goalkeeper. He commenced playing football with the old Ashington Blue Star, which used to play at the Ashington Recreation Ground. He later moved to Ashington FC when in those days the pitch was situated near Ashington Cricket Club. From Ashington he joined Wellington Athletic Club.

Tanner's father, old Jackie Milburn, started off the family on his road to football fame. Known as the 'Old Horse', Tanner's father was a stalwart in the Ashington FC defence. Four of Tanner's sons have made their mark in the footballing world: George and Jack were full-backs with Leeds United for eleven years; James is still with Leeds as a full-back, having thirteen years service with that club. When George and Jack were full-backs for Leeds their brother-in-law Jimmy Potts was the goalkeeper and the three became known as the Milburn Defence. The youngest son Stan is with Chesterfield, having joined them three seasons ago (1946) from Ashington FC. His brother Jack is now manager of the Chesterfield Club, while George is manager at Bradford City.

The Milburn family is well known, but it became more famous this year when Tanner's nephew, Jackie Milburn of Newcastle United became England's international centre-forward.

St Aidan's School Log 23rd July 1948

"School closes today for the mid-Summer vacation. The extra-year classes had a breaking-up party, and agreed that they had had a very happy year. There were tears on parting, an unusual occurrence in my experience. In spite of the many great difficulties – chiefly through my having two classes during the greater part of the year, and occasionally three, and so not being able to give them my full attention – they have developed a grand sense of comradeship and self-reliance. Whilst I was doubtful at first of the merits of raising the school-leaving age to 15, I must admit that the results have surprised me."

Signed Michael McGough, Headmaster

Countersigned John P Mullarkey (Parish Priest)

I left St Aidan's RC School at Easter 1949, the day before Good Friday. I was fifteen years old. In 1947 I would have been eligible to leave school at fourteen. When I got home for my tea that day – we were then living at No 99 Maple Street - my mother shouted through from the scullery: 'Michael, is that ye? Your tea's on the table, son. By the way, ye are startin' the pit on Tuesday!'

And that was the way it was done. An Ashington lad's whole life was mapped out for him in the blink of an eye by one or other of his parents. The crazy thing is that neither I (nor any of my classmates) for one moment thought to complain or object. For me there were no tantrums. I didn't fling myself on the floor kicking my legs in the air as I had done in Woolworth's as a five-year-old spoiled child each time we entered that shop and my mother had refused to buy me a toy replica of the Lone Ranger aboard his faithful steed, Silver. In the 1940s you did as you were told.

'The Only Way You Could Get Away From Ashington Was to Play Football' by Jack Charlton

"In the days when Jackie Milburn grew up, and then a decade or so later, me and our kid, the only way you could get away from Ashington was to play football. Or, like some of my pals, you could go away to London and find a job and sort something out for yourself. Out of the lads that I knocked around with, maybe half of them left home, the rest are still at Ashington and have been there all their lives.

"One of the things about going away to play football was that you were worried that you might not make it, and get sent home again – then you went back as a failure. This is probably why we worked so hard when we went away from Ashington. In the first two years I was at Leeds, I only played about once in the Central League before I went into the army.

"Me and our kid played for Ashington YMCA. The pitch was at Reyrolles Factory on North Seaton Road and it was like kicking the ball up one hill and down the other. We played in the Under-18 League at the time. I was only about fifteen and our kid would be thirteen. We got murdered every week, and in one season all we managed was one draw.

"We had a football, which was through having uncles who played the game, and we took it over to Hirst Park on a Sunday morning, and got kicked to bits. If you wanted to go home for your dinner they would talk you into leaving your ball and they promised you would get it back, which you very rarely did. I've run around half-a-dozen houses trying to borrow a football so that we could start a game. And that one game would go on all day. Strangely enough, I could get a game in the morning when there weren't many there, but in the afternoon, if me and our kid had gone home for dinner, when we came back they'd probably give him a game and I wouldn't get to play at all.

"I worked at the pit for a short while. It was on 'bank' in the weigh-cabin at Linton Colliery with a lad called Jackie Summers. I enjoyed it there. On the screens and spirals, which every young-un had to go on, you were sat in a little cubby-hole all day, watching little bits of coal drifting by . . . and the noise! It didn't work all the time, and sometimes there was a quiet period when no coal was coming down and that was great. You used to draw pictures with a piece of stone. It was an artist's paradise. There were footballers, goals, nudes . . . everything. Some men worked on the screens and spirals for ever.

"It was a worrying time. I didn't particularly want to leave home, and I didn't mind going into the pit or doing something within the mining industry. It was just that you were glad to leave school and go and get a job. And obviously at Ashington at that time there was only the pits – there was very little else." *(From Jackie Milburn in Black and White by Mike Kirkup)*

Nursing was another option for girls. Ashington Hospital had opened in 1914 with only 30 beds. By 1948 not a lot had changed, and a glance at the balance sheet for that year shows part of the Income was 'Pig Swill' and 'Sale of Hen House', both transactions bringing in a combined total of £14 3s 9d. But then salaries and wages of staff were quite low with a combined total of £6,902 0s 3d for the year.

The Matron during the 1940s and '50s was Miss L Hunter who had trained at the RVI as a staff nurse. Other nurses at Ashington in the '40s included: Mary Patterson, Evelyn Peart, Elsie Wise, Edna Railston and Edith Punton. Another matron was called Milne; surgeons at Ashington included Frank Gairdner and Mr Andrew Bonar; house-doctors were Dr Graham, Dr Jim Hobbs and Fitzpatrick, Miles, and Young; in charge of out-patients was Sister Dixon; in theatre McCallister; Male ward Martin; Female ward Rowley; ambulance driver Tom Ritchell; spare-time driver Fred Young; Porter/handyman Mr Postle.

Visiting time was limited to two hours on three days a week with strictly only two to a bed. During these hours, nurses had to sterilize bed-pans and urine bottles, make swabs, dressings and sanitary towels, wash any sheets or bedding which was marked before being sent to the laundry.

During the war, nurses had to sleep in the hospital in case of emergencies; Mary Robson wrote: "I was there the morning the plane crashed in the Fifth Row, unfortunately, only one of the family survived, the son Billy Cox."

The Ashington Children's Gala of 1948 was sponsored by, among others, the 20 workingmen's clubs of Ashington each of which gave varying amounts between two and ten pounds. Clubs (listed in order of location) were Universal, Hirst Industrial, Premier, Linton and Woodhorn, Northern, East End, Grand Street, Central, Progressive, Constitutional, New Hirst (Mortimer), Comrades, Middle Market, RAOB, Cosmopolitan, Ashington and Ellington, Excelsior, White House, Fell 'em Doon and West End. Children gathered at their individual schools and marched – sometimes behind a brass band – to either the Peoples' Park or Hirst Welfare, depending upon circumstances. At the venue they were greeted by the organisers (Jimmy Middlemiss ran it for a number of years in the 1960s) who handed out a coin (by 1948 it had probably reached two shillings) and a bag of sweets; Toogood's fairground was present and, after some running and jumping events, the cash quickly went on dodgem cars, chair o'planes and candy floss. (Note: in 1948 the Gala was run by Ashington Children's Sports Association with E Clarke of 16 Beatrice Street as secretary and AE Eke and Jack Patterson on the committee).

Although in 1949 neither was considered an 'academic' school, there was always great rivalry on the sports field between Hirst Park Boys and Hirst East. There were some great individual performers, too, as shown in the 1949 School Sports results. For Hirst Park, the Senior individual championship was won by Jimmy Main and the Junior by Bob Duff. The following also won prizes: Walter Harmison, Bill Hall, John Parkin, George Hindmarsh, Percy Armstrong, Morton, Gilmore, Alan Taylor and Andy Patterson; for the Juniors: Steve Davison, John Freeman, Eddie Moran, Lashley, M Dunn, White, Moffatt, and Thompson.

Hirst East Boys Sports that same year produced the following winners: W Buglass, Ray McGee, Norman Watson, V Hall, Roy Tunstall, Bill Southern, J Atkinson, Norman Lowther, Bill Robson, A Blair, M Dunn, B Fenwick, Jobling, Ashworth, Alan Wren, J Atkinson, Robert Brown; the half mile race was fought out between two Murray boys, Benny and

Geoff, with the latter running out the victor and being presented with a silver challenge cup by Miss Simpson, headmistress at Hirst East Girls.

Blake Cup at Hirst Welfare. This was an annual competition held among East Northumberland schools and carried great prestige. In 1949 it was won by Hirst East who trounced Westerhope Boys, 6-1 at the Hirst Welfare ground. Picked out for special mention in the *Ashington Advertiser* were the five goals from Sid Hutton and one from Alan Taylor. Inside forwards John Hale and Jackie Winn were praised, while East had the services of Jimmy Jackson international centre half who was 'a tower of strength' in the home defence.

Heatwave Returns (16th July, 1949) The *Ashington Advertiser* reported the return of the heatwave that had arrived in time for the children's summer holidays and the miners' holiday week. "Taking full advantage of the glorious weather, families have embarked for various destinations throughout the country for the weekend and many more have decided to make their holiday day-trips to country beauty spots.

"For those who are holidaying at home the conditions have been ideal over the weekend for lazing around. The influx of visitors to Newbiggin has been terrific and reached a peak of Monday when the beach was packed with holidaymakers. Early mornings resulted in all bathing tents and deck-chairs being booked for the day. The large crowd, however, did not seem as large as last year's Whit holiday, which was a record. Many special buses arrived from early hours in the morning until late afternoon. When it came to depart the local bus and train services dealt efficiently and smartly, carrying away their passengers with the least possible delay."

For Sale Advert
For better listening this year, Dance's have a good selection of radios and radiograms, including Cossor, Alba, Pilot Portadyne etc., all on easy terms, and your old set taken in part exchange. Call today, don't delay – Dance's, Woodhorn Road, Ashington. We also have a good selection of gramophone records, needles and sound boxes. 2/- deposit and 1/- a week will get you an electric iron, so why be without one?

Ashington Agricultural Society Raffle
Winner of Eggs – Mrs Williams, 26 Fifth Row, Ashington
Winner of Cake – Mrs Harvey, 31 Rothesay Terrace, Bedlington Station

Sports News (Ashington Advertiser – 6th August, 1949)
Ashington Cricket First Team versus County Club
Team: J Robinson, Stan Levison, D Tanner, Arthur Teasdale, Jack Watson, Tommy Simpson, Jim Turnbull, J Davison, W Thompson, W Johnson and R Kennedy.

Ashington II v Bedlington: G Sharp, Dave Gibson, W Roberts, J Barnes, J E Gowe, J Chisholm, George Gray, J Hills, H Brown, K Norrie and Bart Conn.

Northumberland Lawn Tennis tournament concluded at the County Ground, Newcastle, on Saturday, when one of the titles came to Ashington. In the mixed doubles final, Mr and Mrs N Howe, of the Ashington Welfare Club, succeeded in winning the event.

Nobbie Poxon (running as F Loss of Ashington, off 55 yards) succeeded in winning the £40 half-mile handicap at the Morpeth Olympic Games on Saturday. One of the qualifiers for the final was another Ashington runner C Mordue, off 70 yards. In the final, Loss just managed to beat A Turnbull of Jedburgh, off 50 yards, on the tape.

Dogs to Watch at Portland Park
Hazel Jubilee, Kilteely, Extra Penny, Pampas, Samba and Emily Hawker.

Ashington United Bus Depot staff has decided to enter the sports arena in a big way. The members are to organise themselves into football, cricket and netball teams, which will operate in leagues to be formed of teams from other depots in Northumberland, Durham and North Yorkshire.

Officials elected are Messrs: Armstrong, T Askew, J Dixon, F Greaves, G Randall, R Wade, R Davison, G Oliver, F Rutherford, L Cockburn, E Gascoigne, W Dodds, J Horne, J Snowdon, R Yellowley, J Lynn, J Innes, J Reavley, W Tait, D Huxley, G Foreman, A Walker, W Thompson and Mrs Cockburn.

Normanton Barron and the Central Hall Choir in the 1940s
Wilma Carr wrote: "I must have been fourteen when Mr Normanton Barron invited me to join the Central Hall Choir, and I was very proud to do so. I had attended Sunday School as a pupil and then as a teacher, taking part in the Anniversaries, but this was a definite step up. I sat amongst the sopranos, next to Eva Worrall, who became a dear friend. After Sunday Evening Service we would walk arm-in-arm for a walk to Sheepwash.

"Other people very active in the life of the choir were the families Allington, Coombs and Brown. We rehearsed on Monday evenings, and afterwards Mr Brown would accompany me on the piano while I tried out a new song or aria. Sometimes we gave concerts in other chapels and I sang solos, but the absolute thrill of it all were the celebrity concerts held once or twice a month in the Central Hall when artistes from London performed: people such as Heddle Nash, Isabel Baillie, Janet Howe, David Lloyd, Kathleen Ferrier and our own Owen Brannigan. I adore Kathleen Ferrier and it was a wonderful thrill and inspiration to hear her in person in March 1945 when she appeared with the dashing, handsome, Polish bass Mario Zigmand (Nowakowski) in his Airforce uniform. What an evening that was! I still have many of the programmes of these concerts."

Of all the employers in Ashington, the Industrial Co-operative Society stood supreme. It was often said *'Aye, hinnie, if ye get a job at the Store* *ye are med for life!'* Apart from the mines, the Co-op was undoubtedly the largest employer in the district in the 1940s and paid the highest wages. There were Co-op stores spread around the town. The 'Top Store' had opened at the end of the 19th century, while the Hirst Co-op (*now Sports World*) in Woodhorn Road came about twenty years later. Newbiggin Co-op opened premises at the bottom of Milburn Road in 1900 while other stores appeared in Hawthorn Road and on the Hirst avenues. So many school-leavers wanted jobs with the Co-op that they had to sit an entrance exam to sort the wheat from the chaff.

Academic qualifications were not necessary to work underground, though you were given an examination paper to sit when joining the Training Scheme at Ashington Colliery. That was to see whether it was worth their while to offer you an apprenticeship, either as a mechanic or electrician. I passed the exam with a high enough mark to warrant being asked whether or not I would like to attend the Mining School for two days a week. That establishment in Darnley Road had opened in 1930, offering the chance for hundreds of lads to progress with a successful mining career, if that was their wish. In the process, the School was responsible for turning out many young men who went on to bigger and better things, both within and outside the coal industry. I had no wish to take on board any more education so I declined the offer and ended up as an ordinary pit yacker. That was good enough for my father and his brothers, so it was good enough for me. Or so I thought.

After a while, the young lads were accepted by the older miners into their close-knit fraternity, though not until all the initiation pranks had been complied with – I was once sent for 'half a dozen rubber dregs' when I should have known that they were only ever made of wood or steel.

My first job underground was at the shaft bottom of the Bothal Pit. It was a place where most young'uns cut their teeth on pit-work as it was brightly lit, whitewashed, and as high as a cathedral. Two other lads were already in place when I started: Alan White and Ernie Eastlake; the three of us worked well together, moving tubs full of coal from the High Main, Middle Main and Bensham Seam workings, and dispatching chummins (empties) along the parallel roadways. Adult workers included Norman Harrison, on the top of the steep Bensham Bank with its post-stone roof; little Hennor Eastlake on the High Main; and Les Common on the Middle Main loader. All easy-going chaps and all on shift-work, apart from Les who was paid piecework, depending on how many tubs he filled from the long conveyor that carried coal from the Middle Main workings.

Onsetters were men at the shaft bottom who sent the coal to the surface in the cage once it had brought all the men underground. Again, this was a piecework job, paid by the score (the number of tubs x 20 that were sent to 'bank'). Bothal Pit onsetters included Frankie Count, Joe Abercrombie, and Andrew Hall, while helpers included big Geordie Robson and Roy Crow, a lad in his early twenties, who was responsible for guiding the tubs as the cage dropped, first at one side then the other. I admired all these men immensely. They were all remarkably efficient at getting the tubs in and out of the cage with minimum fuss, but at maximum speed. It did not do to have the pit 'stannin', for that was a signal for the mine manager, looking out from his office in the pit yard, to enquire why the pulley wheels were not turning. If they were still, no coal was being raised and money was not being made.

Mine Recruits Swamp Training Facilities (Blyth News – 31st October, 1949) NCB Move to Take Over Bothal School

The phenomenal increase in the number of youngsters entering the mines in Ashington and other districts in south east Northumberland in response to the National Coal Board recruiting drive has swamped existing facilities for training recruits. Consequently, negotiations are in progress between the NCB, the school governors and Northumberland Education Committee to transfer the pupils of Bothal Modern School one and a half miles from Ashington to the Hirst East School, and to convert the Bothal into a temporary Mining Training Centre until the new Technical College is completed in Ashington in two or three years' time. *(in reality it was almost ten years later)*

At present, large numbers of young recruits in collieries in this area are pottering on the surface for months, doing any odd jobs which can be found for them, until there is room in the existing centres to give them the educational instruction which they must have before they can work underground. It is understood that the managers of the Ashington group of schools are opposed to the scheme, as it would involve greater travelling distances for their pupils. The NCB, on the other hand, maintain that unless they can have the school, the working of the scores of collieries in south east Northumberland will ultimately be threatened. The scheme will also mean that the Ashington Mining College on Darnley Road would have more room for the large numbers of students of all classes and professions who apply for courses there every year.

£43,000 School Bill for Roman Catholics (Ashington Post – December, 1949)

A bill for £43,000 will have to be paid by Roman Catholics in the Ashington area if they are to retain control of the new schools they have to build for their children under the 1944 Education Act. This is equivalent to the 2,200 Catholics in the Parish of St Aidan's, Ashington, some of whom live in Newbiggin, Lynemouth and other local villages, each having to pay nearly £20 during the next few years if the 300 or so school children are to receive the Catholic education they consider necessary.

A number of St Aidan's parishioners were among many Catholics who were told at Newcastle that the Catholic Church was never consulted in the preparation of the 1944 Act. Father Andrew Sheedy, Parish Priest of Ashington, and Chairman of the Board of St Aidan's School, told the *News Post* that he would ask Mr Bob Taylor, MP for Morpeth, for an answer to these questions on behalf of his parishioners before the next elections. Father Sheedy also said that, according to the development plan drawn up by the Northumberland Education Authority under the 1944 Act, a new Catholic Primary School would have to be built on a new site in Ashington and would cost the people of St Aidan's at least £23,000. They would also have to pay £7,540 as their share of the cost of a new Technical-Grammar School to be built at Whitley Bay to serve Catholic pupils from this, and other areas.

A Secondary Modern School for Catholic pupils (St Benedict's) is also planned for Ashington to be built on a new site, and as this will be a 'special agreement school' under the Act the people of the parish may get up to three-quarters of the cost from the LEA. Even if they get the full grant they will still have to pay £11,000 for the school. Giving these figures to the *News Post*, Father Sheedy said, that if the maximum possible grants were given, Catholics in the district would have to find a total of £42,940.

Although I wasn't officially expelled from St Cuthbert's Grammar, I still found myself back at St Aidan's within three years. This is a class photo taken there in 1948. Back row left Michael Parker, Jim Birchall, Peter Rossi, Kevin Carlin, Len Parkinson, Michael Cassidy, Vincent Lang. 2nd back row Peter Hyde, Sam Goldsbury, John Clark, Ronnie Hunt, Jimmy Robertson. 3rd back row Sheila Coyle, Kathleen Reilly, June Tonkiss, Mary Quinn, Katherine Keagan, Josie Reilly, Mary Mulligan, Elizabeth Stafford, Winnie O'Brien, Moira Clark. 2nd front row Margaret Conroy, Mary Armstrong, Mary Brennan, Mary Tanney, Irene Scott, Emily McGee, Catherine Slavin, Mary Bonner, Mary Ibbetson, Margaret Allen. Front row Ed Brennan, Joe Conroy, Fred Keech, Hugh Barton, Don Guy, Michael Kirkup, Frank Embleton, Clifford Dillon, Joe Parry and Marty Brennan. (Note – it is a sad reflection, but out of 42 class members, at least 13 have not survived).

1940s NEWS IN BRIEF

1940 – A Grand Variety Concert held on 27th March in the Arcade Hall featured Peter Cosimini, BBC Accordionist; Holidays advertised by C Hunter of Woodhorn Road shows" 'Ashington Miners' Holiday Week, 25th June to 2nd July, for 'seven days full board and coach fare' the cost was £6 5s 0d; Wallaw Pictures shows 'Pinocchio' film for first time, price four-pence for children, seven-pence for adults. One of our own planes, a Bristol Beaufort bomber crashes in the Fifth Row; a German plane is brought down at Cresswell; Cosa Maite is undisputed champion greyhound at Portland Park; BSA motor bikes costing £4 10s 0d are sold at Jimmy Main's shop; the Hirst Progressive Club donates £100 to the War Effort; Frank Millican, union secretary, gives talk at Arcade Hall on "*Working after the Siren blows*"; WAAF recruitment begins at Ashington Employment Exchange; Booth Cup Final at Hirst Welfare on Good Friday, Cosmopolitan SC v Fell 'em Doon. Referee D Burt with Alec Anderson and Ossie Sword as linesmen.

1941 - Ashington miners receive no pay on 21st February owing to severe snow storm; two land mines explode at Sheepwash; *Ashington Advertiser* closes for duration; compulsory pit inspections introduced; Coal Mining now designated as 'Essential Work'; bombs drop on Woodhorn Fan House and at Coney Garth Farm.

1942 - Greene Award adds 2s 6d per shift to all underground workers above 21 years; bombs drop at Sparrow House Farm; White Paper says that increased coal output could be achieved by concentrating more men on the more productive seams.

1943 – Secret ballot made in December to decide which men are to be conscripted into UK pits – became known as Bevin Boys; Incendiary bombs drop on Long Row.

1944 – Miners' Hostel opens behind Central Hall to cater for influx of 'Bevin Boys'; Hartford Hall opens as a rehabilitation centre for miners; last of 237 air alerts sirens in Ashington; Priestman Group now includes Ashington Coal Company and seven pits in Durham as well as the five in Ashington.

1945 – Formation of National Union of Mineworkers; Alf Robens elected MP for Wansbeck (later Blyth); Ashington Business and Professional Women's Club formed with Eva Stimpson as first president.

1946 – First post-war Miners' Picnic held at Morpeth; George 'Dusty' Down becomes first Ashington sprinter to win gold medal at Powderhall; Reyrolles Players staged Variety Show in the factory canteen, with performers including Bill McClurry, Ken Galley, George Williamson, Margaret Forster, Jenny Humble, Thelma Jameson, Arthur Standing, Tom O'Hagan, Jim Hunter and Jack Robinson.

1947 - 1st January is Vesting Day when mines are put in the hands of the workers under the Nationalisation act; UK coal owners to get £60 million in compensation; introduction of a five-day week; French children stay with members of Larry Bell's Boys Club; Liz Taylor stars in 'Lassie' at Wallaw Cinema, prices have now increased to ninepence for adults; best selling record at Grierson's Station Road record shop is 'Oh, Mein Papa' sung by Joan Hammond who two years later appeared at the Central Hall, accompanied by Gladys Proudlock, with the West Sleekburn Gleeman, conductor William Newman.

1948 – "Butlins at Filey is favourite resort for Ashington miners," said a spokesman at James Chrisp, booking agent; the price of an eight-day holiday to Ireland at Weatherstone's Travel Agents of 2 Park Road, Ashington, was advertised for £14 7s 6d; aluminium bungalow allocation for Ashington cut from 200 to eighty; homeless women complain of conditions at North Seaton Hall - plans put in place by Newbiggin Council to demolish this stately home.

1949 – Booth Cup Final at Hirst Welfare on Good Friday, Cosmopolitan SC v Fell 'em Doon. Jackie Milburn and Jimmy Jackson, both from Hirst East School, capped for England soccer teams, senior and boys; Rediffusion broadcasting system connected to many Ashington homes at weekly rental of two shillings; Ashington now has 20,000 voters; unveiling ceremony at Ashington Hospital of 1939-45 War Memorial; council members deplore indiscriminate dumping of refuse in Hirst back alleys; Ashington Co-op pays dividend of two shillings and sixpence in the pound.

What was on at the 'pictures' in December 1947.

THE 1950s

Weldon Laing whose shop in Woodhorn Road is seen above in the early Fifties with its Christmas window display of plump turkeys, had learned the butchery trade while with the Co-op at Wooler. Weldon had two sons, Hylton and Ronnie, and a daughter Mary. Hylton eventually took over the family business when the shop moved to No 61 from 95 Woodhorn Road which was re-named Stimpson's Bakers. Ronnie became apprenticed as an electrician with Ashington Coal Company, but later joined the RAF as a navigator during the Second World War; Mary took up teaching and eventually became a headmistress. Hylton Laing was also heavily involved in local football as a director of Ashington FC.

NUM's Wage Claim Move Welcomed (Ashington Post – 3rd June, 1950)
Ashington miners have particularly welcomed the news that the NUM is to negotiate for wage increases for lower paid workers, both on the surface and underground. In an almost all-mining community with no other lower paid industries to offset the sharp comparisons of piece workers, the move is considered long overdue.

Generally there have been two wage rates in this town, high and low. The surface worker on a minimum of £5 has had to buy in the same shops and pay all the prices that face and piece workers earning upwards of £12 a week," said one of the lower income group last week.

The wide wedge between the two income groups in Ashington – the lower paid men are in the majority – has affected social life in the town due mainly to rising prices and shortage of money. Some Social Clubs report very quiet spells during the week, with the poorer miner very careful with his money.

If the wage claims are successful, surface workers will get a minimum of £5 15s a week and those underground £6 10s.

German Visitors come to Ashington (Ashington Post 23rd November 1950)

Miss Valerie Tully, the assistant County Youth Organiser told a meeting in Hirst Park School on Monday evening of the great strides being made by neighbouring Newbiggin in recent years, and altogether painted a favourable picture on the activities of local youth.

She reported there were 47 clubs in the area, and four new groups have been formed recently – the Girls Nautical Training Corps, Newbiggin St John's Ambulance Cadets, Salvation Army, and Lynemouth Methodist Sunday Club.

The balance sheet of the International Fund, which this year took care of expenses incurred by the Youth visitors of the district from Germany, amounted to £76 10s 8d. These expenses covered the party's rail fares from London and back, local transport, and visits to Alnwick, Hexham and Morpeth. The German young people were unable to exchange German money for sterling, and subsequently all expenses were met by the hosts.

In 1951, local youth club members will be travelling to Germany where they will be the guests of the Remscheid Youth Council.

Ashington Councillors claim Council Houses. On 5th February 1950 the *Sunday Sun* ran an article that was to drop a bombshell into Ashington's Council Chambers following an open-air public meeting of 200 angry Ashington residents who signed a petition for an Inquiry to be held into the allocation of two council houses to Labour councillors. The article went on: 'Local members of the Labour Party, to which the two councillors belong, are divided in opinion, but one miners' union branch has expressed disapproval and has asked for a full explanation. Cllr Danny Cole, chairman of the Council, said: 'The NCB informed the Council that six tenants of colliery houses were to be evicted. After a joint meeting it was agreed that consideration be given to each of the tenants for a council house. Three names were then revealed and after each case had been considered they were granted a council house. The names of the other three families involved were not known at the time,' he said. It so happened that two Labour councillors were in the other three. At this, Socialist Councillor George Holliday walked out of the meeting in protest.

This year was proving to be something of an *annus horribilus* for Ashington Council when further embarrassing questions were raised in the Chambers concerning a claim for first-class rail travel when it was declared that the Council Surveyor had claimed for first-class travelling expenses when he had only travelled by third-class to a Torquay conference. Cllr James Tilley, a Co-operative councillor, said: 'I don't think it is right for anyone to put in for expenses that have not been incurred. For three years no official on this Council has put in for expenses on this basis.' Cllr Tilley warned that the Council could now expect the precedent to be applied to every other official of the Council which agreed to pay the Surveyor's first-class rail expenses. (*Journal* 3-8-50)

If the year of 1950 was not a good one for Ashington Council then 1951 was an absolute stinker. It began in February with the District Auditor's Report of the accounts for the year ending 31st March 1950. The District Auditor, Mr HL Stevens referred to 'a claim of £1 made by a councillor for attending at the Council Offices for three hours to open tenders for motor coach transport as having been "found to be untrue and has therefore been surcharged against him."

The Report went on "It is a serious matter whatever the amount involved that a member should submit such claims. The Council will have to consider, therefore, what further action be taken in this case." Dealing with the expenses of *six* other members (whose names were never divulged) , the Report says: "Sums claimed by councillors for subsistence were, in some cases, for longer periods than appeared necessary to perform the approved duties, but on the attention of the councillors being called to the matter, sums of £7 2s 6d were refunded to the audit. Claims for loss of earnings for a councillor for days on which no loss of earnings had occurred, were also reported. It further stated in the Report that "The accounts included other payments of claims for allowances by (7) members amounting to £25 13s 11d for attendance at various conferences, mostly local, which had not received the requisite sanction of the Ministry."

'Ashington won't attract foreign visitors'

An announcement of 'brave proposals' for making Ashington more beautiful, and a clash between two councillors on the advisability of holding Festival of Britain celebrations in the town , meant a lively meeting in Ashington last night. (*Journal*, 19/1/51) It was of more than fifty representatives of miners' unions, social clubs, churches, and other organisations, to consider what Ashington could do towards the Festival. Councillor Arthur Rogers, chairman of the meeting and the local authority, said that a special sub-committee of the council had already made proposals which would have to be approved by the council. These suggestions included tree-planting and general tidying up at the West End of the town, at the North Seaton Road housing estate, approaches at Stakeford Bridge, Woodhorn Colliery, and Booth's Corner (Top Store Corner).

For the Festival season, the Town Hall and historical buildings in the town should be floodlit, bunting hung from houses and shops and window boxes displayed throughout the town. The Festival Fortnight might include carnivals, sports, a shopping week, youth activities, concerts, dances, band parades, combined religious services and the like.

Differences of opinion between the Chairman and Councillor Walter Nunn arose at the beginning of the meeting. Councillor Nunn said that ratepayers already pay twenty shillings in the pound and could not stand any additional burden. He didn't think anyone would be optimistic enough to say Ashington would attract foreign visitors, which, he believed, was the purpose of the Festival of Britain.

Councillor Rogers said that the ratepayers would be affected very little, as the scheme suggested would have to be seen to some time. The Reverend A G W Hunter, Vicar of Ashington, said he hoped Ashington would attract visitors. He liked to think that the festival would show foreigners how the country lived. They should see Ashington people enjoying themselves and he favoured extending the activities suggested over a longer period.

One suggestion at the meeting was that the Coal Board should be asked to beautify their property in the town. It was agreed that the fortnight June 2nd-16th was the most favourable for celebrations and it is possible that Ashington Accident Prevention Council's Road Courtesy Week would be staged then. A committee of the Reverend G P Williams, Messrs. John Oliver, William Downie, Alan Robson and George Ruddick will consider with the Council Sub-committee.

Council Candidate Adoptions 'Staged' Says Socialist Councillor
Allegations were made last night (*Journal*, 6/3/51) by Councillor Arthur Rogers, a Socialist and Chairman of Ashington Urban Council, that certain members of the Labour Party brought relatives to an election meeting to ensure that he (Rogers) was not chosen as a Council candidate. Councillor Rogers, who has been on the Council for eighteen years, is not included in the list of four persons chosen by Ashington Labour Party to contest Hirst Ward at the next local election.

He issued a statement last night, shortly after the list had been published, saying he was concerned about the action of certain members. They had encouraged relatives, he alleged, to make decisions not aimed at the selection of *good* councillors, but to ensure that one councillor was not chosen. Councillor Rogers, who has been Council Chairman and Vice Chairman twice and is present Chairman of the Housing Committee, asserts that this attitude has been adopted since he left the mining industry two years ago for health reasons.

He continued: "I want the public to know these things and to know that I am not one of the councillors involved in the comments of the District Auditor and the authority's finances." The four candidates chosen by the 108 voters present at the meeting were: Mrs H Denwood of Milton Grove; Mr John Oliver of Beech Terrace, Ashington; Councillor George Rogerson of Richardson Street; and Mr B Bell, a former councillor, also of Beech Terrace. It is understood that there were ten candidates for selection at the meeting. Councillor Rogers failed to be elected by a narrow majority. Mr George Holland, Chairman of the local Labour Party, who presided at the selection meeting said last night: "The comments (by Rogers) are quite uncalled for and the statement will probably be dealt with at a meeting of the local Labour Party this week."

In general (apart from on the political scene) the 1950s were among the most stable in Ashington's turbulent history. It was a Golden Age. If you were a teenager (although that term wasn't even coined) then leisure opportunities were many and varied, and I can recall that, like any other youth without a care in the world in this grimy pit town, I fell asleep as soon as my head hit the pillow, safe and secure in the knowledge that a new day would dawn, bringing another carefree 24-hours to savour. And if that day happened to be a Saturday then my joy would be complete.

On a Saturday morning, in the split second of awakening before the senses had time to attune to my surroundings, I'd blink my eyes and wonder where I was, but, more importantly, what day it was. And once the word came back, via my brain cells, identifying Saturday, then a huge grin inevitably spread across my freckled face. After five frustrating days spent underground, I was free to roam. Being a sportsman, my options were open.

First stop before 10 am Saturday was Priestman's Institute on North Seaton Road. A brisk two-minute walk from the family home at 99 Maple Street saw me arrive at the Tute to find a handful of snooker and billiard enthusiasts already sitting on a bench under the glass canopy that kept you dry when it rained and hot when the sun shone. Though, to the best of my knowledge, no Ashington folks in the early Fifties ever boasted a sun tan. A pitman's complexion, by virtue of being locked away from the daylight, was always pallid - some called it 'pasty' - as though suffering some malady. Conversely, a miner's wife or mother was denied the sun, tied by her pinny strings to the pantry – given its coffin-like proportions, you could hardly call it a kitchen.

At ten on the dot, the caretaker/manager would appear from within and unlock the door. Caretakers in my day included the soft-spoken Bill Shell, the sleepy-eyed Wilson Graham and the pugnacious former RAF boxing champion, Sammy Morgan. A management committee that included Tommy Mason, Billy Staines, Norman Scott, Jimmy Henderson, a Mr Fitzpatrick and others, met weekly to discuss day-to-day matters. One day I found myself (aged 15) in front of the committee to explain why I had been 'put on the books' by Sammy Morgan. The way it happened was ... I was playing billiards on No 6 table, next to the office kiosk, when I wellied the red which was on its spot. That spot sometimes had a well-worn hole in it which could cause balls to bounce if struck too hard. How hard is 'too hard'? Well, obviously when it lifts about two feet into the air, crashes into the kiosk bench and smashes two bottles of Vimto that were standing there. I can still hear Sammy, red in the face, splattered in crimson juice, yelling 'Kirkup – you're on the books!'

New Automatic Lighting Plan for Ashington (News Post – 10th March, 1952)

Automatic control will replace the present hand-switching method of street lighting in Ashington if the Minister of Housing and Local Government gives his sanction and his consent for Ashington Urban Council to raise the necessary loan to effect the change-over. This was revealed at a meeting of the Council on Thursday night, when it was stated that the Surveyor had presented a detailed report in respect of the proposals for the change-over. The North Eastern Electricity Board had quoted the figure of £7,868, which would cover the cost for the provision of the necessary injection equipment and relays, and for their installation and connection. The surveyor pointed out the estimated saving by the council per annum, if the capital was raised by way of a loan, as compared with the existing yearly charges for switching. *(Note – prior to this, a lamplighter carrying a long pole pedalled his bike around Ashington's back streets and garden fronts switching on the light-bulbs attached to the lamp-posts).*

Where Did All The Shops Go? by John and Betty Freeman
During a recent visit back home to Ashington, my wife Betty and I wandered along the main street and began to recall the names of shops, cinemas, etc, that once graced Station Road around 1952. We also put a few names to faces of some of the people who worked in those places. (Maiden names for girls)

Our walk begins at what was once the old bus station and we travel west to the Station Bridge. First stop is the Wallaw Cinema where Walter Lawson was the *El Supremo* of cinemas in Ashington. The Wallaw was regarded as the 'second best' of the five that existed at the time – the Regal was generally felt to be the 'best'.

Films were so popular in those days that it was common for people to see two films in a week. If you were a 'couple' the lad paid for one visit and the lass paid for the other. There were two houses a night with matinees twice a week. Queues at the Wallaw of three and four deep stretched right round the corner into Lintonville Terrace and around the back of the shops. If you were unlucky enough to be amongst the last admitted, you could look forward to sitting either in the front row or the side seats. Then you came out after two hours with your nose pointing up to the heavens or with your head at 70 degrees to the rest of your body.

Next to the cinema was the **Wool Shop** followed by **Levey's** the wallpaper and paints shop. A few short steps and you were in front of **Donkin's**, one of the most famous bakers in town, which appears to have stood the test of time. Their produce was always of high quality and, if you fancied a cake, you had to be prepared to stand in yet another queue. Anna Meredith worked in that shop for years and must have been their most loyal employee.

The next window to gaze into belonged to the **Laburnum Stores**, a large furniture shop that specialised in fancy goods. Most of the space on that section of the 'Grand Corner' belonged to **Arrowsmith's**, a huge store with clothes being the main feature of sales. Sid Garvie and Cecil Crask were two of the bosses and some of their great assistants included Mary Beal, who the last time we heard (as Mrs Murray) was still hitting a mean ball at Newbiggin Gold Course. Sid Garvie was also chairman of The Ashington Tradesmen Football Club which operated in the Tyneside

Wednesday League.

Crossing the road at Lintonville Terrace, on the corner was **The Meadow Dairy**, a grocer's shop where I, John Freeman, worked with the Best Man at my wedding, Ronnie Staines. Jack Lyall was the manager then and his wife Connie worked part-time; another full-time employee was Rita Straughan who teased the life out of us two young lads, but she was great to work with. Next door was **Brough's**, another grocer's shop where some of our best friends to this day worked, including Edie Curry (Bridesmaid at our Wedding), Vera Mordue, Wendy Cochrane and Joy Adler.

The Linton & Woodhorn Miners' Hall was next – it eventually doubled up as an indoor market. Then a short gap for a road leading into North View and an **Insurance Office**, followed by the **Scotch Wool Shop** which adjoined the **Midland Bank**.

Next en route was **Main's Bicycles** where one of the greatest personalities working there was Ralph Coupland. A smashing lad was Ralph, and Betty and I enjoyed many happy times with him at the Arcade Ballroom, Docherty's snooker hall and on the football field.
Moving down we come to another large shop: **Snow's** which specialised in lingerie, cardigans and hosiery. **Newcastle Savings Bank** was next followed by **Benefit Shoes** and **Anderson's Baby Shop**.

Then came the modern man's outfitters – **Marcus Price** – and all of us teenagers wanted something from this shop because it was 'different'. Mary Carmichael was the boss, ably assisted by another of our good friends, Gladys Robson.

A hat shop (**Lillian Cook's**) was next in line followed by a large concern called **McDonald's** (no, not the fast food chain!) but a ladies outfitters which provided a wide range of goods. This shop joined on to **Carrick's** the bakers and café which is still there today, but under a different name.

A sweet shop, named **M & M**, filled the next space, followed by the first of three gents' tailors, namely **John Collier**. In those days it was not uncommon to have a suit made to measure, and competition was high. The **White Shop Butcher's** figures prominently, and we recall Mr Burgess and Mr Blevins being at the forefront of this business. If ladies wanted to splash out a little more for their clothes, they could often be found in **Miss Walker's**, a rather select shop, providing coats, dresses and blouses. Next came an ice-cream shop, run then by the **Badiali's** and the **Buffalo Cinema**, another popular spot at that time. George Potts, Bob Duff and I used to strut past the queue on Sunday evenings in our new-fangled 'Bop' shirts (square-bottomed and worn *outside* the trousers) to spot who was fixed up and who wasn't. If you 'clicked' you had to scrush in, and this led to many an interesting situation.

A short gap across the opening to Ashington YMCA, and you entered the portals of **Jackson's the Tailor** who many thought was the best in town. The last shop to be reached on this side was **Jas Walten's**, a classy shop with some outstanding furniture.

Crossing Station Road (heading back to the 'Grand') the first shop we reach was **Adeline's** a ladies Hairdresser's which stood next to **Findlay's** the tobacconist. Where Bubbles Wine Bar now stands was the home to the **Portland Printing Works**. Next came the **Army & Navy** stores followed by **Timothy White's** the chemist. The pharmacist at that time was Mr Maughan, the son of Billy Maughan, the Lynemouth Colliery Ventilation Officer in my early days at that pit – Billy taught me a lot about mining.

Moving down the street we visualise **Leonard's Shoes** before reaching the largest department store in town: **Doggarts**. Many people used this store and paid an agent on a weekly basis in return for goods obtained with a voucher. This was known as the 'Club' system and there were a number of Clubmen willing to provide vouchers.

Burton's the tailor came next and this completed the trilogy of gents' tailors on the main street. Lads who worked at Burton's then were Walter Wilkes, Bill Gibson and Eddie Main, who were also members of the Tradesmen football team. Being a member of the same team, Ronnie Staines and I were sometimes persuaded to go there for our next suit with the hint that we might get a discount. But did we get one?

Docherty's tobacco shop came next, followed by the classy **Keith Cazaly's** ladies fashion shop where Nancy Forbes was the manageress with a team that included Colleen Moore and a girl called Joyce? **Playfair Shoes** occupied the next space where Ernest Walker was manager with employees Lorna Whitfield, Freda Ruddick, Betty Cullingworth and Dinah O'Keefe who later married the boss. It was from this shop that my wife-to-be Betty would be sweeping the pavement outside that shop while I washed the windows of the Meadow Dairy. When we thought our respective bosses weren't watching us, we would wave to each other and blow the odd kiss. On such passionate moments the earth has been known to move!

Lipton's the grocer was next, followed by **Lawson's** sweet shop. Above these last-named shops we had **Bobby Gray's Salerooms** and **Docherty's Billiard Hall** where on many a Saturday morning us pit lads would roll in to play 'Crash'. Amongst them were Billy Mack and Norman Taylor, and you had to be reasonably good or you lost your money.

Moving on, we remember **Duncan's** the grocers where Stan Rowe was the boss. Stan was also a speedy footballer for the Tradesmen, and went on to set up his own business. Next was **Dewhurst** the butcher where Tommy Yearham, the Ford? Twins and Ella Moffat worked.

Boots the Chemist then loomed up, followed by **Hardy's Furniture**, another huge store. The next establishment was **Costelloe's Pawnbrokers**. Yes, kids, people really did take articles to pawn on a Monday to obtain cash, and then return on Friday or Saturday to retrieve them. Quite often it was clothes they needed for the weekend. There was a discreet back entrance to this shop which faced on to the Trade Union Hall so that these unfortunate people could conduct their business out of view.

Moving on, we approach **Dunn's Shoes** and then to the familiar **Woolworth's**. Beyond this store was **Aiston's** a gent's outfitters which always had a good selection of shirts and ties. Then to one of the most interesting shops of the main street – **Lewis's Hardware** shop. Just to go in was an education as Dick Lewis sold everything.

Next came **Dampney's** wallpaper shop where Edna Storey was in charge. Edna was also a very good ballroom dancer. Then that bastion of traders: **Shephards**, a store as large as Arrowsmith's which sat diagonally opposite. It meant, of course, that shoppers could visit two huge shops in a distance of a few yards and conduct an enormous amount of business. Crossing North Seaton Road, and still travelling east, we encounter the never-to-be-forgotten **Grand Hotel**. Countless stories came out of this place, and some of them were quite hairy. This could not detract from the splendour of the building and we were sorry to see it change so much.

We are nearing the end of our walk now and we can just about remember **Cooper's** store on the corner of Poplar Street with Arthur Poxton as the boss, followed by **Sanderson's** Fruit Shop and **Pieroni's** Ice Cream Parlour.

Postscript from JF - "Ashington in the 1950s was a thriving post-war town with plenty of employment – the coal mines being the main provider. There were 20 workingmen's clubs, three pubs and shops galore where the emphasis was on food and dress, particularly the latter. Lads and lasses (and mums and dads) wanted to look their best when they went out and didn't mind paying money to do so. On reflection, those were possibly the best times enjoyed in Ashington, and we were proud of our heritage. We still are!"

'Sprinter hurt on motor cycle'. (January 1953 News Post)
A well-known professional north-east sprinter who was strongly fancied for the Powderhall Handicap in January, lay injured in the Newcastle Infirmary last night. He is John Thompson, aged 23, of Katherine Street who was hurt when his motor cycle collided with a lamp post at the Woodhorn Colliery corner. In sprinting circles John is known as J Berwick of Ashington. He was second at Powderhall two years ago (1951). The pillion passenger, Henry McLaughlin of Ariel Street, was allowed to go home after treatment at Ashington Hospital.' (*Note – sadly, John never recovered from his injuries*)

It is Ashington's 'Muggie' Season (by 'Codling' Morpeth Herald – 15th May, 1953)
I was walking down one of Ashington's streets the other day and I came upon a group of youngsters congregated round a hole in the ground. They were mouthing words which seemed to strike a chord in my memory – words that I had uttered so many, many years ago. They were playing marbles and, as is natural, using the peculiar esoteric terminology of marbles. But that was my first mistake – calling the game 'marbles' – for any self-respecting player of the game knows well enough, to the initiated, it becomes 'muggies',

The youngsters paid no heed to me and, for a time, I watched in interest and considerable bewilderment. Time had taken its toll on my memory and I must needs see a demonstration of what they called 'twosy', 'nudgy', 'smudgy' and 'mairky' before their meaning sunk into my brain. So interested did I become that I crept nearer and nearer the hole, until finally I kicked one of the marbles thrown up by a player. The look of complete scorn I received made the courage ooze out of my pulse. How utterly ridiculous for a grown-up person like myself to be indulging in such sentimentalism as to be engrossed in a game of 'muggies'.

'Builders making £500 a week in Profit'
According to the *Newcastle Journal,* an allegation was made in the Ashington Council Chambers in September 1953 that "Some builders must be making £500 a week profit." Cllr McNiven, Chairman of the Housing Committee, reported that as a result of tenders submitted for the building of houses on the Darnley Road estate it had been decided to build them all by private labour. With a view to contrasting prices by direct labour and those by private contractors, Ashington Council recently invited the tenders. Cllr McNiven added: 'If we had accepted the tenders of private contractors, the weekly rent of the houses would have risen by between 2s and 4s, compared to what we will charge.' Cllr Mick Bell said: 'I estimate that some builders are making £500 a week profit out of building houses at those prices.'

At the age of eighteen, my face-training over, I returned to the Bothal Pit as a coal filler. The procedure was that fillers who were not part of a regular set met at the Overman's cabin near the shaft bottom. On that first morning I mingled with half-a-dozen dozen others that included Reuben Daglish and Alan White, trying to blend into the background. Ernie Cobbledick, backshift overman, allocated some of the newcomers to take the place of absentee men. They moved off in-bye leaving three of us. I was eventually placed at the tail-end of one of the Bensham faces. This entailed keeping the conveyor belt drum at the barrier-end clean and free from dross. It was an easy introduction to face work and I was well satisfied at the end of my first shift, and even more so when I learned that I was 'part of the bargain'. It meant I was now on piece-work and earning about ten pounds a week. But I was still far from happy with my underground existence, always aware that there was more to life than burrowing away under the ground, imitating a mole.

'Crazy' Contests may return to the 'dull' Town'
That was the headline in the *Journal* of 10th September 1953. It reported "Is Ashington a 'dull' town? Some residents believe it is much too dull. So a group of local men are considering a revival of the town's crazy contests in the near future.

'This may mean the return of onion, rabbit pie and ham sandwich eating contests; competitions involving blowing up of balloons, drinking pints of beer and smoking cigars faster than anyone else; and even hectic wheelbarrow races through the town.

'Even the horticultural show and children's sports are facing diminishing attendances. The refusal of Ashington Council to allow a fairground at People's Park has been blamed for the loss of the

horticultural show and the children's sports. The Council may be petitioned with a request for a relaxation on the use of the Park.
'Until 1947 when the Park was re-sown and levelled, a fairground formed a big part of the entertainment at the annual flower show and children's sports. Attendances at both these events have been dropping since.'

'Footpaths may be banned to Cyclists.' (Ashington Post – September 1953)
'Seaton Hirst and North Seaton Colliery are only 100 yards apart, but cyclists may shortly have to pedal a mile-long road to get from one to the other.

'An attempt is to be made by Ashington District Council in 1953 to ban certain footpaths in the town to cyclists, and the paths between Seaton Hirst and North Seaton will be among them. Councillors have become increasingly alarmed during the past months at the number of reported incidents in which pedal cyclists using footpaths in the built-up area as short cuts have knocked down pedestrians. One of the paths likely to be banned is at Hirst Park where youths are reported to hold cycle races.'

'Deserved what he got' – Lawyer. A man said to have associated with another man's wife, deserved what he got when the husband hit him and broke his false teeth. This view was expressed by Mr William Craigs, defending solicitor at Ashington Magistrates Court in September 1953.

'Bus and Engine Crash at Crossing' Twenty-eight members of the Ashington YMCA Gleemen narrowly escaped serious injury late last night (8-10-53) when the bus in which they were traveling was in a collision with a locomotive and guard's van at Ellington Crossings at Ashington. The bus was bringing the Gleemen back from Widdrington where they had been giving a concert. It approached Ellington Crossings near Portland Terrace at the same time as the engine which was about to go into sidings. The buffers of the engine went through the side of the coach. Only one person, Mr Fred Bennett, a former chairman of Ashington Council, was injured, but his injuries were so slight that he would not go to hospital. Mr R Rickaby of John Street, Ashington, said afterwards "We were all very shaken, but thankful that there was no more serious injury." The bus, belonging to Bedlington and District Luxury Coaches, was driven by Mr J Hunt of Newbiggin.

'The Shoveller-in is Raking It In – as yet, the tax man doesn't know'. (Journal October 1953)
Without recourse to arbitration, Union negotiations or strikes, a fifty per cent increase in pay has been obtained by a class of wage-earners whose activities would probably surprise many an Inland Revenue Inspector. One of these days, some clerk in the tax department is going to get a surprise, for he will open a letter containing a statement of earnings from some conscientious person and will find on the line reserved for "occupation or profession" the term "shoveller-in". The surprise clerk will undoubtedly ask: "What is a shoveller-in?"

‘Shovelling-in has been a recognized job in mining villages for many years, but until recently nobody had been known to tackle it on a full-time basis. The shoveller-in, with shovel and advance knowledge of the movement of trucks delivering concession coal to miners, goes around offering to transfer the coal from street into the coalhouses. In Ashington there is a group of such men with regular customers and almost a regular weekly income. They regret that all coal is not dumped on the street, for the use of bags does them out of a job. Like most other costs, the price of shovelling-in has increased, but now these workmen are starting to charge 1s 6d per load instead of the shilling that has ruled for some time. At this new price a good shoveller-in with regular customers can, in an area like Ashington, Newbiggin and Lynemouth, earn over £5 for a 24-hour week with only the maintenance of a shovel as overhead costs.’

‘Collier Joins Sunderland’ Ashington FC last night (13-10-53) transferred to Sunderland their 21-year-old West Sleekburn goalkeeper, Gordon Mason, at a fee described by the Ashington Club as “very satisfactory”. Mason, who is 6ft 2ins, has been attracting the attention of First Division scouts all this season. Sunderland officials watched him at Blackhall last Saturday, and negotiations were completed last night, so that he would be able to play for Sunderland Reserves at North Shields tomorrow. Mason, who has been with Ashington for two seasons, signed professional forms for the club only two weeks ago.

‘Ten hurt in Ashington Bus-Train Collision’ Ten people were taken to Ashington Hospital yesterday (1-11-53) when an Alnwick-Ashington bus with forty passengers, was in collision with the rear part of a train which was going over gateless level crossings at Ellington Terrace, Ashington. It is understood that a large hole was torn in the side of the bus by the buffers. The accident was the second on the crossing in a month. The driver of the bus was Mr H Latimer of Guide Post, employed at the Ashington depot of the United Automobile Services Limited. The crossing is over a main road between Ashington and Ellington. When used by rail traffic, road vehicles are usually held up by large red disks labelled “STOP” installed at each side of the crossing. British Railways, who have already inquired into the first incident, are making another investigation into what happened on Saturday.

‘Now Only Ashington Women Use Tin Bath – Coal Town lacks modern amenities’. Following the opening of the pit head baths at Ashington Colliery in 1952, the days of the miner bathing in a tin bath in front of the fire are no more – only his wife and daughters have to do that now. Friday night is generally bath night in the town, when father and sons – fresh from a bath and sunray treatment at the colliery – are confined to the sitting room while mother and daughters take turns to wash in the kitchen. This lack of modern amenities at Ashington’s colliery houses is referred to in the annual report of the Medical Officer of Health, Dr C B McGregor, issued today (6-11-53).

'She says that most of the colliery houses are sub-standard. "According to modern ideas, but few of them are likely to merit demolition." They could be modernised and brought up to a reasonable standard by the provision of bathrooms and other amenities and while Dr McGregor hopes that this may be done at some time in the future "there is no immediate prospect of these improvements taking place." It is estimated that nearly half of Ashington's 8,000 houses are without baths and similar modern amenities.

'According to a report by Dr J B Tilley, such housing conditions are a contributory cause, making Ashington a county black-spot for infant mortality. One in every 24 babies born last year died before reaching one year. Such reports are causing concern among the people of Ashington. They view with envy the fortune of the miners' wives of Newbiggin where bathrooms are being installed in colliery houses. It is understood that no similar plan is yet contemplated to modernise colliery houses in Ashington, although the NCB will shortly embark on a scheme to provide front gardens and tidy paths to more than 1,000 colliery houses in the Hirst area in fronts which are at present merely expanses of mud and water with the occasional garden fenced in. Owners of the few houses in the Hirst which do not belong to the NCB will be asked to fall into line by contributing towards the general scheme.'

Christmas Bustle on the Coal Front (Advertiser – 24th December, 1953)
The pre-Christmas bustle of activity at the local pits has produced some noteworthy output figures. On Monday last, the 4,000 miners of Ashington Colliery broke their daily production record of 6,299 tons when they recorded an output of 6,479 tons.

Last week, No. 3 Area, comprising the Ashington group and the collieries in north Northumberland, broke the area record with an output that was 20% above the output for the same week of last year. The feat of the Ashington Colliery miners is surprising as Monday is normally considered as being the 'black' day of the week, when output does not normally touch the weekly average.

To add to this achievement is the fact that at the colliery the seams are much narrower than they were in years past and therefore record breaking could hardly be expected. Last week was 'Bull' week for the area miners who will be paid their Christmas wages this Thursday. It will provide a useful bonus in many workmen's pay packets. Mr Donald Hindson, Area General Manager, said this week: "I should like to thank all the miners and officials who have thus increased the output and contributed to the record-breaking achievements. It proves that there has been some hard work done throughout the area."

Community of Pioneering Blood by Norman Shrapnel (The Times – June, 1953)
They call Ashington the Biggest Mining Village in the World, with its 36,000 at the dormitory centre and thousands more round the satellite pits at Linton, Woodhorn, Lynemouth and Ellington. Any suggestion that

they have not moved with the times would be resented, and rightly. They have done better. They have gone on mining into the quite exceptional virtues of their past, rich seams of enlightenment which made their pioneers, in matters of welfare, pit safety, technical training, and – more disinterestingly than many would think proper today – general education. Yet Ashington stands, in the physical sense, roughly where it did. Just as the output from its three shafts have been pretty steady for half a century, so have the dark crowded lines of its miners' cottages seen little change but extension.

The idea of a ruled-off community standing fiercely apart is naturally frowned on by those who can see farther than the gleam of their pit lamps. Yet it is little enough, except statistically, that the non-mining world knows of what goes on beyond the grey frontier mountains of pit waste: the strange country with its private network of railways known mysteriously as the Tankey, moving the coal to the undiscovered port of Blyth on its way to Scandinavia or coastwise to London. Between the dark lines is the brightness of proud little gardens, tomatoes growing in greenhouses. It is a country both congested and spacious: there are sixty acres of playing fields around Ashington, huge rooms in some of its twenty Working Men's Clubs, and in the Institute – provided by what is claimed to be the only self-supporting Miner's Welfare Scheme in Britain – a main hall so vast that they used to play bowls there in the winter.

Nobody would believe that it is all study and song, drama and quartets, higher thoughts and flower shows in this brave old world. What of the mighty pie-eating contests, once so famous in these parts? These seem to have died, though the Onion Eating Championships are still talked about with a surreptitious awe. But more famous here than any onion eating or leek growing champion is Mr Harry Wallace, a retired miner with a crushing hand grip and unextinguished eyes, who for sixty years has been producing wood carvings of remarkable vitality, his subjects ranging from ploughmen to Mr Aneurin Bevan.

It is its painters, however, who have more than anyone else carried the name of Ashington over the grey mountains. Working miners are among the best painters in the Ashington Art Group, which can claim to be a 'school' with more truth than usual.

One member explained: "Right from the start we tried to splash the paint about and keep clear of the academic rules." The results? Hundreds of paintings are stacked in the studio hut which members bought from their sales and sheer liveliness of fish-and-chip shops, holiday camp and similar uninhabited scenes nearly knocks you down. There have been shows at Newcastle Laing Art Gallery and in London, too, and people pay £3-£15 for a picture. At first, all the money went to the group; now it gets two-thirds and the painter the rest. Sometimes a member will sneak off into the country and paint a conventional landscape 'for a little light relief.'

A Home That Leeks Built (Journal 1950s)

The man they call 'King of the Leeks' is hoping to crown his career by winning a dining room suite. It is the only item of furniture in his house that Mr Jimmy Eke has not won in the 36 years of growing prize leeks. Next month, 59-year-old Mr Eke, a colliery foreman at Ashington, sets out to put this right.

He will compete against 24,000 amateur gardeners for a share in the £250,000 worth of prizes to be won at leek shows in pubs and clubs throughout Northumberland and Durham. Prizes like suites of furniture, TV sets, refrigerators, washing machines, crockery and cutlery. In Ashington alone prizes valued at £25,000 are at stake.

At his home in Hawthorn Road, Mr Eke listed his past winnings: a bedroom suite; kitchen suite; writing bureau; settees; fireside chairs; piles of bedding; about twenty sets of tea and dinner crockery; fridge; dozens of canteens of cutlery; a made-to-measure suit; shoes and a few hundred pounds in cash. Mr Tom Drysdale, Secretary of the local Social Club's leek section said yesterday: "There is no doubt that Jimmy is the best leek grower in the north. If he gets first prize again – he's already done it three times in the last four years – I'll see to it personally that he gets the suite."

Ashington lads in the 1950s were becoming eligible for National Service and a compulsory two years spent in one the Armed Forces. Coal miners were exempt from this by virtue of working in a 'reserved occupation', so it was only a small minority of youths working in the retail trade who found themselves, at eighteen years of age, serving King (later Queen) and Country. Suddenly, working underground seemed a far better proposition than fighting wayward Koreans or squaring up to the Mau Mau in Kenya, so some young shop-workers were lured down the pit. The ones who did brave National Service came back, saying that "it was an experience they would not have missed". Even today in 2006, there are those who would like to see some form of conscription brought back. For myself, it didn't affect me one way or another. At twenty years of age in 1954, I had been down the pit for five years, progressing from my shaft-bottom job, via timber leading and putting on to coal filling. Like hundreds of other young men, my life was mapped out for me. This would be my lot for the next fifty years. But would it? Towards the end of my coal-filling days, the conveyor on which I was working stopped - the rubber belt had snapped, and that meant at least a half hour delay while the deputy spliced it back together. As you sit on a wooden chock at the coalface, you have time to ponder, to view your surroundings. The nearest man's cap lamp, ten yards away down the face, threw a sharp beam into the goaf, revealing tons of rock ready to fall when the Drawers came in to take out the planks and chocks that held it up.

You would think there is silence down the pit when all the machinery driving the belt grinds to a halt – not so. The roof is constantly on the move, strata laying on strata, wooden props crackling and popping under the weight. And there I was: a twenty-year-old with all my life ahead of me. I looked down at my hands, counting the scars – thirty-two in all – incurred by man-handling sharp pieces of coal. And for what? In those days young men 'tipped up' their wages: gave them to their mothers who, in turn, provided board and lodgings, and even paid for their clothes and holidays. I was making 'canny' money on filling in 1954, probably around ten pounds, but all I was getting back was thirty bob pocket money. I thought it unfair. But apart from that iniquity, there was the fear of the job itself. I seemed to take on the mentality of a Lancaster bomber pilot during the war, flying into Germany. It was well known that the more sorties they flew, the less chance they had of coming back. The odds were stacked against them. That was me! I thought *'Hey, Michael, get yorsel oot o' here, bonnie lad, or the next time ye gan doon the pit ... ye might not come back up again.'*

My mother was furious (strange how my *father* never came into the equation). Even more annoyed were the gaffers at Ashington Colliery. For anyone to leave their pit was an affront – how dare you go away when we have trained you into a highly skilled miner? For punishment they put me in the nightshift – four pm until midnight – the graveyard shift, fit only for old men who had given their all for coal and country. I was determined never to let myself get into that category. In the end, I didn't even serve out my two-week's notice, but threw away my hard hat after lasting only four days. *Good riddance to the pit,* I thought.

'Whey, waat are ye ganna dee noo then, Michael? Ye canna sit aroond the hoose, deein' nowt, ye knaa.'

'Aa knaa that, mother – Aa'm ganna join the Air Force.' I had seen an advert in the *North Mail* saying that the country was short of airmen. And so it was that in August 1954, I became Aircraftsman 4157295 Kirkup with a trade of Radar Operator. I had opted for this job although, at the time, I knew nothing of what it entailed. I knew that there were radar aerials just up the north-east coast at Boulmer, wafting away in the sea breeze on grassy hillocks. But what I did not know was that the radar cabins where I was to work were situated in bunkers fifty feet *below* the ground. I had enlisted to see the world and had signed on as a Regular for five years. But having spent five years 'doon the pit', I discovered that I was to spend the next five years underground – the only difference from being at the shaft bottom was that the radar station floor was covered in linoleum.

My first posting of any length was at RAF Seaton Snook, at Seaton Carew, near Hartlepool. It was a twenty-minute train journey from Hartlepool to Newcastle Central and then another hour's ride on the bus from the Haymarket. Regular twenty-four and forty-eight-hour leave passes issued at the camp meant that I was still able to keep tabs on what was happening on the home front at Ashington where I spent most of my weekends.

After a couple of years I had reached the rank of senior aircraftsman – only two steps up from the bottom – when it was suggested that I go on 'Advanced Training' which would make me eligible for promotion to NCO ... a Corporal. The course lasted six weeks in various parts of the country, one of which was at Portland Bill, overlooking the high cliffs. It was here in early 1956 that the songs of Elvis Presley were on everyone's lips, and I recall getting up on a stage in the NAAFI, in front of a few others, and gyrating my hips while miming to *All Shook Up*, blasting away on the jukebox.

Towards the end of the course, the examiner – a Flight Sergeant – commented: 'You have done very well, Kirkup. You really surprised me with your theoretical knowledge and application." Now I thought at the time that this was a real compliment. But having had time to reflect, what he was really saying was: *"With your background as a pitman, laddie, I gave you* no *chance at all of passing."* I was to find it was almost universally perceived in the 1950s (and probably still is) that if you had a background in coal mining then that was all you were good for.

I passed that course exam and was duly promoted to Corporal, but that, too, brought its problems. For a start, you couldn't mix socially with the 'other ranks'. You had to use the Corporals' Club and not the NAAFI for relaxation purposes, so splitting you up from any friends you might have made. Naive youth that I was, I suddenly began to understand that there was a class system operating for practically everything in the UK. Most folks I knew that were born into a working-class environment, like Ashington, accepted their lot and rarely, if ever, moved up the social scale. They didn't feel deprived – everyone in their back lane was the same. A line from *'Song of the Coal'*, a musical I wrote many years later went: *'Doon the pit, you're doon the pit, there's not much lower ye can get'*. And that was true. If you were a pitman, it was thought that you couldn't get any lower down the social ladder.

"He plays a church organ in Ashington" by Sentinel (Ashington Post September 1954)

"Once a journalist always a journalist," they say. On the whole that is true, for journalists are a strange tribe, and few are gifted with the golden quality of versatility unless it applies in some way to our craft. And so we remain in the only world we really know and understand. This briefly is the story of a living exception to the rule of 'once a journalist always a journalist.'

"He was born and bred in Ashington and knows almost every nook and cranny of his native heath. He knows an army of people, too. And even more know him – by sight. He plays a church organ in Ashington during much of his off-duty leisure. He is passionately devoted to the music of Bach and Beethoven. He is 24-year-old John Mordue, of 100 Beatrice Street, Ashington.

"In slightly less than a month from today (Sept 1954), Mr Mordue will have severed his connection with journalism, and will embark on a course of study which he hopes will bring him degrees in Music, leading eventually to a happy life as a musical 'GP'. Assuredly, he will succeed as a teacher of Music, for he is himself an ideal pupil with a temperament superbly attuned to the task he has set himself.

"His cheery grin and good-natured humour will be missed in the police stations and fire stations in Ashington and Bedlington and in other establishments of officialdom which are reliable sources of information. John will go to a college in Leeds to study, and with him will go the sincere good wishes of all who know him."

(Note – many of the articles in this book were penned by journalist John Mordue who went on to become a headmaster – he now lives in Oxfordshire)

Ashington Sunday School Decline – Methodist Report on Fall in Numbers

Figures and first visual observations clearly show that all is not well in the youth work of Ashington Methodist circuit. Of the 562 young children in the Sunday Schools eight years ago, and who are now 15 to 16 years old, fewer than 46 remain, it is stated. These facts are disclosed in the report of the activities of the circuit of 1954 by the Circuit Youth Secretary, Mr W Lamb, of 124 Maple Street, Ashington. "In addition," continues the report "the inflow of young children aged seven years has dropped by over 200 per year in the same period."

Mr Lamb points out that the number of children who are lost between the ages of eight and sixteen raises a very serious problem which cannot be ignored. To help stimulate interest among the young people in the churches, the first Circuit Youth Festival was held in April 1954. The success of this first festival shows that the children are quick to follow the lead given by some of the circuit officials, and the festivals make the first step to arrest the alarming decline in numbers. It is now learnt that Dr Jim Hobbs will be the Chairman of the Youth Festival Concert on Saturday 13th April, the last event in this year's festival at which two handsome trophies awarded to the successful churches will be presented by Mrs Winnie Hobbs. It is felt generally that the festival may, in future years, become the biggest event of its kind in East Northumberland.

Ashington Miners are Satisfied but Watchful (Advertiser – 1st April, 1954)

It took two hours on Sunday morning to tell a thousand Ashington mineworkers - representing eleven thousand men – the story of the interview of their five-man deputation with the Minister of Health concerning ways and means of improving the efficiency of Ashington General Hospital's services, and what the men heard they liked, for they passed a resolution saying "We are satisfied" and urged their officials to carry on with the good work.

The story was told at a meeting in the Pavilion Theatre by Mr George Corbett, Secretary of the Ellington Miners; Mr Bob Scott, an official of the Woodhorn Administrative Workers' Union; The Rt Hon Bob Taylor MP from Morpeth; and Mr Tom Fox, Secretary of the Mineworkers' Federation. The meeting was told of regulations made for the staff at Ashington Hospital as a result of the representations of the miners. These include:

- An extension to the present phone has been installed in the nurses' home at the centre so that in future emergencies communication will be speeded up.
- In case of serious injury, the consulting surgeon on duty must be notified before any person is refused admission to the hospital.

- As soon as it is known an emergency case has to be admitted, the surgeon on duty has to be informed.
- A bed must always be kept empty and available somewhere in the hospital for an urgent case.

In a written reply to the verbal arguments from the deputation, the minister has informed the Mineworkers' Federation that:

- A Consultant Anaesthetist, recently appointed, is now required to live nearer to the hospital than his present home at Gosforth.
- The successor to the Registrar, who has resigned, will be required to live near the hospital.
- The Newcastle Regional Hospital Board will shortly consider the case for appointing a Senior Casualty Officer at Ashington Hospital.
- The NRHB has been asked to submit claims for a further allocation of capital towards large building projects. They are fully aware of the needs of Ashington.

The Minister concluded his reply: "I shall, of course, continue to keep in close touch with the position at Ashington Hospital and I hope that the various measures I have referred to would result in a steady improvement in the service available."

The disquiet about Ashington Hospital all came about when the Ashington Mineworkers Federation complained about the lack of treatment to an injured miner. This is the way the *Sunday Sun* covered the topic:
'Pitmen accuse a hospital' The 11,000 strong local miners' union have sent a letter of complaint to the Wansbeck Hospital Management Committee, expressing 'deep concern' about the alleged lack of facilities to treat 34-year-old Mr David Scott of Beatrice Street, Ashington, injured at Ellington Pit.

The Federation alleges that when Scott had an arm caught in a machine 'more than 20 minutes were spent in trying to contact the hospital by telephone and finally the local police had to be asked to go to the hospital and request someone to answer the phone.' In reply, it was stated that Ashington Hospital was short-staffed, but two vacancies for surgeons were expected to be filled 'in the near future'. Mr Scott was eventually sent to Newcastle RVI, fifteen miles away, because no surgeon was available at Ashington Hospital. The patient's arm was later amputated.

Two new surgeons soon arrived at Ashington Hospital; they were Dr Alan White, a senior house surgeon, and Dr Averil Charles – a woman doctor – a part-time house surgeon.

Later in the 1950s, medical staff at Ashington Hospital were arriving in mini cars or riding on Lambrettas.

In 1955 Jackie Milburn grabbed another FA Cup-winner's medal to add to the other two he had won in 1951 and '52 and in doing so scored the fastest goal ever in an FA Cup Final. A record that was to last almost to the millennium. Jackie left Newcastle United in 1957 to join the Irish team Linfield as player coach, winning for the Irishmen many trophies in his three-year stint, while himself picking up Irish Player of the Year. In the meantime, Jackie had cajoled, his old United colleague, Albert Stubbins, into taking on the role of player manager of Ashington FC. Said a bewildered Albert later, 'I only popped into his new fireplace shop on Station Road to say "Hello" and before I knew it I was Ashington FC's new manager. Did I say that Jackie Milburn could be very persuasive?'

Ashington Old People's Mangle is Mended (Ashington Post – 24th March, 1955)

Repaired at last is the old mangle which Ashington Urban Council's tenants in Woodhorn Villas subscribed to buy. They bought the mangle because the hot-air dryers in their communal laundry would not operate properly, but the mangle broke down too. The council have given the tenants a new wringer also, and have fitted posts into sockets on the grass to which the clothes lines can be tied. But the drying poles may be used only *once* a week. They remain in the laundry the rest of the week. Still, the old folk are well pleased.

YMCA Bulletin (Ashington Advertiser July 1955)

The famous cricket match between the Toc H and a team composed of the 'old men' of the YMCA took place on the Library Field last Friday. Toc H managed to win by by the narrow margin of three runs.

The following scored points for the Ashington Association of the Divisional YMCA at an atheltics and sports meeting held last Saturday at Bedlington Grammar School: Jim Waugh, B Glen, Mel Trevethick, J Charlton, A Laws and J Pringle. Our thanks to competitors and to Albert Laws and Cyril Gittins for their work in organising the team.

Letter to the Editor (Ashington Advertiser 29th July 1955)
From RW - 23 Rutland Street, Ashington.
"As I write, the sun slides down the shimmering blue bowl of sky, down to the cool level of far horizons. Those who toiled in the heat of the greater glory of Ashington Athletic fame have once again gurgled down their gullets a deep drench of victory, at Langwell Crescent Cricket Ground.

"But, sir, the smile on my face is a wry smile for I have just bumped my bottom on the Kenilworth Road entrance to the cricket ground. This entrance was imaginatively conceived as a rustic arch, but, alas, its dimensions are niggardly. It allows of no more than 2 ft 4 ins of headroom and its width is a paltry 1ft 10 ins. Moreover, partly obscuring the wayleave, is an iron protuberance at a low height from the ground. It was on this obstacle that I bumped my bottom.

"I beg the members of the cricket committee that they should recognise the experience of supporters who wish to enter the Kenilworth Road corner, and provide there a gateway of fair width and infinite headroom similar to that recently constructed at the Park Road East side of the ground."

Playing for Ashington Seconds that week at Langwell were J Robinson, W Roberts, Tom Glasper, Dick McLaughlin, Tom Eke, George Gray, E Hall, Peter Hollings, J Hill, F Robson and Brian Thain. They triumphed over a Lynemouth Eleven comprised of A Brotherton, W Kidd, E Murray, T Whillis, Alan Simpson, T Foster, A Anderson, J Simpson, Tom Laidler, Raymond Poxton and Eddie Straker.

Problems at Dangerous Railway Crossing (Ashington Post – 14th November, 1955)
The *Ashington Post* understands that factory employees at the North Seaton Trading Estate are unlikely to approve any suggestion of staggered hours to alleviate morning and evening congestion at North Seaton Railway Crossing. This suggestion was the outcome of a special representative meeting called by Ashington Council some time ago to seek a solution for the congestion at this traffic 'blackspot', and it is understood that the employees will not agree, and adhere to the belief that another crossing or footbridge should be provided.

Since 1953, this problem has been alive. In that year, it is understood, factory employees requested consideration of provision of a footbridge, which in their view, would decrease the daily danger. The suggestion went to Ashington Council who had been investigating the provision of a sub-way at Green Lane crossing, north of the estate. In view of the continued congestion, the council went ahead with plans for a special meeting to thrash out the question and seek a solution.

Staggered hours while operating from the management's point of view, is linked up with the provision of special buses to take employees to places like Newbiggin, Bedlington and Blyth. The managements say that with staggered hours more buses will be required. Information has now reached Ashington Council to the effect that the transport commission has considered the question of a crossing at a point about 150 yards south of Messrs Reyrolles crossing, but they did not favour this proposal. The view is now held that another crossing would be more satisfactory than a footbridge. And if such a crossing were provided, the factories, it has learned, would agree to providing a patrol man at peak periods of the day. Another aspect of the problem is that a crossing would be less costly than a footbridge. While a footbridge would cater for the pedestrian employee, the view is held by some authorities that it would not solve the problem of pedal cyclists.

Ashington Headmistress for Twenty-Six Years (News Post – 1955)
When she retires this week after more than twenty six years of Headmistress of Hirst East County Modern Girls School, Ashington, Miss Elizabeth Simpson will be saying goodbye to teaching, but her influence will continue to be felt in the school, which reflects so much of her own buoyant personality. She became head when Hirst East was changed for an all-standard to a modern secondary school, and under her it has become known as one of the best girls' schools in the district.

It might be thought that giving up an absorbing and satisfying career would come as something of a wrench, but Miss Simpson is looking forward to her retirement with the same interest and enjoyment she has put into teaching in the last forty years. She said last week: "I never regret leaving any stage in life, for I find there is always something to look forward to in the next." Hundreds of women living in the Ashington district are old girls of the school, and over and over again Miss Simpson has seen daughters of former scholars in their turn become pupils at the school.

Miss Simpson was honoured at a ceremony in the school attended by former pupils and past and present staff, when she was presented with a cheque from the Hirst East Old Girls' Association. A member of a well-known Morpeth family, Miss Simpson was education at Morpeth High School, now Morpeth Grammar School for Girls, under Miss E Morgan. From there she went on to St Hild's College, Durham. She began her teaching career in London, remaining there for five years before returning to the north. After a year on the staff of the Hirst North School, she went to what is now Bothal County Modern School, where she taught for eight years under Miss N Dixon.

It was in 1928 when the schools in the Ashington area were reorganised that she became headmistress at Hirst East, which was then to cater for pupils from eleven to fourteen. She paid tribute for the help she received from Miss E Coils. "We have got on very well together and Miss Coils' help has proved invaluable to me," she said.

"The importance of domestic science is stressed at the school, for Miss Simpson considers it valuable training for any girl. Here at Hirst East pupils spend one day a week at the cookery centre and study also laundering, needlework, tailoring and housewifery. "I don't think people realise just how much of the technique of domestic subjects girls learn now," she said "especially the older girls who are more mature and benefit from the extra year at school. I wish you could see Christmas cakes made by the pupils or a really beautiful display of garments tailored by them."

Miss Simpson confesses to being a feminist, but hastens to add that she deplores any suggestion of a battle between the sexes. "I think women have proved themselves just as able in executive positions as men and I feel most strongly that they should receive equal pay for equal work."

Lynemouth Coal will keep Men Busy for Sixty Years (Ashington Advertiser – September, 1955)

Everybody knows that a bold and exciting development story is being written day by day at Lynemouth Colliery, but not everybody – even on Lynemouth's doorstep – knows just what is cooking. The story was told in details to Prime Minister Sir Anthony Eden when he visited the 'Mechanical Marvel' pit recently.

Output at Lynemouth was 913 tons daily in 1947. It is now running at 2,160 tons per day and is expected to increase to 6,000 tons per day in 1960, at which level it should remain for another sixty years. To clean this greatly increased output and to serve neighbouring collieries, a new washery has been built, costing over one million pounds. The washery can take 800 tons per hour.

The purpose of the scheme is to work the large reserves of coal available to Lynemouth – 102 million tons, mainly under the sea – by the 'horizon' mining method. In the Lynemouth scheme this requires main roadways driven from the bottom of the two shafts to underground 'staple' shafts, where the coal can be lowered by chutes from the workings in the seam above. The coal is loaded into five-ton mine cars from the staple shafts and drawn by diesel locomotives to the shafts. Manpower at the colliery has increased from 787 men in 1947 to 1,591 today and is planned to increase to 2,107 in 1960.

United Bus Traffic Supervisor retires. (November, 1955)

After working for United buses for forty-two years, Mr J Gray of Rutland Terrace, Ashington, retired and will be succeeded by Mr Tommy Hall. A native of Cromer, Mr Gray was one of the first drivers in 1919 at United's Darlington depot, after which he was sent to Northumberland, initially to Blyth. He recalls that he went to Blyth with two buses running on solid tyres. At first he had to park the buses in the streets of Blyth at night, but later he got the use of a shed at Newsham Farm.

As the United bus service grew, he was sent to Ashington in 1930. At that time he combined the position of depot foreman and traffic supervisor. He remembers when United brought buses to Ashington they were parked in a field near the Old Road (North Seaton Road) Later, however, garages were built down Lintonville Terrace and in 1937 the United company built their first well-known depot on farmland next to Ashington Co-operative Arcade on Woodhorn Road.

Mr Gray told a *News Post* reporter (3-11-55) that in the early days at Ashington they ran a shuttle service to Newcastle at Bedlington Bank (Hairpin Bend) because the Bedlington Furnace Bank Bridge could not take heavy traffic. Passengers travelling from Ashington to Newcastle had to leave the bus on one side of the bank and walk up the other side to get another bus to complete the journey.

Ashington Miner's 'Fairy-tale' Success (Ashington Post – 13th January, 1956)

Mr James Bowman, who started work in the mining industry as a pit boy in Ashington, is to succeed Sir Hubert Holdsworth as Chairman of the National Coal Board. The appointment takes effect from 1st August. For the past year, Mr Bowman has been Deputy Chairman of the NCB, a post he took over at the start of a big NCB reorganisation scheme in February 1955. Aged 57, Mr Bowman has had nearly forty years in the mining industry and has worked at practically every level. He spent his early life at Haltwhistle, where his father was a blacksmith, and when he was fifteen the family moved to Ashington. His career followed the familiar pattern: putter, hewer, filler and conveyor worker. During the 1914-18 war, at the age of eighteen, he joined the Royal Marines and afterwards returned to his work at the pit.

Jim Bowman became a Pit Inspector and an officer of his Trade Union. He had a hard time during the difficult years of the 1920s depression and was, for some time, out of work and on the dole. In 1936, he came out of the pit at Ashington to become General Secretary of the Northumberland Miners. A year later, he was elected Vice-President of the Miners' Federation of Great Britain, a post to which he was returned unopposed during each of the ensuing ten years.

Ashington Top Town Team Home After 'De-Lovely' Time (Journal May 1956)

"*It's delicious, it's delightful, it's de-lovely,*" sang Sheila Armstrong, Ashington's 13-year-old star-in-the-making in the television engagement with Bournemouth on Saturday night. These words sum up the joyful feelings of the entire Top Town team as they were royally received back home last night.

The brass band struck up as the coaches entered Newbiggin Road, and people tumbled out of their houses to greet their 'giant killers'. A large crowd had waited for nearly two hours to greet them at the council chambers. Ashington showed it was proud of its team, and there was no doubt from their singing that the team were more than proud of Ashington.

With their coaches bedecked with flash and paper banners, the Ashington artists made a hand-waving return across Durham and

Northumberland. "Stop the traffic! Let the Top Town team by," was the cry at the crossroads.

The excitement is not over yet for Sheila Armstrong who has been offered a BBC contract that promises her at least two broadcasts a year. Her mother has already rejected an offer of a summer show contract at Butlins Filey because she thinks her daughter is too young. She is still considering a second offer.

And what does Sheila herself think of this fuss? Avoiding the waiting crowds, she jumped off the coach at the Grand Corner and went straight to the pictures. The children of the town were well in evidence during the triumphant entry into Ashington. A green-ribboned horseshoe, which they presented before the team set out, rested proudly on the front of the bus throughout the trip.

During the return journey, Mr Alan Robson, producer, Mr Arthur Leonard, secretary, and Cllr George Rogerson, bus-driving council chairman, were presented with a lighter, briefcase and cigarettes respectively. The presentation in a Leeds hotel was marked by an impromptu floor show to which Dick Slaughter, Tom Camsell, The Five Beaux and a Belle, and Dave Thompson set the waitresses and staff applauding.

The Ashington performers strongly deny that they were responsible for the disappearance from the Bournemouth dressing room of the black cat mascot. In fact, after an intensive search, it was 72-year-old Ned Shearer of the YMCA Gleemen who found the cat hidden between the partitioning.

Another singer who will remember her television debut is Lillian Turner. One of the judges, Dorothy Ward, said "This is a young lady who will go far." The team will go back to Manchester for the quarter finals in August.

(Note – unfortunately, the Ashington team was knocked out in the next round)

£128,000 Extensions Make Ashington Hospital centre for Emergency Cases (Ashington Post -6th December, 1956)

Work started this week on the first stage of turning Ashington's cramped little fifty-five bed General Hospital into a modern building, capable of accommodating 170 patients from all over East Northumberland. When the whole scheme is completed, in about five years' time, the hospital will be able to deal with most emergency cases in a wide area, taking in Blyth, Bedlington, Morpeth and Seaton Valley, with a population of 150,000.

Mr J Brennand, secretary of the Wansbeck Hospital Management Committee, which has its headquarters at Blyth, told the *News Post* yesterday "We consider it will adequately cover our medical and surgical needs. Ashington will be the principal hospital in the Wansbeck group."

To some extent, the big new extension at Ashington will also compensate for the indefinite shelving of the proposed 300 bed hospital at Bedlington. The full project also includes a training school for nurses, which will enable the students to get practical on-the-spot experience.

The land which is being used for the extensions is the three acres to the south of the present hospital. The site was formerly used as allotments.

The extensions have come about as a result of continued pressure, both by the Hospital Management Committee and Ashington Mineworkers' Federation. While the builders are busy on the outside work, the Ashington Hospital's League of Friends will be busy inside the present building completing the work of having all the beds in the hospital in cubicles.

Already the male and female wards have been put into cubicles by the League. Now plans are in hand for providing cubicles for the remaining Memorial Ward, which is used by males. When this work is completed early next year, nearly £700 will have been spent by the League on cubicles alone.

Looking Back at (1950's) Ashington by David Bean (from an article in the Guardian)

'For an outsider, one not born, bred, and raised in this unlovely town which produced not only coal but Jackie Milburn and the Charlton brothers, it may not be easy to understand why men should not bow to the seemingly inevitable and let Ashington Pit close. It was in 1956, the year of Suez and Hungarian Uprising, I found myself one afternoon in Ashington. That main street stretched away empty, its tinny shop signs clanging as they swung in a gritty, cold nor'easter. Only a dusty collie slunk along the shop fronts, glancing over its shoulder as it went, as if it found itself caught out after a curfew. I had made a dreadful mistake, for I had come here to be an ace reporter on the local weekly paper (*Ashington Advertiser)* and there was nothing happening.

'Behind the main street, up towards the colliery itself, there was a little more life. A few groups of young children were playing in the back lanes behind the rows of squat terraced houses that seemed to stretch on, straight as military ranks, into infinity, a classic exercise in perspective. First Row, Second Row, Third Row they were named, and so on, right up to Eleventh Row. Miners, it appeared, had not been worth the bother of having their streets decorated with names.

'And then all hell was let loose. One moment the street had been empty, the next it was flooded by a great tide of humanity. It was like the build-up to a vital football match: men in rough clothes, bait satchels slung over their shoulders, hands in pockets, heads hunched, were moving down the street like a Lowry painting come alive, if not so colourful. From the other direction another army was on the move, similarly uniformed, except that some wore helmets and had faces daubed with black, so that their eyes stared out white like what were called nigger-minstrels in those days before the race relations act.

'It would be an exaggeration to say that I had to stand back in a shop doorway to let the twin tides mingle and pass, but the changing of pits at Ashington collieries then was something to behold, heightened, no doubt, by the silence in the streets immediately before. But it was typical of the place. Everything there was done in extremes. If Ashington people decided to take something up, they took it up with an enthusiasm seem nowhere else in the land. Hula Hoops were all the craze at the time, and I remember a shopkeeper telling me that more had been sold in Ashington, per capita, than anywhere else in the kingdom. Or maybe it was the world.

'My initial assumption that alcoholic solace was nowhere to be found proved erroneous to put it mildly. Certainly there had been no pubs – and I mean pubs, not the two rambling Victorian Hotels (Grand and Portland) that propped up the main street like bookends. But there were Working Men's Clubs. Not just one or two, but twenty of them, constituting together the largest concentration of boozy, self-help to be found anywhere.

'By the time I arrived in Ashington there was something of a boom in mining and the clubs were turning posh. One week, the place to be was the White House Unique, because it had just acquired fitted carpets, the first in the town, and everyone was queuing to see what the old men would do without the benefit of spittoons. A month later it was the Excelsior or the Fell 'em Doon because one or the other had installed tropical fish tanks or had hung its walls with maroon fabric at thirty bob a roll.

'The clubmen did not spend all their time admiring the new décor. To say that a fair amount of ale flowed down Ashington throats each evening is like saying that a fair tonnage of coal spewed out of its pits every day. You didn't see drunkenness – not the rolling, retching, flat-out-in-the-gutter kind anyway – but you did see drink. Those clubs were full every night, and no-one was exaggerating when he talked about such-and-such, a face worker, being a fifteen-pints-a-night-man, twenty on Saturdays. After a shift at the pit, they reckoned you didn't even feel the first three pints go down.

'In my time in Ashington in the 1950s, none of the clubs would allow women in unless accompanied by a man, and some would not even allow this. The Middle Market Club, a pokey little affair with sawdust on the floor, held out the longest, although it apparently had no objection to letting horses in. Its nickname – the Kicking Cuddy – derived from the night a pit pony entered and was promptly served a bucket of beer. Women's Liberation would doubtless have not approved of the sexual set-up in a pit town like Ashington, but they might have missed the point. These were not down-trodden fearful ladies. They were as strong-minded as their men-folk but in different spheres and they shared the men's overriding trait of enthusiasm. There was a lot going on in Ashington in the evening and at weekends and by no means was it all club-orientated.

'Their five cinemas, all showing films in those days before the Bingo boom, and their nightly crowds were a smaller repeat of the shift changes at the colliery, flooding the street whenever the film ended. There were male voice choirs and amateur dramatic societies and there had once even been a Miners' Theatre, their very own, but taken over in the late 30s as another picture house (Regal). There was an amateur orchestra rehearsing weekly in the Harmonic Hall, and a regular series of organ recitals and celebrity concerts at the big Methodist Central Hall. The Ashington Group of Artists, mostly primitive painters of their own

Photographer Alan Dixon's panoramic view of Ashington Colliery in late 1950s.

environment, was formed before the war and reached international fame. There was also the Milburns and the Charltons . . .

'But the great boast of the people themselves, fostered by generations of politicians and music hall comedians, was that they were the warmest hearted people in the world. They could certainly be the noisiest of the noisiest, but what attracted me was their sheer enthusiasm. Life was too short, they reckoned, to be anything but enthusiastic, but where they got their extra energy from after a shift at the pit I do not know. There was a pride in the job all right, but a miner would usually tell you that no son of his was ever going down the pit. If they had their time over again, a chorus would say, they'd never have gone down themselves. "Trouble is," someone would be sure to pipe up, "we knaa nowt else but pit work" and they all nod their heads in mutual regret.'

Town Plan for Ashington Changes (Morpeth Herald 1957)
A Town Plan for the development of Ashington Urban District in the next 20 years is being considered with keen interest and some concern by the town's civic leaders. If the plan is made effective the whole face of Ashington will be changed by 1971. It is forecast the Ashington population will be drastically reduced because 4,000 people will live in the projected satellite town of Broadlyne, to be built between Ellington and Lynemouth. Another 880 folk are likely to re-settle in the Newbiggin area. The transfer of Ashington workers and their families is thought to be necessary because of the acute shortage of house-building sites in the Ashington area due to the sterilization of land by coal working, and because the limited land available will be required for schools and colleges.

A significant omission from the planners' "shape of things to come" is the proposal put to the Boundary Commission some years ago that Ashington become the centre of a larger area to include Newbiggin and substantial areas of Morpeth rural district. Far reaching proposals are made for the progressive demolition of old house property in the town.

"In Ashington," it is stated, "the oldest housing is that in the long terraces between Station Road, High Market and the Colliery. These colliery houses were already there in 1890 ... the condition of buildings in Ashington is generally good. The worst houses are naturally those built before 1890 (Long and Cross Rows), but those often have far more light and space than the later buildings. The accommodation is, however, sub standard by modern criteria."

Existing shopping facilities in Ashington are considered adequate. There is one food shop for every 115 persons and one other shop for every 165 persons. There are 105 food shops in Ashington and 117 non-food shops.

Apart from the revolutionary changes for re-housing workers outside the town, the most impressive development is promised in the field of Education, the timing of which is not yet established. There is a proposed Nursery School and Clinic on the site of the Hirst East School; plus Nursery blocks at the proposed Wansbeck Infant School, Hirst South Infants and St Aidan's Primary School. At Hirst North there is a remodeling scheme for the provision of a Junior School for boys and girls in separate departments, and the Hirst North Infants School would be closed when a new school is erected on an adjacent site. A new school is to replace the present Roman Catholic School (St Benedict's) and Bothal School will also be replaced.

Ashington Council Protests against Town Map 1957

The *Ashington Post* reported that 'Ashington Council is protesting the proposal to build a new satellite town at Broadlyne which would provide a community of 9,000 people with all modern facilities. The Council argues that any emigration from Ashington would seriously affect the town's finances. They feel, too, that there is further room for development in Ashington; this they would prefer to participation in a new scheme which would be within the boundaries of another authority. However, the County council, in a précis of the Development Plan to cover Ashington, Newbiggin, Linton, Ellington and Lynemouth, points out that the main problem in the future arises in connection with coal mining. They say: "The National Coal Board is engaged on a programme of re-organisation likely to cause major changes in the places of mining employment. Newbiggin Colliery is expected to close and a new drift mine is developing at Longhirst. These changes and the present daily movement of miners to work raises the problem of the future location of new housing areas to accommodate those employed in mining."

They further stated that large scale building in Ashington and Newbiggin would sterilise valuable coal reserves, the loss of which would seriously affect the length of life and, consequently, the employment at adjacent collieries. The NCC is pressing its claim that the only sizeable site available was between Ellington Village and Lynemouth – known as Broadlyne – and this would provide a convenient location for new houses to accommodate people employed in the mining industry.

Ashington Council has given very careful consideration to the full content of the Town Map and they do *not* favour a new satellite town, hence the strong possibility that a public enquiry will be necessary before the Development Plan can be finally approved. The Plan for the area makes provision for an increase in population from 42,300 to 45,000 in 1971. To house this population 2,000 new houses will be required. It is pointed out that while Ashington is busy with new housing estates, and Newbiggin is contemplating a housing estate of Newbiggin Moor, the bulk of the remaining need for houses would be at Broadlyne, where it was hoped to provide a small, compact township of 9,000 people, which would have within its confines a nursery, primary schools and secondary modern school.

While Ashington Council has shown its dislike 'for Broadlyne', Morpeth Rural District Council has shown great interest in it and they have, in fact, taken steps to build a new estate in that vicinity. This proposal is for some 600 houses of which 400 will be let on first tenancy to the NCB, which is anxious to obtain accommodation for mine workers serving the Linton, Ellington and Lynemouth collieries which are subject to some measures of re-organisation and development.

Ashington Singer Does Well (Ashington Post Oct 1957)
By day, Miss Ruby Fotheringham handles figures and pay sheets at Ashington colliery offices, but her evenings are devoted to singing. A contralto, she holds a very high position in north-east musical circles, and her fame has now spread to more distant fields. Her contralto voice has been heard in many north-east halls and at northern musical festivals, but her biggest chance comes in December this year when she appears at the Festival Hall, London, as contralto lead in Handel's Messiah.

Miss Fotheringham who lives at 198 Hawthorn Road, Ashington, has worked at Ashington Colliery since leaving school, but throughout her life singing has played a very important part. She was educated at Hirst North and Hirst Park Modern schools where she sang with choirs. Her voice was pleasing and it was no surprise when she began taking lessons with Dr T E Hutchinson of Jesmond with whom she has been for many years.

Ruby's association with Dr Hutchinson she recalls that this eminent north-east tutor was closely connected with the career of the late Kathleen Ferrier, who herself visited Ashington in 1944 and 1948. Through her London agents, Miss Fotheringham will also appear in the Messiah at Stirling, Blackpool Tower and at Cheltenham. It is one of the biggest steps in her career.

Miss Fotheringham told the *Ashington Post*: 'I am delighted with these engagements, particularly the London one as it will be my first appearance in the capital city. During my career I have made three radio broadcasts, and on each occasion I was accompanied by Miss Gladys Willis of Morpeth, and I have been accompanied by many of the country's leading soloists at the Ashington celebrity concerts at the Central Hall in conjunction with Mr Normanton Barron.

Snow was Falling in Ashington as well as Munich (6th February, 1958)
Cissie Charlton had a premonition when she left her Beatrice Street home to call on a neighbour to explain how anxious she was. Not long after she trudged back home through the snow, local newsagent Ted Cockburn entered her back yard. It was as if Cissie knew what he was going to say.

"It's Bobby, isn't it?"

"Yes, but I wanted you to know before it went on the placards. The *Evening Chronicle* has produced our bills about Bobby being in a plane crash in Munich and I wanted to make sure you knew first before I put them up."

Probably the worst thing for Cissie was that the first radio and press re ports to reach Ashington had said there were no survivors. She headed for the nearest telephone box but the lines were down because of the snow. Fearing that Bobby now lay dead in the Munich snow she began crying and screaming out his name, before being helped home by the friendly newsagent.

Down in Leeds, Jack Charlton had also received news of the tragedy and went up to the club office to see if anyone had any more information. There was none, so Jack then decided to come back to Ashington, though, because his parents had no phone, he couldn't let them know he was on his way. He had been married for less than a month to his wife Pat who he telephoned to meet him at the station for the grim journey north, still thinking that his younger brother was probably dead.

On arrival in Newcastle, Jack and Pat went to the Haymarket to catch the bus to Ashington. On their way they saw a newspaper vendor selling late editions of the *Evening Chronicle*. Though he dreaded what he might find inside, Jack decided that he had to buy a copy. Then, as he approached the stall, he could see a folded paper on the vendor's arm bearing the Stop Press news: '*Charlton among the survivors.*'

Unsurprisingly Bobby could not face the plane journey back to England from Germany, so he took the train and boat to London. At Liverpool Street Station he was met by Jack and his mother who was shocked at his dejected appearance. Jack ushered Bobby and his mother into a car and drove them north. It was during this journey that Bobby recalled the painful memories of his crash, concluding "That's it. I don't want you to ask me about it again. I want to forget all about it."

It was while he was back at the family home in Beatrice Street that Bobby received the news that his best friend Duncan Edwards had lost his fight for life. His despondency became greater.

Ron Routledge, a former Sunderland and Ashington FC keeper, who had grown up with Bobby recalled: 'He was particularly upset about Duncan Edwards. He just locked himself up and wanted nothing to do with anyone. It was terrible. After about a fortnight of this his mother came up to me and asked: 'Has he mentioned anything to you about football?'

I told her, 'Not really. He seems more concerned about what's going on in the hospital at Munich.'

Then Cissie replied, 'He said to me that he doesn't want to play again, that he won't go back to Old Trafford.'

"I wanted to do something so I went to the Park School, got a football and said to Bobby, 'Right, let's go to Hirst Park.' He didn't want to go but I pushed him. So we went to the park and we were there for a good three hours. I wasn't going to leave it there, and I decided that I was going to keep pushing him. Over the next week or so we did that a few more times and he gradually opened up. At first he had been really down, hated the idea of kicking a football around, but eventually he got into it, and after a few sessions, he told his mother, 'Look, I want to get back. I feel like getting back to United.' But he never mentioned the crash once during our kickabouts, not once.'

The year of 1958 ended with a lady Chairman of Ashington UDC, Wilhelmina Duffin, who wrote in the *Ashington Advertiser* of 26th December: 'During the past year, many problems have confronted us. We have tried to solve them in a way which would benefit you all.

'Due to the far-sighted policy of past and present councillors we have been able to continue to beautify our town by planting trees and shrubs grown in our own Nursery. We have sometimes been disheartened by the wanton destruction of these, but will continue to carry on with the work.

'The plans for road improvement schemes still occupy our time very much, and we hope to see the work completed for our mutual benefit in the near future. We all realise that houses are our greatest need. Our aim is to have every resident adequately housed, and we welcome the energetic steps taken by the National Coal Board to bring the old-type colliery houses up to date.'

Mr Will Owen MP for Morpeth sent out festive greetings to his constituents by way of referring to the new grammar school that was being built on Green Lane. He had this to say 'The children who have not secured a place at the grammar school want the year of 1959 to open with the hopes of just another chance, and parental hopes regard this prospect as the very best of Christmas greetings.'

Mr Owen also looked in on the temporary mail sorting office in the Central Methodist Lesser Hall which Ashington Post Office was using to handle the sorting and distribution of an avalanche of festive season letters, cards and parcels. He was received by Mr J Furmston, Postmaster at Ashington. Mr Owen said: 'This is the time of year when the postman's knock is eagerly awaited in every household.'

A 'rich and rosy future' for Ashington's football team was forecast by Mr Owen at a get-together dinner party given by the directors of the Ashington Football Club in the West End Club. To members of last season's North Eastern League team, runners-up trophies were presented and they were congratulated on their performance in their first season in the Midland League. Mr Dave Davidson, team manager, in his reply said:' Everybody connected with the Club has reason to be proud of what has been achieved, but a disappointing feature was the failure of the sporting public to provide the attendances the excellent team displays deserved.'

He went on 'You will see as good football at Portland Park as at Roker Park, Sunderland, yet our gates are still hovering between three and four thousand.' Mr Walter Nunn chairman of directors presided the evening and there was entertainment by Jack and George Shepherd, a father and son vocal act, and Jax and Nena, a husband and wife conjuring team.

Another 1958 Christmas Party went with a bang at the Ashington Senior Citizens Friendship Club in St Andrew's Church Hall in Hawthorn Road when the fun and games included a double act burlesque of the part song '*Nymphs and Shepherds*'. Club leader, Mrs N Alderson, welcomed the guests including the civic head Cllr Mrs Wilhelmina Duffin, and representatives of the local authority, also Mr George Holliday, Mr George Roll, and Mr Thomas Wood of the Linton and Woodhorn Miners Hall Committee, who provided gifts for the oldest male member, Mr George Sweet aged 77 and the oldest woman member, Mrs L Wright, aged 85; he also distributed packets of confectionery to all members and the workers who support the Club. Bouquets were presented to Mrs Alderson and Mrs M Allington (pianist) for services rendered.

A Christmas Party was also held at the Ashington Miners' Welfare Institute (top Tute) when a treat was provided for 240 aged people. Tea was provided and entertainment was given by the Five Beaux and a Belle with Florence Thompson, accordionist. Mr Jack Kirkup, institute secretary presided and also present were Councillor Larry Lavelle, NUM's Mr George Nelson, Mr Will Owen MP and Mr Billy Riches, NCB Group Manager.

One of the town's leading charity fund-raisers, Ashington Round Table, in a festive season drive for the welfare of mentally handicapped children, pulled in £160. The money was raised by means of house-to-house collections and by comic costume entertainment, stunts in clubs and pubs, and a football match appeal. The chairman, Mr Eric Bird, expressed grateful thanks for their generous support.

If you didn't hand over your money to these cut-throat pirates you were in trouble. Prominent local businessmen include from left auctioneer Louis Johnson, Norman Brotherton dentist, ?Armstrong, Bell Bros carriers, ?, Jimmy Main bike-man in glasses and beard, Jefferys optician, Hindhaugh chemist and another Bell's brother.

Standing at the top of the Midland League in December 1958, the Colliers took on their arch rivals Blyth Spartans on New Year's Day, fielding the following team: Gordon Mason, Lindsay, Humble, Newton, Smith, John 'Pat' Patterson, Linnaker, Gibson, Bobby Cummings, Hewitson and Oliver.

Ashington Rugby Club continued to field three teams and entertained Vickers when tries for the Thirds were scored by Bob Beddard and F Bates. The first XV for the next game was chosen from MJ Green, J Jackson, D Bannister, I Jackson, S B Matthews, Sid Waddell, Archie Moffatt, J Sidney Kirkup, R Self, JM Davison, K Wake, J R Bell, C Graham, A Harper, J Patrick and J Baxter.

In the Ashington Welfare League Subsidiary Cup, the Hirst East End team to play Lynemouth Mechanics was chosen from Les Weddell, Ronnie Scott, Alan Hayton, John Hale, Law Weddell, Morgan, Davison, Percy Armstrong, Les Common, Joe Smith, John Freeman, Eddie Tibbs and Jimmy Milburn.

Billiard matches over the 1958 Christmas period saw these results: Lynemouth Welfare drew 2-2 with Ashington West End Club. The former fielded Davidson, Moscrop, Tarbit and Brown, while Riches, Rainey, Bill Shiell and Bruce Butters were West End players. Priestman's Institute went down 3-1 to the Excelsior Club. For the 'Tute', Charlie Wendt, Jimmy Henderson, Ron Devon and Joey Emery took on Moody, Smith, John Sinclair and Davey Home. The Billiard League placings to date had the Ex on top with Ashington YMCA still without a win.

Veteran Scout, Mr Jack Dorgan of 18 Third Row, Ashington, the 1st Hirst Group Scoutmaster and founder of the troop, received a surprise when he attended the 'Feast' in the Lintonville Terrace Headquarters. He found himself the guest of honour and the recipient of awards to mark his 50th year in Scouting. Also present were his son Nicholas, 36-year-old Scoutmaster of the troop who lives at 93 Castle Terrace, and his grandson Michael, aged 10, who is a Cub. The three Dorgan generations have between them 83 years' service to Scouting.

Brass Band Contest Awards were given out a few days after Christmas 1958 held by the Northumberland Brass Band League; soloists and quartets had performed in Newbiggin with the following receiving awards: Soloists under 15s – A Cummings of Ellington Band , P Bell of Mickley and A Thornton of Pegswood Band; soloists under 16 – Denis Wright of Newbiggin, and Miss Ann Mackintosh of the North Seaton Band (daughter of Ashington police inspector). Senior soloists – Jimmy Shepherd (then playing for Pegswood), Denis Carr (playing for Bedlington) and William Lister of North Seaton Band.

1950s NEWS IN BRIEF

1950 – James Bowman is now the chairman of Northern Division of NCB with Frankie Millican appointed Labour Director, while Bobby Main, secretary of Ashington Mineworkers Federation became General Secretary of the Northumberland NUM; Ashington FC go out of FA Cup 2-1 to Rochdale in front of almost 14,000 fans at Portland Park, beating the previous attendance record set against Aston Villa in the 1920s; Longhirst

Hall earmarked as an approved school for young law-breakers.
1951 – Second Increase in Wages Agreement – miners now head the table of industrial workers' earnings; but Seaton Hirst Vicar, the Rev J Morton, warns that the 10d meat ration for miners: 'Will hardly produce enough energy to burst a paper bag'; Arrowsmith's department store fined for 'Offering Utility goods for sale at prices exceeding the Board of Trade maximum.'
1952 – Inception of Mineworkers' Pension Scheme; transfer of Welfare Schemes to Coal Industry Social Welfare Organisation (CISWO); Ashington population now 28,470; Ashington Co-op Arcade offers 'Dainty Blouses in Nylon and Voiles, black, pink and white, from 21/-'; it was announced that there will be 'work for a thousand miners' when the proposed Longhirst Drift get under way.
1953 – Television set installed in Excelsior Club; Longhirst Drift opened; a Blood Bank was made available to the public at Ashington Hospital, technician in charge was Mr F W Stoker - Ashington blood donors were then giving 400 pints per year.
1954 – Will Owen elected MP for Morpeth; John Minoughan wins Ashington Flower Show sprint at People's Park; the English Schools Athletic Championships were held at Hirst Welfare; although not officially on holiday, many Ashington children were kept away from school because of the newly-introduced *two*-week miners' holidays between June 18th – 28th .
1955 – Jackie Milburn scores goal in record time as United beat Manchester City 3-1, picking up his third gold medal in four seasons; Prime Minister Anthony Eden visits Lynemouth Colliery; River Wansbeck blocked by ice in January.
1956 – James Bowman appointed Chairman of National Coal Board and is knighted the following year; Ashington's home-grown talent goes on TV Top Town trail; Bothal Drift opens in Ashington Colliery pit-yard.
1957 – Ashington's Old People's Festival and Exhibition begins; Area Workshops begin to clear site near Ellington Road Ends; fire guts Grand Street Club on 1st March; Walter Nunn appointed as a JP after having lost his council seat as Co-operative in the local election - Mr Nunn was then Vice-chair of Ashington FC.
1958 – The Redheads Concert Party was booked for Excelsior Club on Christmas Day; and Billy Mason's Band played on Christmas Eve at the Clayton Ballroom, admission 3s 6d; a 15-day holiday at Catollica cost £35-10-0 at Weatherstone's Travel Agents;. two pianos were offered to the new old people's home (Essendene) as a result of appeal by Cllr Wilhelmina Duffin, Chairman of Ashington Council.
1959 – A Compensation Scheme is introduced for miners compulsorily retired at 65 or over; Ashington lad Billy Gray wins FA Cup medal with Nottingham Forest and goes on years later to become grounds man there in the Brian Clough era.

Ashington Ladies Football team played in a charity match at Hirst Park in aid of the Easington Pit Disaster Fund in 1951.

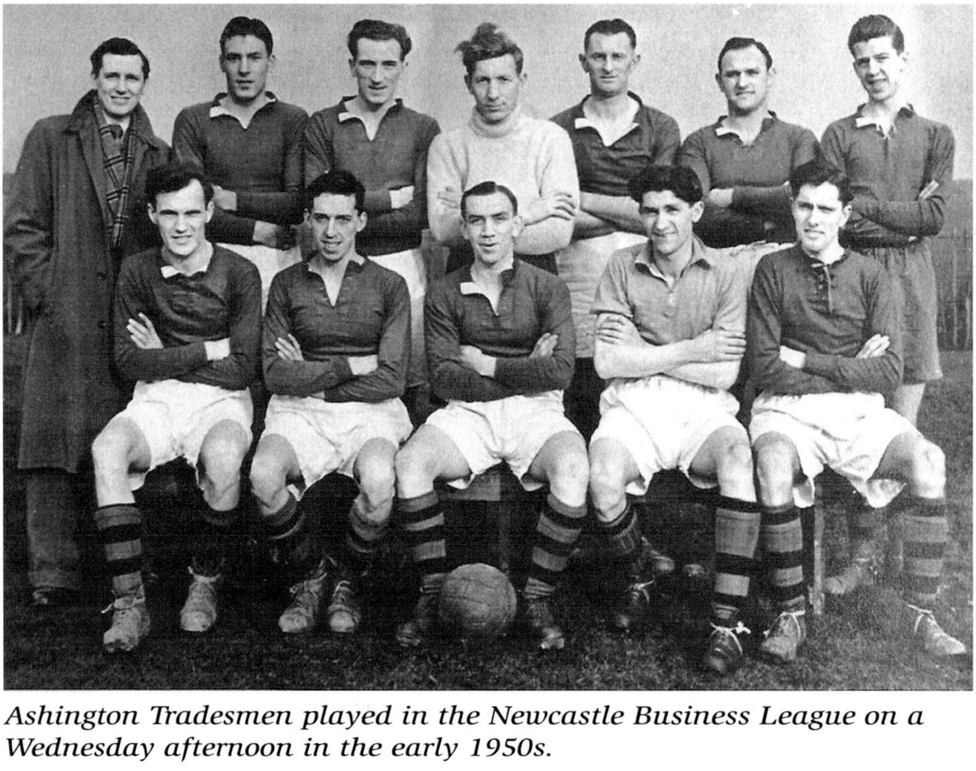

Ashington Tradesmen played in the Newcastle Business League on a Wednesday afternoon in the early 1950s.

THE 1960s

An Ashington Hospital development in the early 1960s is visited by the then Conservative Minister for Health, the Right Hon Enoch Powell (in homburg). Man in white coat on right could have been the hospital's first Asian, Doctor Dee.

In the Sixties, popular coal merchant cum-singer/compere, Eric Nichol became well established at the Harmonic Hall (and at the newly-opened Hirst Welfare Hall) after several successful years with Joe Gray and his Arcadians at the Arcade Hall. In a way, it was the end of an era when dances such as the Foxtrot and the Modern Waltz were overtaken by the frenetic phenomenon of the Twist and the Locomotion. However, Al Cummings, who was then tenant at the Harmonic, still performed with a trio that specialized in the more sedate dances preferred by the older or middle-aged set; and the Walton Assembly Rooms was a popular venue for *Strictly Ballroom Dancing.*

It was probably the antics of Boppers and Jivers that sounded the death knell for the Arcade dancehall – Joe Gray thought that the old floor could not stand too much vibration and he called for the *'Last Waltz'* to be played at the Arcade in the early 1960s, leaving the way open for Bingo nights.

As the bigger dancehalls bowed out, there opened a spate of smaller, more intimate venues, for boy to meet girl. The Cellar Club opened on Station Bank, frequented by the youth of the town; Bill Kell gave up one of his rooms at the Portland to allow small combos to come in and play the latest 'pop' music; a group of like-minded folk formed the Rio Grand Cavern in the basement of the Grand Hotel with a cowboy-style décor; St Andrew's Church Hall on Hawthorn Road began to pull in the kids when a certain home-grown pop idol performed there – it was the dark-haired, good looking, man-about-town Neil Dixon.

Was it just a mirage or were the teenagers of the '60s getting a little more sophisticated than those of the previous decade? Just looking at many of the school photos from the 1950s – especially those not in school uniform – it seems that 15-year-olds were adults before their time; boys in dark suits or sports jackets; girls with drab, loose-fitting dresses, sporting Andrews Sisters' hair-dos.

The Sixties signalled the boom of the package holiday when you could book 10 days at Benidorm for only £39 at Dawson and Sanderson travel agents. The canny folks of Ashington wanted more sophistication than that offered by the regimentalised Butlins and Pontins – Spain became their target. Yet in spite of professing to want 'to get away from it all', once Ashingtonians arrived on the Costa del Fish and Chips, all they wanted to do was to lie on the beach with their friends all morning; take an excursions to the local market in the afternoon; and find a pub that sold *Broon Ale* in the evening.

Entertainment at home at Hirst Ashington was changing, too. As television got a foothold, Ashington's cinemas began to close to be replaced by Bingo halls, such as at the Piv and the Hipp, both taken over by Jack Richardson, a local showman, who also took out a lease on the Arcade Hall and began Bingo sessions there in the early 1960s – sounding the death knell for dancing at this popular venue.

Workingmen's clubs like the Comrades went up-market, attempting to get rid of the spittoon and sawdust image by decorating the bars and lounges with red flock wallpaper, while one-armed bandits replaced the customary domino cards. The clubs took on huge debts in renovation work as they vied with each other for the custom of the miner and his lady. It might have provided lots of employment for Ashington Co-op and other building firms, but the expense was a huge albatross around the necks of successive club committee men.

'Ashington Grammar ... girls had vivid imaginations" by Brenda Chatteron (nee Reid)

A strong-minded girl who rebelled against conformity in the Sixties was

Brenda Reid, one of the early intake at Ashington Grammar school. In her autobiography (A Pennorth o' Scranshums), she wrote: "At sixteen I cropped my hair with a pair of nail scissors as I had heard Mia Farrow had done when she married Frank Sinatra. I just grabbed clumps of hair as long as the width of two fingers, shut my eyes and snipped ... after that I bleached it as blond as it would go, and feathered it forward from the crown. Sometimes I used to put an ash-grey rinse through it ... I rather liked that.

"Mr Hoodless of the Scouse accent and not long out of University, was the youngest male teacher at Ashington Grammar (in the early 1960s). As is usual for a fellow in his position, many of the girls thought he was 'dead sexy' and fluttered their eyelashes in his direction. They used all their feminine wiles to try to get round him and constantly demanded his attention. He showed remarkable restraint. At one point, Miss Hazel Richardson, the girls' mistress, had to assemble all the senior girls and give them a lecture about rumours they were circulating concerning some of the young male teachers. Then, as always, the girls had vivid imaginations. Of course this only served to increase the curiosity of those who hadn't heard the rumours. The gathering then merely served to inflame the situation rather than diffuse it.

"... When I first arrived at Ashington Grammar, I became friendly with a girl in my class called Joyce Long. ... she showed me the ropes in that strange place, helping with directions, names and customs. Joyce lived in Ashbourne Crescent and a few times she invited me to stay over the weekend so that we could go to the Cricket Club Dance on a Saturday night. Quite a lot of kids from the Grammar used to meet there and it was always a good night out."

Successful Scholarship Girls from the Hirst North School who might have been at Ashington Grammar with Brenda, included those girls who passed in 1958/59/60: Alice Athey, May Smith, Avril Hodge, Heather Massingham, Helen Kent, Maureen Jackson, Ann Newton, Helen Whillis, Jean Harvey, Marjorie Bolam, Nancy Allsopp, Elizabeth Laing, Janice Lillico, Margaret Leonard, Heather Keeso, Carol Darling, Fiona Willis, Norah Renwick, Eveline Bradley, Denise Douglas, Leni Mitchley, Thelma Shaw, Anne White, Dorothy Foster, Judith Cox, Joan Coulson, Kathleen Curran, Glynis Owen, Jean Batey, Phyllis Parkin, Nancy Anderson, Kathleen Lille, Ann Simpson, Vivien Anderson, Jean Bradford, Ann Gibson, Margaret Irving, Linda Marshall, Ann Langdown, Patricia Evans, Eleanor Doyle and Margaret Taylor.

'Changing Face of Ashington' (Newcastle Journal, 1960)
'Faith in the future is expressed in the investment by the National Coal Board of substantial capital – with the aid of local authority improvement grants – in a major scheme for re-modelling and modernising hundreds of sub-standard colliery rows. Now well under way, this imaginative project has changed the face of Ashington and given hundreds of mining families better living conditions.

'Of the 2,500 colliery houses, 450 have been reshaped and work has started on another 125. Recently-erected self-contained houses and flats give working class families middle class status at a reasonable price. Extensive tree planting and the laying out of ornamental shrubberies has improved the appearance of a town originally planned with all the emphasis severely on utility.

'Whatever the rest of the world may think, 28,000 Geordies are sure that Ashington is a top coal town. And they believe they are top people for the millions of tons of coal they have produced – and will produce in the future – have contributed to the wealth and well-being of the nation.

'Now the "biggest mining village in the world" is an aggressive, prosperous, forward-looking town with its income for years ahead heavily invested in public development and individual status symbols. To date Ashington's civic chiefs have resisted the temptation to jump on the bandwagon and have firmly declined to co-operate with development firms and consultants who want to tear portions of the town apart and create a brave new shopping world with all its expensive frills and trimmings.'

'What Ashington's First Lady Thinks', (Evening Chronicle, 1960s)
Ashington-born Mrs Lydia Robson, the colliery town's newly-appointed civic chief, had this to say: "To be first citizen of a town like Ashington is a great honour and a heavy responsibility for a councillor. I am deeply conscious of both. Ashington is a top coal town and its great annual output is vitally important to the economy of the nation.

'But it is no longer just a pit town. The character of the community, through education and the achievement of a higher standard of living, has changed in recent years. We are no longer isolated pit folk, but have become almost a cosmopolitan community open to outside influences, such as the important development in educational field. These have brought into the town an influx of county technical college students from all walks of life in all parts of the North."

"Ashington seems to have grown up piece-meal" – Sir John Hall
Sir John Hall does not appear to agree with the above assessment. Talking about the changes which have come about in Ashington over the years, he said: "If Ashington appeared never to have changed, it was because it had a static business when the pits were going strong, and there was no need to change. Had they (the Council) looked ahead, they would have seen that there should have been changes long before the pits started to close. Ashington never had a lot of private housing. Whether they were wanting to keep political control I don't know. But all the new housing was based at Stakeford, which was where I bought my first house, on Leech's Estate. That was the first mass exodus; the houses were sold up overnight, with people queuing up to buy. The whole Ashington area was static for a long time and change was forced upon them in the end. You have got to know where you are going, but unless you have strong leadership you will fall behind until change is forced upon you.

"Ashington seems to have grown up piece-meal - a little piece added here and another piece there. I think that Ashington as a town should be telling the world about its successes. If they stand up and moan that the area has 20% unemployment, that will do no good at all. Businessmen don't want to hear about a town's failures, they need to be told of all the good parts."

Where are the Tops of Yesteryear by W A W (Blyth News 1960s)
There is lots of talk these days about juvenile delinquency. Why not turn the discussion to juvenile grievances? There are plenty of them, though the children themselves don't realize it. They don't know what fun their mothers and fathers had at low cost. Take tops, for instance. Some of us who are 'getting on' sympathise deeply with youngsters in having to put up with such miserable specimens. The only ones I have seen are small, shapeless things, such as can be turned out in a minute of two on a carpenter's lathe. The whips, too, are 'cheap and nasty' – with some doubt about the word 'cheap'.

One remembers those of one's own boyhood, nicely turned and grooved ones, with iron points, for a penny or tuppence, and the majestic 'Big Ben' which cost sixpence and would keep any healthy boy happy for hours on end. And where have the peg-tops got to – those pear shaped tops round which you would a string and then, with considerable skill, cast to earth, where they wound continue spinning gaily for minutes on end? We used to play a form of conkers with them, slinging one at another, in deadly combat.

Then again, where are the hoops – wooden ones for the girls, iron for the boys? 'Gourds' they were called - with iron hooks to guide them, we would run for miles and organise thrilling races, both sprints and marathons. What happened to kites, which helped many a summer afternoon pass so enjoyably? It's ages since I saw one, whereas I can recall when, on suitable days with a light breeze blowing, scores of them could be seen soaring brightly aloft on every open space and even from back yards.

Doubtless other grown-ups can add to this list of humble pleasures of childhood that are no more, but without being able to explain why, I see no reason why such provision for the amusement and exercise of the younger generation should not be supplied now as then. Moreover, someone is missing a very remunerative business. Some enterprising man will, sooner or later, realise that a good regular market has been lost, and can be regained. I offer the suggestion that there is quite big money on tops and whips and hoops and kites and all the rest, and that the boys and girls of today are overdue a 'break' in their availability.

"More of a coal house than a coal depot." When the Sixties got underway (I was demobbed out of the RAF in 1959), I was already four months into my next new job as a clerk at Duke Street Coal Depot. Jimmy Little was in charge, though his health was clearly failing. Assistant manager was Billy Mason and the staff also included a young lad called John Foster and Tommy Tinkler who had transferred from Woodhorn Depot. The office was dusty and small - more of a coal house than a coal depot. In one corner stood a huge, round-faced, red weighing machine, and on the opposite wall was an open coal fire which young John had to light when we opened up at 7 am each morning.

Even before the staff arrived, a straggling queue of vehicles was lined up from the depot's wooden gates as far back as the Harmonic Hall clock. Drivers needed to get an early start in order to make the maximum number of deliveries. The depot yard, with Larry Bell as foreman, was filled with railway trucks holding every size of coal you could imagine from Doubles, Trebles and Cobbles, right up to Wallsend Best, which, indeed, was the 'best' that money could buy.

As well as large-scale hauliers such as Theo James of Bedlington and Thompson of Christon Bank, the smaller, local coal delivery firms of W J Nichol and Sons, George Beatty, Derek Tweedy, Bob Mercel and Ramm of Newbiggin made up a line of about twenty vehicles, all with their engines running, polluting and pestering the residents of Duke Street with noise and fumes.

Jimmy Little was one of the old Coal Company men, trained not to waste one penny during their working day. One of my tasks entailed sitting at a sloping wooden bench and recording data by pen and ink into a massive ledger, rather like the one used by Bob Cratchett. To keep up the Dickensian connection, I was required to make entries with an old-fashioned pen that had a steel nib attached. After a few months into the job, the pen had started to leave ink blotches on the pages. I thought the nib might be 'cross-pointed' so I took it to Jimmy who sat dressed in his brown, knee length, dust coat on a swivel chair next to the weighing machine.

'Do you think I might have a new nib, please, Mr Little? This one is starting to get a bit scratchy.' Jimmy took off his glasses and held the pen up to the light, squinting as he did so. He gave it back to me, saying 'Here, lad, you'll get another three months out of that nib.' And that was the whole ethos of Ashington Coal Company wrapped up in that one little cameo: keep costs to a minimum.

Sadly, Jimmy Little died about a year later and, as we were cleaning out his desk, Billy Mason opened one of the drawers that Jimmy had always kept locked. And inside we found a *dozen* boxes of pen nibs, each containing 50 nibs. I later found that the ACC's frugality would all change once the National Coal Board got into its stride and began to spend lavish amounts of money on each of the Ashington Group of Collieries.

Stock Car Racing Proposal by Local Motor Club (Ashington Advertiser – 26th May, 1961)

Ashington Motor Club are giving serious thought to the idea of running either stock car racing combined with grass track motor cycle events or on its own. Discussing this last week, members commented on the popularity of stock car racing in the neighbouring county. It was felt that interest in this type of event could provide an alternative to the club's popular scramble meetings, now held up owing to lack of suitable ground. The ground required for stock car racing must be flat, it was stated, a point which might facilitate securing a site as opposed to the club's difficulty in securing one for their popular, but at the present defunct, scramble meetings.

The club's first lady member has made application for membership. She is Mrs N J Ross, wife of Mr S Ross, a long serving club member. Arrangements were made for the club's camping holiday at Whit, which took them to Melrose in Scotland, a 69-mile run from Ashington.
In reply to questions from members about statements in the press recently, the Secretary, Mr J W Reed, said it was quite true that no replies had been received from Ashington Council to letters of complaint. Members urged that a letter should be written complaining of the congestion caused by cars parking on the First Avenue corner at the junction with North Seaton Road. Complaints about the road conditions from the North Seaton Hotel to the Green Lane level crossing, and also the number of street lights that were not operating, were asked to be included. This Sunday, a run to a secret destination leaves at 1:30 pm from Castle Square, opposite the Universal Club.

Firms Still Rush to Build New Shops But The Council Says "No" (Journal 1961)
A new shopping centre, which would be traffic free, is included in the Town Map Development Scheme for Ashington. It is sited from North Seaton Road east to Poplar Street and includes the Grand Corner. Within that area are some 100 houses, all privately owned, with some tenants paying rent. The problem is re-housing if development is allowed to take place.

Ashington Council is adamant that it will not allow development to the detriment of housing accommodation, and is not prepared itself to undertake development on the suggested new shopping centre. Some property trust firms have indicated they are prepared to go ahead with a re-housing scheme, but the problem would involve re-housing until the new project was completed.

One firm has already suggested the provision of maisonettes and has even contacted house owners for their views. This, two years ago, has not brought any fresh information to light and those tenants approached are 'still in the dark'. It is understood that another objection of the local authority is that while multiple stores could afford the possible high rents, small traders might not be able to do so. Although the County Planning Authority has scheduled this area for redevelopment, it is now apparent that Ashington Council looks on the plan with some disfavour and is not prepared to commit itself to any such project.

Local traders within the Ashington Chamber of Trade are interested in this project, not because they want it, but because they feel it would be detrimental to the present shopping centre, which has been described as 'one of the best in the north'.

New Road Gets 'Go-Ahead' (Ashington Advertiser – February 1962)
Regular users of the Ashington road which runs from Cooper's Shop to Sheepwash Bank will welcome the news that a new road – in a straight

line from the corner to the top of the bank – is to be built. The cost is to be nearly £25,000, of which the Ministry of Transport will pay £18,742, and the County Council Highways Committee is recommending that the work go ahead.

This means that one of the road projects visualised by Ashington Council could materialise this year. The old turning and twisting road will be done away with and the new scheme should do much to speed summer traffic to and from the coast in the summer. Another scheme of considerable interest to Ashington is the rebuilding and improving of Pegswood Railway Bridge and its approaches at a cost of £35,000.

Ashington also has hopes that this year may see the fulfilment of future road schemes. Due to the building of an Old People's Home (Essendene) at the south end of the library field, and completion of the 'link' road from Station Road to Kenilworth Road is also expected. Another scheme in the 'possibility' stage, which is being held up because of financial consideration, is the road diversion at the Store Corner, Ashington. This provides for a new road, straight from the fire station (on Station Bridge) through to High Market, but will entail the demolition of 27 colliery houses in the Seventh Row. These, however, are planned to be replaced by council-built houses. The widening of the footpath on the south side of Station Bridge, for the safety of pedestrians, is also proposed and planned. In the interests of safety, rails on this side are also under consideration. *(Note - obviously, plans for demolition of Seventh Row houses did not go ahead)*

Interest by property trust development firms in developing a new traffic-free shopping centre for Ashington has not waned. At least six firms have written to Ashington Council asking about the scheme

Congratulations Begin for Wor Jackie in his New Job (Journal – January, 1963)

Jackie Milburn, soccer pride of Ashington and the greatest idol in Newcastle United's history, was last night appointed Manager of First Division League Champions, Ipswich Town. Milburn, at thirty-eight-years-old, succeeds Alf Ramsay, England's new team manager, and takes over full control on 29th April. But for weeks before that he will be working at Portman Road in close association with Ramsay, his old England buddy, and the man with whom he shared a hotel room when both were picked for their first representative game in 1949.

Wor Jackie was picked from sixty applicants for one of the plum jobs in football – there have been only two managers at Ipswich in twenty-five years and neither got the sack. Milburn, thirteen times capped for England, said: "I don't want any contract. I think it is up to a man to prove himself." So impressed were the directors by Milburn during the interview that the Chairman, Mr John Cobbold, an old Etonian, said: "In the case of Jackie Milburn, we were overwhelmed by the personality of the man."

Jackie Milburn drove home to the Berkshire village of Crowborough late last night and found on the mat a telegram which said –

'Congratulations on appointment as Ipswich Manager; great news – Bobby Stokoe'.

Residence for Students to be Built This Year for £60,000 (Ashington Advertiser – March 1963)

The County Technical College at Ashington is to have its Hall of Residence this year to allow up to 60 of their students to live near the college instead of travelling large distances or living in 'digs'. The college playing fields will also be completed at the same time.

The building will be sited about 400 feet south east of the main college building on the proposed extension of Hawthorn Road, but in the college grounds. Playing fields layout, costing £9,918, has already been planned and includes hockey, rugby, cricket and soccer pitches, plus an athletics track, with discus, shot, high and long jump sites. Future proposals include practice wickets and tennis courts, and spaces available on the college site for additional classrooms, workshops and a proposed swimming pool. These projects and the playing field layout will fill in the area bounded by Seventh Avenue, Hawthorn Road and its extension, Monkseaton Terrace and Richardson Street.

Ashington Station Bridge Face-lift (Ashington Advertiser – 26th April, 1963)
Railway Plans Fly-over Shops

Ashington Station Bridge will have a new 'face' if proposals by British Railways, approved by Ashington Council on Tuesday, go through. The BR plans to build shops from Clydesdale Stores, 200-feet deep, bridging the railway line to the Post Office and fronting onto Station Bridge. Ashington Council Surveyor, Mr George Boundy, explained that the plan resulted from an idea he put to the authority for widening the railway bridge on the south side. The Railways and Development Company decided to propose these plans for building shops, running from the present three shops on Station Bridge, which are set back, doing away with the two shops on the west side of the lines, to the Post Office. The shops would extend 200 feet back into the goods yard and station, bridging the main lines. They would extend backwards as far as the shelter in the library field. Councillor George Holland thought the Beeching Plan was being applied before it had been accepted.

The Plans Committee also agreed to receive a letter from the development company who were interested in redeveloping land north of Station Road. The firm now offered to build multi-storey flats to re-house displaced tenants. Councillor Jim Freathy said the council would have to acquire and clear the site by compulsory purchase at capital cost. He said "The plan leaves a lot to be desired, but we don't want to knock houses down, that is not the way. It would be a tremendous undertaking and the Council would have the Chamber of Trade around its neck." Councillor George Holland said "I am alarmed at some statements seen in the press. We do not know the full story and the full expenses involved have not been revealed." Alderman George Duddridge said "We don't want the lease of a block of flats. We don't need any. If there are any flats built around here, we will build them."

Big Field in Election Stakes (Ashington Advertiser – 26th April, 1963) Nomination for election of councillors in Ashington and Hirst wards closed on Tuesday. The elections will be held on 9th May, the following are candidates. Ashington Ward: Albert Bramley (Labour), Miner, of 67 Green Lane; Thomas Dawson (Liberal), Shopkeeper, of 98 Station Road; Annie Evelyn Eke (Co-op), Married Woman, of 24 Aln Street; John Grierson (IND) Work Study Engineer, 'Brentwood', Green Lane; James Herron (Liberal) Shopkeeper, of 2 Darnley Road; William Patton (Co-op) Butcher's Foreman, of 5 Ellington Terrace.

Hirst Ward: Ronald Ainsley (Liberal), Milk Roundsman, of 21 Bamburgh Terrace; Anthony Davison (Liberal), Printer, of 28 West View; Elsie Dodd (Labour), Housewife, of 7 Milton Grove; Ellen Dodds (Labour), House Worker, of 68 Pont Street; Alfred Forster Gray (Labour), Storekeeper, of 3 Alexandra Court; Tommy Harkness (Labour), Civil Servant, of 23 Welfare Crescent.

My School – 1963, by Brenda Reed (nee Locker) then aged 9
I go to Hirst North County Primary School in Ashington. We are on the corner of Second Avenue, opposite the Salvation Army Church. We are in a tall building, painted green, and we have a large yard to play in. To get in to our school you have to climb some stairs. The girls are upstairs and the boys are downstairs. In our school we have ten classrooms and we have a dining room and a music room. In the music room we have a piano, it is fawn, we have also got some new curtains up, they are blue ones. They are up so if we want a film then we can draw the curtains and get a better film.

In our school we have two porches, one for the Junior end and one for the Senior end. Beside each cloakroom we have some washbasins. In our classroom we have three bookshelves. We also have two calendars, one is on the little cupboard and one is on the wall. We have three blackboards, two wall ones and one on wheels. In the classroom we have many flowers to make it look gay. On the wall the teacher has one big map of the world and one of castles.

Viewing Television Sunday I like to watch The Magic Boomerang, it is about two boys, Tom and his friend Wampy. Whenever Tom throws his boomerang everything stops still. Blue Peter is an interesting programme which is at 5 o'clock on Monday evenings. Also at 7.30 Coronation Street takes place in an ordinary street where someone is always in trouble. Wednesday night my Dad (Jimmy Locker) lets me stay up to watch Z Cars, where someone is always involved in a crime. Friday evenings I like to watch Crackerjack. Each time Eamonn Andrews says 'Crackerjack' everyone gives applause.

Saturday evening I like to view Dr Who. He lives in a Police Box and discovers different countries and planets. In the comedy series I like to watch the Flintstones, and Harry Worth, Beverley Hillbillies and Eric Sykes. My favourite actor is Jack Warner on a Saturday night. He is a police constable in Dixon of Dock Green. My favourite actresses are Ellie

May and the Granny in Beverley Hillbillies. My favourite pop singers are Paul McCartney, Cliff Richard and Lonnie Donegan.

Two Welfare Veterans (Ashington Advertiser – December, 1963)
Sixty-six year old Mr John Fairfax retired this week after forty-two years' service with Ashington Joint Welfare Organisation. On Thursday night his colleague Mr George Murdie, who has forty years service with the Welfare, presented Mr Fairfax with a chiming clock.

Mr Fairfax told the Advertiser that he commenced working for the Ashington Group of Collieries Welfare Scheme after starting out as a miner. He, along with Mr A Watson and Mr George Clementson, and his present colleague Mr Murdie, were among the first men to be employed full-time on this type of welfare scheme in the country. Mr Fairfax has been at all four Welfare centres in the area and spent over thirty years at Lynemouth, where he lives at 18 Jersey Square. A machine-gunner in the Machine Gun Corps in World War I, John Fairfax saw action in France in several major battles. His two sons are both Lynemouth Colliery miners and he has three grandchildren.

Future Looks Grim for Men at Woodhorn Pit (Ashington Advertiser - 10th May, 1963)
Discussions with the Miners' Unions and the Coal Board over the future of Woodhorn Colliery are taking place this week, following the weekend meeting held by the Unions concerned to explain the proposals to the 370 men affected by the move for single-shift working in the sixty-nine-year-old colliery. First news of the moves afoot was going from mouth-to-mouth in Ashington on Friday, and the weekend meeting confirmed the rumours. The 370 men affected are mainly younger craftsmen and face workers and the move to single shift working will create these redundancies.

Alternative work at other collieries will be found for a large number of these men, but it is expected that about fifty will be jobless. It is hoped that before the move to single shift working becomes effective, some of the older men at the pit will be retiring and places may be available for those without jobs.

An NCB spokesman said: "Proposals regarding the organisation of Woodhorn Colliery are under discussion with the Unions at the present time and we can make no further comment until talks are complete." A reduction last year meant a move to other collieries for 270 of Woodhorn's men. This time, however, an indication of saturation point in these collieries is that no more than 300 men can be accommodated. The men fear that the redundancy moves will probably mean a wage drop for some, and regard this as a sign that the pit may not last much longer. Some men feel like looking for other employment while there is an opportunity. One man told the Advertiser he had been at Woodhorn for over forty years and if the future was as grim as it looked to him, he wanted out.

Coal reserves at Woodhorn are estimated at 36 million tons, but neighbouring collieries, with mechanisation, may be able to work this more economically. The colliery was sunk in 1894 and began drawing coal on 5th February, 1898.

Scout Award for Ashington Woman (Morpeth Herald – May, 1963)
Mrs Elizabeth Tomlinson, Secretary of the Ashington and Newbiggin Boy Scouts' Association, will be presented with the Silver Acorn at the annual meeting of the association on 20th May. The decoration was awarded by the Chief Scout in the St George's Honours list.

Mrs Tomlinson's notable service to scouting has included making large quantities of toffee to raise money for scout troop funds. It was in 1914 that Elizabeth joined the Girl Guides, becoming a Patrol Leader for two years and a Captain from 1935-1940 when the company was disbanded for the duration of the war. The first scouting service Mrs Tomlinson attended was in 1919 when she helped to raise funds for the 2nd Hirst Scouts to make the trip to the First World Jamboree in 1920.

At her home in Sycamore Street, Ashington, she has entertained scouts from all over the country and from overseas. Local association Secretary since 1944, Mrs Tomlinson still serves as Chairman of the 2nd Hirst Group Committee of which she was previously secretary for ten years. All her committee meetings are held at her house.

During her long service, Mrs Tomlinson, already holder of the Medal of Merit, has missed only one Local Association and County Executive meeting. The two successful Gang Shows in the 1950s which raised 1,400 for scouting in Ashington and Newbiggin, owe much of their success to her secretaryship. Her husband, Mr George Tomlinson, is District Commissioner for Scouts in Ashington and Newbiggin.

Expansion Plans at Ashington Factory (June, 1963)
Factory reorganisation, which eliminates cramped working conditions, has been completed at the cake manufacturing establishment of G T Culpitt Ltd at North Seaton Road Trading Estate. And the 10,800 square feet extension to the building could mean introduction of new lines of manufacture, possibly plastic, and could lead to an increased number of operatives.

The business started in London in 1921 and in 1945 they obtained premises in Ashington. After occupying temporary premises at the Coronation Bar, next to the Portland Hotel, the firm moved into its present building in 1948. Engaged in the export trade, Culpitt's gave a boost to the employment position in Ashington and District, especially in the employment of women. Now the factory employs some 370 operatives.

Mr Ernest Jameson, manager of the Ashington factory, told the News Post: "This extension will enable us to reorganise the factory and to dispense with some of the cramped conditions under which we have been working." The new extensions will be officially opened by seventeen year old Miss Margaret Maxwell of 8 Linden Close, Stakeford, who is the 1963 Personality Girl at the Ashington factory. Mrs Charlotte

Cullpitt will make an unusual presentation to the girl employed in the factory who draws the one millionth pound paid in wages in Ashington.

Ashington Faces a 'Dead Town' Threat – Ashington Post 8th November 1963

'Population down by 1,000 in ten years'. Unless urgent action is taken, Ashington may become a 'dead town' because the district pits have an estimated life of only twenty years. This was the news which Mr Gordon Boundy, engineer and surveyor, broke to Ashington Council members on Tuesday night.

Mr Boundy was presenting to the council extracts from the Town Map review of Ashington, which also shows a 4% drift of population between 1951 and 1961. The news that Ashington pits had an estimated life of twenty years and of the steady drift of population, prompted Mr Boundy to comment that action needed to be taken well in advance to deal with "a declining and vulnerable economy. The Plan gives a life of twenty years for the pits, therefore we have to face the prospect of Ashington becoming a dead town with no future", stated Mr Boundy.

"The situation for Ashington is far from rosy, and the report says that the introduction of new industries must be accelerated to give a new balance in which the traditional industries will be less dominant. Action needs to be taken well in advance to deal with the declining and vulnerable economy. I feel that while new towns are very nice in a way, some planning energy should be diverted to older urban areas like Ashington. A lot of people are drifting from Ashington because of lack of residential accommodation and, in view of the estimated life of the pits, I can not see why the NCB should continue 100% coal sterilisation of land." Councillor George Holland said that if the Coal Board was not going to develop it they should give the Council the opportunity to build. Alderman George Duddridge said that the 4% drift of the population had gone to Bedlington and Morpeth, but he hoped that they would eventually get people back.

NCB Kill Rumour That Pits Will End In 20 Years (Ashington Post – November 1963)

The Northern Divisional Coal Board said yesterday it was incorrect to say that collieries in the Ashington area would last for only twenty years. Some of the pits of Ashington, Lynemouth, Linton and Newbiggin "should last more than twice as long," said the Board's statement to the News Post. It added "The life of a colliery depends, not only upon its mineral reserves, but on the skill and management of all employed in the mines, and the co-operation which exists in making the best of them, not only of those who work in the pits, but of the many others who live upon the spending power the pits provide. While no-one at the present stage could guarantee that the Board would succeed in its object of maintaining the Northumberland output at its present level for a great deal longer than twenty years, everyone would agree that undue pessimism at the present time could be a major factor in defeating that object."

An Ashington councillor, on Tuesday night, used the words 'ridiculous' and 'untrue' in refuting estimates by planning experts that the local pits have a life of only twenty years. He was Councillor Larry Lavelle, who complained that a statement made last week at a Council Committee Meeting had caused despondency and gloom among the working population of the town. He said "I can assure you that the figures are entirely wrong. There are considerable coal reserves in this area for much more than twenty years and where this figure came from I don't know."

Book Demand Grows at Ashington (Ashington Advertiser – January 1964)
What is it that makes Ashington folk read 200,000 books per year? Despite television, the number of readers and the books they read have increased astonishingly. Increased leisure time, modern educational methods, the opening of the new Technical College, and an absorbing and inexpensive hobby for retired folk, are some of the reasons for the increase in reading in Ashington.

It seems by far the most avid readers are the children, who use the library to its limits and vary their reading all the time. Not for them the safe world of the western novel or the murder mystery. Two of the Saturday visitors, Linda Oswell (7) and Carol Cossar (8) told us they prefer adventure books, but they read books on history, geography and travel and vary their reading all the time. Mr Tom Chicken, father of two small children, said he and his wife try to see that their children get the best use out of their books that they can. "The library does provide them with an extensive range of reading matter, and we try to get them to read the books for themselves."

The Branch Librarian, Mrs Peggy Kilbourn, agreed with her staff, Mr Bill Harrison, Miss S Davies and Miss S Bell, that travel books head the list of popular non-fiction reading. Stories about the wars are still popular said Mr Harrison and technical books were in great demand. There is much more to library work than is seen by the public, Mrs Kilbourn told us that work commences an hour before the library opens. New books have to be catalogued, an average of 800 book tickets have to be sorted into their proper places, incoming books put in alphabetical order on the shelves, and quite an amount of paperwork. Library assistants have to have a flair for their work, an ability to deal with people, and indulge in quite a bit of detective work to ferret out books requested by readers.

The County Council plan to build a new library on a larger space, but on the same site as the present building (Station Villa). It will cost £28,000 and double the floor space, and there is to be a branch at the eastern side of the town. This branch is something Ashington councillors have agitated for as an amenity for new housing estates.

Business was Brisk in the Ashington Council Chamber during the first quarter of 1964. There was some dismay expressed by councillors that the closure of Ashington's railway passenger service had not occurred on the 6th January as hoped. Plans were already well advanced to use the goods yard as part of a new shopping precinct on Station Bridge, and it was no secret that the council wished to use the extra space to widen the footpath. The railway station in Ashington dated back to 1878, six years after a line had been laid to Newbiggin. Then called Hirst Station, and renamed in 1889, it formed a vital link in the chain of Blyth and Tyne Railways. But Dr Beeching's axe, provided by the Conservative government in the name of progress, severed the Ashington artery and, like dozens of others, the little station stood shabby and derelict for a number of years, destined, as were many of Ashington's historical landmarks, to become a concrete car park.

- It was announced on 14th February 1964 that the East Villas housing estate was to undergo a massive facelift over the next two years at a cost of £40,000. The estate, one of the first to be built by the council after the First World War, had become very run down.
- On 21st February it was reported that an end was in sight to the problem of communication around Ashington. A five year road plan was approved that would eventually see a new spine road bridging the River Wansbeck. A plan to build 216 more council houses on Moorhouse Lane was passed, rents to be charged range from £2 3s 7d for a three bedroomed, centrally heated house to £1 0s 0d for a flat. It was also agreed to put up the rents of nearly 2,000 other council properties by one fifth.
- As Ashington housing estates encroached ever nearer upon their fisherman friends on the coast, a merger between Ashington and Newbiggin, with others, was 'fast approaching', according to a council spokesman. Another improvement scheme was scheduled for the west end of town with the proposed demolition of the Long and Cross Rows. This was to be the first step in a massive redevelopment of Ashington's Top End.
- It was announced that the proposed old folks' home in the library park would be opened in the autumn. The name was to be Essendene, once the ancient name for Ashington. Residents would be asked to pay £2 14s 6d towards their keep.

Builders Find Bones – January 1964
Human remains have been found at the Glebe Farm, Sheepwash, and were stated by experts to be over 500 years old. They were found as workmen were erecting a barn on farm land. Other finds have been made in this area, and it is believed by some local historians that there was a burial ground in this area in the Middle Ages and possibly later. The site of the old Rectory at Sheepwash and references to a Church of the Holy Sepulchre are also clues to the existence of a burial ground. Sheepwash was mentioned in records before the year 1300 and keel boats were said to come up as far as the present Sheepwash Bridge; the roads leading to the river Wansbeck were once known as Thieves Bank. The two skulls are to be used as specimens in the biology department at Ashington Technical College.

Rail Bridge Second Refusal – February 1964
Refusing to consider a previous decision, Ashington Council are having nothing to do with the erection of a footbridge at Darnley Road Railway Crossing. British Railways want them to pay three-quarters of the cost (£3,350) and maintain the bridge afterwards. Last week councillors decided to stick to their original decision

New School Changes Right of Way
On 6th March 1964 it was reported "In order to make the satisfactory layout to the new Roman Catholic School's playing fields, on the school site east of Sixth Avenue, the county council are seeking authorisation to divert a right of way which crosses the proposed layout. The school is to be known as St Benedict's." The *Ashington Advertiser* also went on to say that the County Education Committee hoped to provide two swimming pools at Ashington Technical College with a view to swimming being taught there. Authorisation was also given for a new laboratory at Hirst East School.

Bus Fares Up – 30th March 1964
Some Ashington bus fares will be affected by a rise successfully negotiated by the United Bus Service at a traffic enquiry. The company are trying to leave their smaller fares alone on the 2d and 3d fares. Prices from Ashington to Newcastle will go up by 3d to 2/3d. A bus ride from Newbiggin to Ashington will now cost 8d – an increase of 1d.

Fashion Parade – March 1964
Shephard's of Ashington are arranging a fashion parade to aid the YMCA's new building fund. The staff members of the store which dominates the Grand Corner will act as models. They are: Carol Bell; Heather Highmoor; Ann Carruthers; Pat Woolton; Joan Squires; Joan Russell; Ann Skinner and Brenda Young.

Council Housing – 30th March 1964
More homes are expected in a building boost as Ashington Council hope to double their output of council housing during the building programme this year. They are expected to tender for 260 houses in 1964, and private builders may be used to boost the figures. Worried about the slow rate of housing progress in the last few years, councillors had a report on the matter compiled by their surveyor. House building over the past few years has fallen to sixty per year.

Councillors will not Paddle in the Wansbeck
Alderman George Duddridge was referring to the pollution of the lower reaches of the river and the danger of contamination when he said: "Everyone knows it is a dirty river." Councillor George Holland replied: "I blame it all on Bedlington Council for indiscriminate tipping."

Thirty acres of land at Black Close Bank was set aside by the council on Jubilee Industrial Estate 'primarily for female labour'. Two months later an advert appeared for Hepworths, asking for women to apply for jobs at 'our brand new, ultra-modern factory'.

On 1st May 1964 the Council approved planning permission for a five-storey NCB headquarters to be built next to the new fire station opposite Bothal Terrace. Following amalgamation, Ashington Colliery had ceased to be part of Number Three Area of the northern division.

In the May Council Elections, Ashington had a smaller than ever turnout at the polls. Only 25% voted at the Hirst where John Brotherton, Labour, topped the poll with 1,464 votes; and 30% turned up in the Ashington Ward to make Arthur Gallagher top Labour man with 1,570 votes. The Liberals, making their second attempt to break the Labour strangle-hold, failed to gain a seat, but vowed: "We will be back next time."

More affluent than at any time in the town's history, Ashington residents demanded more and more amenities. A taxi rank was established on the piece of ground next to the Grand Hotel. Two enterprising young men, John Richardson and Charles Grint, took advantage of a TV western to start a new taxi business, calling themselves 'Paladin'; their catchphrase motto was 'Have Car Will Travel'.

One of the more zany suggestions at that time came from Tom Dawson of Ashington's Chamber of Commerce who advocated that "Ashington's slag heaps be transformed into dry-ski slopes and become a tourist attraction." The idea might not have been so crazy given that Woodhorn Colliery is now pulling in crowds as a museum, and who would have forecast that in 1964?

The Swinging Sixties caught Ashington up in its frenetic lifestyle. The long hair as worn by men was highlighted by G W Raffell, local official of the Hairdressers' Federation, in 1964 when he said: "Ashington men get their hair cut far cheaper than anywhere in the country – two shillings and thrupence – I think it only reasonable that those youths with longer hair should pay more to have it cut off."

In May 1964, the town got itself a genuine nightclub for the first time when Ronnie Harrison, former centre forward for the Colliers, took over the lease of the Harmonic Hall. Named 'The Three Ones', because of its address of 111 Station Road, the opening night cabaret featured Tyne Tees songstress Ethna Campbell.

Ashington Council Break with Tradition (Ashington Advertiser – August, 1964)
In a month's time the administration of Ashington from the Town Hall will be directed by a full-time clerk for the first time in the history of the urban district. Arising from a recommendation by a team of organisation and method consultants, the council has ended the era of the part-time clerk. The new man, who will be Principal Official, is 33 year old Mr

Roy Rushworth Nuttall, a Lancashire man who has been Deputy Clerk of Aldridge Urban District Council in Staffordshire for twelve years. He is a married man with two children and the family will live in Cresswell.

Mr Nuttall was the only applicant for the full-time job, which was declined by Mr John Kent, who held the position on a part-time basis for twelve years.

Mr Kent, who is deputy coroner for South Northumberland, will stay on for a month in an advisory capacity to show the newcomer 'the ropes' as Ashington's first full-time town clerk.

Ashington Student Russia Bound (Advertiser 28th August, 1964)
Included in the party of twenty British graduates who sail for the Soviet Union tomorrow (Friday) to do a year's post graduate work in Russian universities is twenty five year old Michael Singer of Park Villas, Ashington, whose father is a journeyman grocer with a Blyth firm. The studentship awards have been made available by the Soviet authorities under the terms of the Anglo-Soviet Cultural Agreement. Soviet graduates will arrive in this country in mid-September.

Michael Singer, the Ashington member of the British Party, has been at Edinburgh University for three years, where he is studying bio-chemistry. He recently obtained his Doctorate of Philosophy. He attended the Wansbeck School, Ashington, and Morpeth Grammar School, then went to Reading University and afterwards studied for a year at London University. He will work in his own subject of bio-chemistry in Moscow under an eminent Soviet professor he met at Edinburgh University. Michael, who studied the Russian language for his PhD examination, said "I am looking forward to meeting the professor again, and working under his guidance."

Ashington Council Scrutiny (Evening Chronicle - 1st October, 1964)
A decision to bar the Press and members of the public from certain Council committee meetings prompted this article:
Mr Roy Nuttall, Ashington Urban Council's newly appointed clerk, has attempted to clarify his attitude to a proposed re-organisation of council procedure by saying that the admission of the Press and public to committee meetings is a side issue. Evidently he forgets that the citizen values his right to a proper account of the stewardship of those he has elected to represent him in the conduct of community affairs.

The preservation of that right cannot possibly be regarded as of subsidiary importance to other considerations – even those as vital and urgent as improving the operational efficiency of the council. Because Mr Nuttall, very properly, recognises that he has a duty to enable the council to function more efficiently, he has apparently allowed himself to be persuaded that the admission of the public and the Press to committee meetings is of little relative consequence.

Unfortunately, his single-mindedness has precipitated an unfortunate situation in which, once again, there is implicit a threat to individual rights. The streamlining procedure which may be adopted and the reduction in the size of certain committees so that they can be held concurrently with others, could effectively prevent both Press and public from attending all meetings hitherto open to them. But this accident of organisation must not be allowed to be interpreted as meaning that their right to attend should disappear.

Any attempt to limit the freedom of the Press to inform the public on municipal matters must inevitably raise grave doubt over the motives that inspired it. The conduct of public business in private, for whatever reason, must always be suspect, and cannot possibly improve the quality of confidence in a local administration. The suppression of information to which ratepayers are entitled, the stopping-up of sources of information, the creation of the 'official spokesman' and the inclination to obstruct reporters are all alien to democratic principles.

When councillors and their officers lose sight of the fact that their primary function is that of service to the public, a retrograde step has been taken. The Public Bodies (admission to meetings) Act of 1960 made a brave attempt to persuade local authorities of the prudence of frankness in dealing with the public. Unfortunately, it is too often and too easily flouted.

It has been said at some point that when justice goes behind closed doors it withers and dies. Much the same may be said for the conduct of public affairs. The aim today should be complete trust in dealing with the local electorate, and adherence to practice which shows conclusively with what honesty and purpose elected representatives pursue their chosen vocation as members of a local authority.

Cost of New Library Zooms Upwards (Ashington Advertiser – 1st January, 1965)

Ashington's new library, adjoining the present building, is to cost £5,000 more than was thought. The original estimate of the cost has gone up from £28,000 to £32,832. The reason given by the county for the increase is that the new cost is based on the tender accepted. The new library is to be built this year, situated on the ground adjacent to the present library building, on land that was bought from Ashington Council. It will be reinforced by a sub-branch library, scheduled for 1966, to be built opposite the County Technical College. The cost of this branch library, to be built in conduction with a child welfare clinic, is in the region of £14,000.

Looking Around Ashington with Mack (Ashington Advertiser – 12th February, 1965)

An Expensive Necessity

Ashington Council are in the process of gaining money to build some 49 houses on the Newbiggin Road site at a total estimated cost of £107,335. This works out at well over £2,000 per house, a reasonable figure compared with that of privately constructed houses sold locally. However, the cost doesn't seem quite so reasonable when held up against that of other local authorities throughout the country. A figure of £2,800 is quoted for a house in Battersea, which is fair enough since it entails all sorts of expensive items which crop up when building in a city like

London. Other councils outside this type of zone can build houses for as little as £1,800, on land that is not so easy to obtain and with more difficulties than we of Ashington face.

No-one wishes council houses to be any less modern and well fitted than private homes, but there are items in private dwellings which are not added to the cost of a rented housing unit. In an area where land values are not inflated, where wages are not as high as in metropolitan areas, it seems a little expensive for the erection of ordinary houses built by a specialised labour force. Not that there is very much to be done about a remedy is this estimate is one of the lowest. There are undoubtedly some aspects of the affair which are not common knowledge. For all I know the houses may be for sale. But one thing is certain, if an economic rent is to be charged for them, prospective tenants are going to feel a draught around the purse.

Concert Programme Attractions

Bass singer Owen Brannigan's programme for his appearance at the 120th Celebrity Concert at the Central Hall on Sunday (14th February, 1965) includes some perennial favourites and three wonderful Songs of Praise. Yvonne Proudlock, a local pianist of outstanding ability, who is a pupil of Norman Spowart, includes in her piano recital Nocturne in A flat by Chopin. The Choral Union with Ada M Davidson on organ and Audrey Stimpson on piano will contribute choral music to the concert.

Ashington Operatic Society Perform 'La Belle Helene' (Ashington Advertiser – 19th February, 1965)

Rehearsals for this production at Ashington Tech College, are now being directed by Madame Forster, musical direction by Miss Audrey Stimpson and choreography by Sidney Jeavons. "I would like to mention that, without the rehearsal and committee rooms kindly loaned by the Hirst Premier and Middle Market Social Clubs, and the funds realised by the society's own supporters' club, the modest entrance price of 12/6 would not be sufficient," said Mr Charles Sewell, producer.

Headmaster Retires at Hirst North School (Ashington Advertiser – March, 1965)

An Ashington Headmaster, who has spent forty years at the same school, retires at Easter. He is Mr Redvers Trueman, Head of the North School, who lives in Ariel Street, Ashington. For many years he rendered valuable service on the East Northumberland Association of the National Union of Teachers, in official positions. Another of his interests has been in school savings. He retires as School Heads' Representative on the Ashington Local Savings Committee, this year, a position he has held for many years. "I became interested in school savings forty-five years ago and have retained that interest every since," he said. Mr Trueman, known as 'Ted', began teaching at Wheatley Hill in County Durham. He came to the North School in Ashington in 1925. For a short time he was headmaster at St James' Church School in Morpeth and in 1946 was appointed headmaster at the North School. He will be succeeded by Mr

Nat Graham, a Newbiggin teacher, well-known in sporting circles as a FIFA Referee.

More North School Memoirs by Nathaniel 'Nat' Graham
I applied for the Headship at Hirst North in 1965. When I arrived for the interview I found that the other four candidates were already Headmasters. I was then a Deputy Head at Hirst South School, where I had been for fourteen years. I thought I was just there for the run-out, but when I was offered the post I was really pleased. If asked to choose the highlights of my time spent at the North, I would select six:

- An early change was the abolition of all streaming. From the very beginning I was determined that the three-form entry would no longer be 1A, 1B and 1C. All classes would be comprised of mixed ability. I would also have liked the school to be mixed in a co-ed situation. I felt it was terrible for brother and sister to be separated and often saw them having conversations over the large fence which kept the boys and girls apart. However, my policy of non-streaming met some considerable objection, and co-education was ruled out completely.
- The success of having the outdoor toilets in the far corner of the yard and indoor toilets provided.
- I couldn't accept that we would have no Assembly Hall. Within a short period of time, two spare classrooms were converted into a good-sized hall.
- I was quite proud of what I thought was the sensational effect the newly introduced school uniform had on the appearance and ethos of the school.
- We were often asking for support in fund-raising, and I would like to mention the wonderful support we had from the ladies of the Beetle Club who met weekly at the school. My thanks would go to them, and in particular to a Mrs Routledge who helped to organise this event which went a long way towards paying for the installation of the new library in one of the classrooms.
- A highlight after England won the World Cup in 1966 was putting on an exhibition of Charlton memorabilia supplied by Jack. I often picked Cissie Charlton up when I was refereeing a football league game at, say, Bolton, and on my way there I would leave her at Jack's house in Leeds and pick her up on the way home. Jack Charlton was great with all his stuff – he threw England shirts, International Caps and World Cup Replicas into a suitcase, saying: "Here ye are, tek as much as ye like." He was a great lad. The exhibition of his mementos at Hirst North was staged and supervised by Cissie and we made a lot of money for our school funds.

On returning to Hirst North in 1968, after two years at Teacher Training College in Alnwick, I was still a little disappointed at not being able to establish the school on a co-ed basis. Miss Florence Buck, Head of girls, didn't think that mixing girls and boys would work, and I did. So when I was offered the Headship at newly-built Coulson Park First School I jumped at the chance to run a mixed school, and I was there for twenty five years until I retired.

Bob Wedderburn's moving from Hirst North, 1968. Left Miss Taylor, Mrs Enid Wedderburn, Bob and Nat Graham; two boys Brian Robinson and Roy Henderson.

Comedy Thriller at Hirst Welfare (Advertiser 14th May 1965)
Despite its title, the Welfare Players production this week is anything but a 'Dead Loss' The group have cleverly handled a comedy thriller with sinister overtones to entertain. Eileen Patterson was impressive as the dizzy Amanda who turns into a hard and vicious woman. Douglas Dickson as the TV producer loped about like Groucho Marx; Bill Backburn changes character from London van-man to smooth TV type easily; and Albert Johnson as the fatuous Lord Wickersley, acts the titled blockhead in comedy vein. The rest of the cast, all fitting easily into their parts, are Olive Proctor, Pat Foggan, Brenda Wood, Brenda Nevens, Ian Collinson, George Mordue, and Bill Furness. The play is produced by Sally Wood and backstage staff are Margaret Horn, Ian Collinson, Joan Cardno, with stage settings by Joe Grieve and his Welfare staff.

Ashington YMCA News (May 1965)
There was a good gathering of parents and friends for the Boys and Girls Club evening. Club leaders Albert Laws and Enid Stewart arranged a most interesting and enjoyable evening and with the help of their

assistants demonstrated Scottish Dancing, Gymnastics, and Rhythmic Exercises. David Lyons narrowly defeated Eric Williams in the Boys Club table-tennis final. During the evening, parents watched an initiation ceremony and two boys were admitted. The highlight was the presentation of the Boy and Girl of the Year Award, made by Mr Isaac Smeaton, Ashington Colliery manager, to Barbara Reilly and Raymond Bunn. YMCA organiser, Mr Charlie Mills, paid tribute to the leaders and assistants for their hard work. Bob Darling ended the evening by showing slides of the boys at Lakeside Camp.

Ashington Hairstylists at YMCA (May 1965)
Five Ashington hair stylists waved and combed and cut in the YMCA on Tuesday night to show their skill before an attentive audience. Miss P Pape, Mrs B Price, Ron Hedley, Steve Brannigan and George Price showed their latest hairstyles for men and women. The five are in a hairstyling artistic group who compete, and their experience is being used to promote fashion-conscious hairstyles in Ashington. In a remarkable demonstration, Ron Hedley took a 'long hair' and styled him in a magical fashion that evoked oohs and aahs from the birds – and that decides how the well-groomed man – in this case David Scott – gets his hair cut. Mrs B Price showed off her 'Parisienne Chic' style, as modelled by Vivian Cook.

Development Scheme 'Yes' – Where and When to Come (June, 1965)
Redevelopment of Ashington Town Centre will have to come, decided the Planning and Development Committee councillors at Ashington last week. But where and when have still to be settled. The committee under Chairman Councillor A F Gray resolved the Town Centre Development should be carried out, but they have not decided where, or how, this will be done. A special meeting to consider this question is fixed for later this month, which will consider the various methods and sites available for carrying out the development.

Ashington's Town Map, defining the roles of town areas, is due for review in the near future. Other areas previously considered and turned down by Ashington Council include the site bordered by the Grand Hotel, Ashington Co-op, First Avenue and Woodhorn Road, and one that included Station Road, Lintonville, North View and the Portland Park entrance road. The first plan was dropped because it meant that 250 houses *(in Myrtle, Sycamore and Maple streets)* would have to go, and the people re-housed in flats. The second plan was also dropped, though it meant taking over only 18 houses because Ashington Council were expected to clear the site by compulsory purchases.

Redevelopment of Ashington is nothing new. Fourteen years ago a Government Planning expert reported that Ashington could be 'put right' by 1971. The report summed up by saying that Ashington could become an important educational and technical mining centre. But railway closures were not foreseen, and when an airfield was planned for Ashington and Morpeth it is easy to see why some of the plans flopped. (*Ashington Advertiser* – June, 1965)

New Ashington Tory Branch Interest (Advertiser June 1965)
Of great interest to Morpeth Constituency Conservative Party, at their annual meeting, was the establishment of an active branch at Ashington. In his annual report, Mr A Armstrong, Party Chairman, after paying tribute to the work in the recent election, mentioned the new Ashington branch. He said: 'An event of great interest in the past year has been the establishment of an active branch at Ashington under the chairmanship of Dr John Noble. With a nucleus of willing helpers, there are prospects of growth in this stronghold of Labour.'

Presentation marks 25 years' service as Head (Ashington Advertiser 30th July 1965)
Miss Elizabeth Joisce, headmistress at Wansbeck Junior School for twenty-five years, retired from her duties last Friday. School pupils gave her a tea service, past pupils a tea trolley, and the staff an onyx clock. She said: "In teaching you never know whether or not you have done a good job. Things made by hand could be seen, cakes baked could be eaten, but teachers had very little idea of what you had done for your pupils. But once in a while one comes back and mentions something that shows you how you had done something for a particular boy or girl." Miss Joisce has been headmistress at Wansbeck School for over 25 years. Her father was Head of the old Bothal School, and she taught at Hirst Park Modern, a Blyth training centre, and a teacher-training college in Bristol before coming to Ashington. She is succeeded by Mr J Barlow from Tweedmouth, Wansbeck School's first male headteacher.

Their handiwork is all around the town (Advertiser July 1965)
A man whose work is seen all around Ashington in green spaces, trees, flowers and shrubberies, Parks Superintendent Mr John J Stewart looks after his charges with a patience born of his calling. He and his staff – twenty in all – have 100 acres of grass, trees, shrubs and flowers to tend, including two parks, the town's open spaces and land at Sheepwash and Black Close Dene.

They look after paddling pools, the cricket field, football pitches in the parks, plant trees, flowers and grass seed, run a new nursery, work in potting sheds and greenhouses, and plan for the future. Mr Stewart who has been with the Ashington Council Parks Department since 1937, has been Superintendent for 14 years.

He said: 'One-third of our time is spent on necessary work in order to keep a reasonable standard. And two-thirds of the time is laying out shrubberies, open spaces, roadside and estate planting. Our work expands as the town gets bigger, and biggest problem is the weather - a good winter ensures us of a good spring. '

Work is now going on with the preparation for the spring and summer faces of the parks and open spaces in Ashington. Hirst Park is the showpiece for flowers and shrubs, and Mr Stewart points out: 'From what I've seen of other places, Ashington compares highly with them, and even with some larger authorities.'

Hirst Park developed over the years from what was an ash-tip in 1910 and is now a much-admired flower and rest enclosure, which is a popular place in Ashington.

Parks Department staff has been busy re-planting into the cosiest atmosphere of open spaces under the direction of foreman, Mr Bill Taylor. On the staff are gardeners, apprentices, labourers and youth labourers. John Stewart paid tribute to all his men for their enthusiasm and interest in their work, saying: 'In recent years, I've been very pleased with the number of youngsters using the parks at Ashington. It keeps them off the roads and away from the dangers that abound here. Under my eye, here at Hirst Park, they are under some sort of supervision at night. The playing fields have been improved this year, and those at Ashington People's Park and Hirst Park are being well used.'

New Principal for Ashington Technical College (Ashington Post – 8th July, 1965)

Mr Alan Davies, a forty-year-old Welshman, comes to Ashington from Aberdare College and he succeeds Mr Charles Pulford, who retired earlier this year. The new Principal told the *News Post* this week: "Mr Pulford and his staff have played a major part in planning the existing college buildings and envisaging the proposed extensions and establishing the pattern of occasional courses now organised. As a result, the College is now poised and ready for further educational growth and extension. This College should emerge as a 'powerhouse' of further education in its widest sense."

Mr Davies explained that there were complex factors which would affect further education in the near future, one of which was the future raising of the school leaving age to sixteen and the possible introduction in the county of a comprehensive system of education. The present college session is drawing to a close and in the past year there have been 3,000 students, of which 600 have been full time, 1,600 part time and 800 for evening classes. The teaching staff for the next year would number 90, assisted by a number of visiting lecturers.

New Admin Block for NCB as Ashington (Ashington Post – 19th August, 1965)

A centralisation scheme, which will bring the administrative department of the north Northumberland area of the National Coal Board under one roof, is now making steady progress at Ashington. The Area is being equipped with a new modern-style building which is under construction at the west end of Ashington. When completed, the office block will house about 300 members of the staff.

At present, the area administration is scattered in offices at Ashington Colliery, on the top of a shopping block at Station Road (Burton's Buildings) and at Linton Colliery. By bringing all the departments into one building, the NCB will streamline its administration. The new building will have a large conference hall plus a dining hall. It is ideally sited in an area which in recent years has been the provision of a new fire station, new secondary school and a new depot for the North Eastern Electricity Board. The electricity depot is on a site which once housed

Ashington Colliery Granary, which served the old Ashington Coal Company and later the NCB farms.

Town Rubbish – Plan for the future is sought (Advertiser 21st January 1966)

To burn or not to burn, to pulverise until we can afford to burn, or to suffer the stink of town tip refuse a little longer, was the difficult problem Ashington Health Committee councillors waded into last week. The committee recommended that Ashington have a £140,000 incinerator, but while waiting until the town can afford one, they are going to look into pulverisation methods which compress rubbish into tight blocks. Councillors examined a report by Ashington's Chief Public Health Officer, Mr Sam Musk, on the problems and use of pulverisation methods of rubbish treatment. Cllr Isaac Jackson said he had been pressing for an incinerator, and he was not the only one, but he stated: 'Money is the bar. The business of chopped-up rubbish may be alright, but we are not going to remove the causes of danger and disease from our rubbish tip.'

Cllr A F Gray described the present refuse disposal methods at Ashington as 'crude'. He said the scene of the town tip was one of' 'utter disgust' and said it looked like a nuclear aftermath. Town Clerk, Mr Roy Nuttall, said that it might entail seven years pulverisation, and an incinerator could mean a seven-penny rate increase. 'But pulverisation is certainly better than what we have now.' Cllr Arthur Gallagher said it was very important that something was used for refuse disposal that burned everything. He stated: 'It's the only way out.' The Health Committee agreed on the purchase of an incinerator, but is studying pulverisation methods.

Four-Lane Spine Road Starts North Trail – (Advertiser 11th February 1966)

The first two stages of the County Plan for a spine road arrowing north from the Tyne Tunnel to Alnwick, passing through Ashington's *western* end after bridging the River Wansbeck, got under way this week. But it will be well after 1970 before the dual carriageway to the north will get into Ashington. And before it crosses the River Wansbeck, a new bridge will have to be built.

Some of the schemes for the spine road should have started this year, but staffing difficulties have held them up. Stages One and Two, at an estimated cost of over two million pounds, will start the road on its way north. The entire road plan will cost about seven million pounds eventually, and will tie in with the industrial development all along its route – Cramlington, Kitty Brewster, Ashington and Ellington – in the immediate locality.

Ashington Town Clerk, Mr Roy Nuttall, said of the 72-page Town Map book: "It puts forward a picture of what the town could look like in 20 years time. The spine road running north from the Tyne Tunnel will make a big difference to Ashington as it will mean that a journey to Newcastle will only take 15 minutes." The road is not expected to reach Ashington until the mid-1970s.

Cheering News for Local Industry (Ashington Advertiser – 13th May 1966)

Cheering news for the local industrial front came this week when the President of the Board of Trade, Mr Douglas Jay, announced in the House of Commons that Ashington was among towns scheduled to get a 25,000 square feet Government advance factory. This is in addition to another Government advance factory of 10,000 square feet, already planned, and the town's own factory, of 11,500 square feet, now almost ready for building.

Councillor A F Gray, in welcoming the news, said: "This is very good news indeed. It is an added spur to our own efforts in the fields of industrial expansion. The type of industry is immaterial as long as it caters for the male labour." Ashington Town Clerk, Mr Roy Nuttall, said: "This is three up. Now we have to see how many more (factories) we can get to keep our young people here."

Ashington Council, faced with three of the areas five pits having a 'doubtful future' category, last year decided to build a factory of their own. All four factories on the town's Jubilee Trading Estate use mainly female labour. Two pits in the 'doubtful category': Ashington, with its one million ton of saleable coal a year, and Woodhorn, once again on double-shift working, might be able to lengthen their lives. Though the present unemployment figures for Ashington area are 345 males and 99 females, the coal industry situation provides a possible future headache if the doubtful pits go under. With this in mind, the Council have been pressing for employment assurances for the town's labour force.

Main Road Toll Shock Warning (Ashington Advertiser – 20th May 1966)

Ashington traders were told this week that despite the low traffic volume on the town's main streets, compared with other centres, the accident rate was appalling. Mr C Smith, a County Planning Authority Senior Assistant, told the Ashington Chamber of Trade that unless something drastic was done the situation would get worse. The county proposals for traffic improvements were already outlined and they favoured a Town Centre Plan with development behind the Grand Hotel, and leaving the main shopping area where it is but leaving it traffic free.

On migration of families from Ashington, Council investigations showed that the bigger percentage were in the younger age group. People, on moving to new estates at Stakeford, found that once they had made a break with Ashington, and changed their style of living, they could more easily move away from the district and were lost to Ashington altogether. Percentages of Ashington people on the Stakeford estates were high. A check on Leech's showed 37% from Ashington, and on Bell's 40%. He stressed the county's role in bringing Ashington up-to-date as a fit place to live in the future, leaving the question of alternative industry to the local authority.

Mr Smith spoke at length on the County Report on the prospects of Ashington to date, and illustrated his talk with copies of the Town Map. The possibilities ahead for the town's traders and their assistance with the town centre project were also mentioned. Members questioned

Mr Smith at great length and covered considerable ground. Chamber of Trade chairman, Mr Jimmy Herron, thanked Mr Smith for his efforts and pledged the support of traders for future schemes.

Ashington Living Space Forced East (Ashington Advertiser – 8th April, 1966)

In its search for living space, Ashington looks as if it is going to be channelled eastwards towards Newbiggin, councillors were warned on Tuesday. The Housing Committee were told on Tuesday that redevelopment of the town's west end would take three or four years before anything was seen. And councillors were also warned that if the thirty acres promised east of Moorhouse Lane in the Newbiggin area, for council housing, was not settled quickly, the housing programme would be put back two years.

Warning the Housing Committee, the Town Clerk, Mr Roy Nuttall, stated that it was obvious from the first review of the Town Map that the County Council intend all future housing land requirements to be met from land lying between Moorhouse Lane, Summerhouse Lane, Newbiggin Road and Woodhorn Road. He stated that there were only 40 acres of land released at the moment, for industrial purposes at Black Close, though more may possibly be released. "As far as land allocated is concerned, I think you will find it is all lying east of Moorhouse Lane," said Mr Nuttall. He added that the land released for industrial purposes and possibly another 30 acres there, was only land south of the Stakeford Dyke and free from subsidence.

Alderman George Duddridge said he still stuck to his original statement that, though there was ten million tons of coal on the Green Lane/Sheepwash site, not one ounce of it would ever be seen. He added: "I would rather we build within our own boundaries than in the areas of another authority." Councillor Jack Mather said the Council should go ahead with the 30-acre site east of Moorhouse Lane, and continue the policy of building houses to rent. The Town Clerk said that he would not advise building for sale by the council. They would be in competition with private builders and no good would be done for either. Councillor George Holland urged the committee not to forget about the west end of the town, where redevelopment was planned. "We will get a bit of land there," he suggested. Mr Nuttall replied that houses were being checked for unfitness in the west end as they were being vacated. Out of the 320 houses, 180 were reported as unfit, and they were not being re-let, as promised by the Coal Board.

West of the Bridge Face-lift Suggested for Shops (Ashington Advertiser – 21st January, 1966)

A face-lift for Station Road, west of the bridge, has been suggested on the lines of a Civic Trust Scheme, provided traders can get round a table and talk to the local council on the matter. The Planning and Development Committee were told last week that the stretch of Station Road from the Post Office to the Police Station could have its shops 'face-lifted' making the street more presentable.

Explaining some of the points in the Civic Trust Scheme, Mr K Taylor, a County Planning Officer, said it took the form of shop repainting to a pattern, with possible modernisation, the re-planning of signs, street lights and litter bins. Mr Taylor said: "One of the ways to get an attractive town centre is through a scheme like this. Now that Ashington is a development district we are trying to get industry here, and a first impression can mean a lot."

Councillor John Murphy said: "We have no attractive and historical fronts. I think the Civic Trust concerns itself with that sort. The street from the Post Office to the Police Station is crying out for something to be done. I am not saying that we can make Ashington into a well-known watering place, but we can improve it." Councillor Isaac Jackson commented that the Council could copy the example of Lloyds Bank and clean up the Town Hall stonework.

Councillor Arthur Gallagher said: "Because we all would like to see Ashington brightened up a bit, I think we should go out and get the views of the tradesmen of the town." Councillor Jack Mather said: "Some of the tradesmen might be deterred by threatened development in the town, but that shouldn't stop us from trying to get an agreement with the trades' people."

Ashington in Spotlight (Ashington Advertiser – 6th May, 1966)
Ashington Councillors made some tough comments on the County Planning Department's Town Map Review last week when they discussed what the county were proposing for Ashington in 1981. The special meeting of the Planning and Development Committee got through part of the proposals, and recommended retaining the West End of Ashington as a residential are; dropping plans for 'environmental development' of part of the Hirst area; redevelopment of the undeveloped part of the area behind the Grand Hotel; and the acquisition of thirty acres of housing land east of Moorhouse Lane.

Mr K Clayton, Assistant County Planning Officer, told the councillors that the Town Map they had before them was an obligation on the planning authority. He stated: "We have gone into this with great detail and thoroughness and the proposals take you to 1981. It was worthless producing a plan to last for just five years and they had been asked by the minister to make 1981 their target year."

Councillor George Holland, commenting on the first part of the town plan, said the council agreed that a change must take place in the old residential quarters of Ashington, in the west end. "I am alarmed," he said, "to find this area marked for light industry, as we intended to develop it in our own way. The road coming from the Spine Road *west* of Ashington looked as if it would interfere with some colliery rows and buildings, and whether there was a mine or not there would always be a use for the buildings. I feel that this, as a project, would be very expensive and it is really unnecessary. I think the County should let Ashington councillors plan our own town, our way. We agree that changes should take place, but this is not necessary and there has been no desire expressed for this."

On the road planned to lead into the town centre ring road, the Planning Chairman, Councillor A F Gray, said he had doubts about the road, the position was bad. Councillor J T Barras stated that he could not see the need for a road, yards from the main street. There was no justification for it.

Mr Clayton explained that the allocation of the west end for light industry was a matter of policy. "The major reason in allocating the land is because it is not a good environment for housing," he stated. "It is too long and too narrow and divorced from the rest of the town. To re-use it for housing is a poor suggestion; used for light industry it could provide an attractive entrance to the town, as industrial layout is today more a matter of good design. What we are trying to do with regard to the roads is to take Ashington as a whole and the overall context of roads in the town. This will eventually provide you with a traffic-free town centre. We are fully aware of the desirability of a road running from east to west, but our desire is to provide you with a long-term road structure for Ashington."

Alderman John Brotherton thought the road being talked about was superfluous and said: "Ashington is going to be in the middle of a spider's web of roads when the Tyne Tunnel comes along. I think this idea is absolutely ridiculous and a better connection would be a link between the Four Plantations and Newbiggin." *(Note: and this is exactly what transpired)*

The Town Clerk, Mr Roy Nuttall, replied that the only land offered was eastwards in the Newbiggin area. He told councillors enquiring about the land between Cooper's Shop and Bothal Cottages to the river that this would not be stable until 1981. Mr Clayton stated they had been studying comprehensive reports on subsidence from the NCB in that area and concluded that a road like the Spine Road was possible, but not housing.

Councillor Arthur Gallagher said he was more at sea than when they started discussing the review. "If you are going to say there is no more land for housing on the one hand, yet on the other hand you are going to ask for clearance of some houses for trees and grass verges, when we are looking at a plan for 1981, it all revolves around how long collieries are going to remain open," he stated.

Milburn goes back into Training, Doug Wetherall, Daily Mail, May 1967

'The fashion is different – shorter pants and a slim-line jersey rather than the old shirt – but the style of the player and the colours are unmistakeable. It is Jackie Milburn, back in the famous black-and-white at St James's Park, Newcastle the ground where he thrilled regular 50,000 crowds in the '40s and '50s.

'Jackie, now 42, yesterday began training for his last playing appearance at St James's – his own testimonial on Wednesday 10th May. He will play in two matches that night – the 30-minute game between ex-Newcastle Cup stars against former internationals, and then for a combined Newcastle/Sunderland team against current internationals.

'He said: "I am itching to play at St James's again. I'm training because I want to do myself and the fans justice ... and I want a goal or two."'

As a postscript to the above, Jackie Milburn was presented with a cheque for £8,200 for his testimonial match that night in 1967. Alan Shearer's testimonial in 2006 on the same ground brought in over one million pounds.

The Last Colliery House to be demolished in Ashington's west end in 1968, was number 95 Fifth Row, built around 1890. Rising like a phoenix from the ashes came the new estate named after southern counties such as Devon, Sussex etc. It was a far cry from the unimaginative names thought up by Ashington Coal Company: First Row, Second Row, right up to Eleventh Row, including Cross and Long Rows. But the colliery raas had a certain ring to them. Someone would say: "D'ye knaa owld Jack from up i' thi Cross Raa?" And everyone knew immediately who he meant. Today in 2006 that's all gone and now people don't even know who lives next door.

Hirst North Girls' School Log Entries for 1967

- February 2nd – The Girls' School was reduced from a Grade 3 to a Grade 4 school. The average number of pupils for the preceding three years had dropped to 273. Salary of Head and Deputy Head to remain the same.
- February 21st - Mrs Iris Cape, school meals, dropped a dining room bench on her right big toe. No serious damage was done.
- March 1st – The Year Four girls, with their teachers Mrs Johnson and Miss Clarke, attended the Regal Cinema to see *The Ten Commandments*, at a cost of two shillings and sixpence each.
- June 20th – Miss Clarke took 20 girls on a visit to Culpitt's Cake Decoration factory.

Colliery That Made a Profit gets the Axe from NCB (Newcastle Journal – 27th June, 1968)

A giant Northumberland Colliery, employing 780 men, is to close down, it was learnt last night. The National Coal Board has decided that Linton Colliery, near Lynemouth, must shut down by October. But the miners can take consolation from the fact that the redundancies will not be too great. In fact, 450 of the men will be offered jobs at Lynemouth Colliery, and the miners who will lose their jobs will mainly be over the age of sixty.

Mr Bob Main, Northumberland Area Secretary of the Miners' Union, said: "Linton pit did make a profit quite recently when the men hit a good seam of coal. But the quality is now so poor that the coal has been selling at ten shillings a ton below the normal price. We knew that in the long term this pit would have to go."

Town Honour for Sheila – July 1968
Ashington-born soprano, Sheila Armstrong, was accorded the recognition of her home town on Monday for her achievement in the world of music. Council Chairman, Councillor Mrs E Dodds, told the assembled audience of councillors and friends of the soprano: "Whilst we produce the best footballers in the world, we also have attained great achievements in the world of art and music."

Sheila, thanking the town for the gift in mark of her achievement, said Honour and gratitude were words that had gone out of fashion. People seemed embarrassed to use the words today but she wanted to use those words. In a simple and homely speech of thanks she referred to her family and friends and the help they had given her. She said: "Wherever I have travelled I have been asked about where I came from and I'm proud to say I'm a Geordie from the North-East."

Ashington FC Shareholders Agree to Sell Portland Park (Advertiser – August 1968)
With debts of nearly £5,000, Ashington Football Club Shareholders, by a majority vote, agreed to sell Portland Park to Ashington Council for £10,000. The decision, however, was close. The football club, on terms suggested by the Council, will have a ninety-nine years' lease on the ground at a peppercorn rent.

Meeting in the club offices, the shareholders were asked to give approval to continue negotiations with the council for the sale. On a show of hands, approval was immediately given by twenty votes to fourteen. This immediately prompted a demonstration from Mr Norman Stafford, an ex-director who recently resigned from the board, for a poll vote of shares.

Tellers were appointed and the final result was approval for the sale by 1,465 votes to 1,158. Mr Louis Johnson, a director, explained at the meeting leading up to the offer of £10,000 said this was the District Valuer's figure.

When a shareholder asked if the Cricket Club had a good deal from the council, Mr Charlie Chisholm replied 'yes'. Mr Sammy Scott, another director who agreed with Mr Chisholm, commented: "I think this Council will play fair. They want a good football team in the town. They want people to come to Ashington for shopping."

Ashington Welfare League Season Gets Underway on Saturday (15th August, 1968)
With a full complement of eighteen teams in the set-up, the Ashington Joint Welfare Football League gets underway with its programme on Saturday, and goes on to have a full programme of games on both Monday and Wednesday of next week. Fixtures include:

- Central Club v Premier Club at Hirst 1
- Hirst East End v Linton and Woodhorn at Hirst 2
- Cosmopolitan Club v Universal Club at Hirst 3
- Grand Street Club v Northern Club at Hirst 4
- Ashington YMCA v Central Workshops at the Rec

Teams for Saturday: **Hirst East End**: Les Alderson, Tom Randall, D Desmier, Morris, Farnham, Eddie Tibbs, Gowland, P Cummings, Carr, Fear, Terry Orkney. Reserves: Ronnie Scott and Cummings. **Northern**: Rutherford, Gascoigne, Fieldson, R Johnson, A Johnson, T Thompson, Brown, M Thompson, Cook, Elsdon and Doyle. **Linton and Woodhorn**: W Johnson, R Johnson, G Drysdale, K Armstrong, R Hetherington, L Freeman, G Nelson, A Soppit, M Coulson, G Thirtle, A Evans and W Thirtle.

Travel Advert for Dawson and Sanderson, 98 Station Road, Ashington RETURN FARE by sea to AUSTRALIA AND NEW ZEALAND from £299 for parents of emigrants.

1960s NEWS IN BRIEF

1960 – New cricket pavilion is opened at Langwell Crescent, Ashington.
1961 – Divisional Engineering and Mechanisation Centre (Area Workshops) opens at Ashington; Alf Robens takes Chair of NCB on retirement of Sir James Bowman; ace gardener Dickie Freeman wins four individual club Leek Shows.

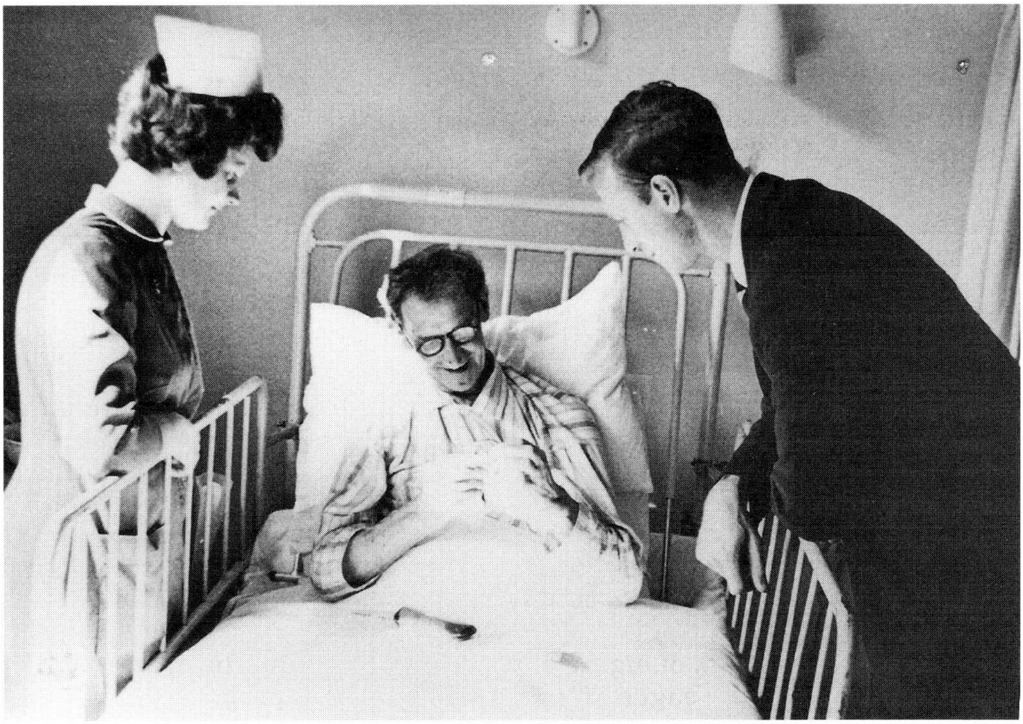

Jack Charlton pays a visit to Ashington Hospital in August 1966 to show patients the gold watch he had just received at the Council Chambers together with brother Bobby. The Ashington lads had set a record by being the first set of brothers to play and win a gold medal in the World Cup Final when they beat Germany 4 – 2. On left is Sister Sheila Pattison with patient Joseph Wood.

1962 – Inception of Inter-Divisional Transfer Scheme for Miners, and many pitmen decide to leave the area for what were then considered the more prosperous and job-secure mining jobs in Yorkshire and the Midlands; Ashington and district Mechanics go on unofficial strike; new legislation sees dozens of 'little men' opening betting shops on Ashington street corner-ends; new road from Cooper's Shop to Sheepwash Bridge opens at a cost of £25,000; 27 houses are demolished in the west end of town as part of a new town development; Fred Trueman brings international cricket to Ashington with an all-star team; proposals made for a new Wansbeck area to merge Ashington with Newbiggin and Bedlington.
1963 – Universal Club renovation costs £30,000, featuring the futuristic *Apollo Lounge;* new Midland Bank opens on Station Bridge with manager Alan Proud; work begins on colliery house modernization in Hirst; new post office built, it has been on present site since 1923.
1964 – Over 3,000 cricket enthusiasts crowd into the Langwell ground to see Rohan Kanhai testimonial; local Ashington shop-girls – apart from the Co-op – win a five-day working week; the Three Ones becomes Ashington's first nightclub on 6th May with Ronnie Harrison as manager; Ashington FC allowed into Wearside League, local players included Ron Routledge, Peter Hollings, Bob Taylor, Tom Baird, Ron Heckley and Ron Singer.

1965 – Rohan Kanhai (*seen above with Bill Kell and one of his Portland staff*) and Colin Cairns set record opening stand of 242 at Langwell Crescent; new houses advertised by Dawson & Sanderson for sale on Coulson Park Estate, semi-villas up for sale at £2,710 and terraced with garage £2,650.
1966 – The Charlton brothers, Bob and Jack, get a civic welcome on return from helping England to win the Jules Rimet trophy and the World

Cup; MP Will Owen is returned with increased majority; a major fire in November at Lynemouth Colliery closes pit when everyone is evacuated; it was reported that the NCB was to dump 400,000 tons of waste from coastal collieries, such as Lynemouth and Newbiggin into the North Sea; after the closure of North Seaton Colliery it was announced that the whole village was 'unfit for human habitation'.

1967 – The Buffalo Cinema closed and became a shoe shop; NCB had plans to spend £780,000 on a new coal preparation plant at Ashington, but the pit itself was still classed as having a 'doubtful future'; in July a new Maternity Unit was opened at Ashington Hospital; and the Princess Royal opened the new YMCA building costing £10,000

1968 – It was announced that Linton Colliery was to close, the first of the Ashington Group's big five pits to fall under the mell of 'rationalisation; Milburn Motors have new Vauxhall Vivas for sale for £770; Pegswood Central Kitchens which cooks meal for all Ashington schoolchildren gets a new set of steaming ovens, costing £800.

1969 – Ashington's station bridge was strengthened costing £41,000; the last shift was worked at Longhirst Drift on 14th March.

Jackie Milburn seen here leading out a veteran Newcastle FA Cup team in May 1965 followed by full-back Bobby Cowell who married Elsie Prior an Ashington lady once living in Duke Street.

THE 1970s

Usually to be seen at Ashington's workingmen's clubs in the 1950s, it wasn't until the Seventies that Alan Millican and Tommy Nesbitt (above) really hit the 'big time' when they were propelled into stardom though the medium of Thames Television's Opportunity Knocks, hosted by Hughie Green. The two lads from West Sleekburn won the show week after week and then went on to win a platinum disc for their rendition of '*Via Con Dios*' a song that gained them a spot on Top of the Pops. Seen here with another Winnin' lass, May Willimot, when the pair appeared - not at the Piv in Ashington - but at the Pavilion Theatre in Cromer.

'In 1972, (Ashington Colliery) manpower was cut to 1,200'
by George Hetherington, former Colliery Manager

I went to Woodhorn as Manager in 1969. Unfortunately the colliery was a strong candidate for closure due to the thinness of its seams and the prevailing weakness of coal in relation to other fuels. However, it survived until 1981 by continuing to extract the very thin Lower Plessey seam, using *gleit hoble* ploughs with a high degree of skill and dedication.

December 1971, I was appointed Manager of Ashington Colliery. This was just before the National Strike. My first impressions of the Ashington miners was somewhat distorted because they were in the process of demonstrating to the NCB the seriousness of their militant threats by overtime bans and go-slows.

At mines like Ashington and Woodhorn, which had been struggling for years under the threat of closure, the average workman gradually closes his mind to the possibility and adopts a *'don't think about it'* attitude.

The most common response when the subject of closure is broached: "They have been going to close us for years, we're still here."

A change of emphasis on the thinking of the men in control of the coal industry had a profound effect on Ashington Colliery. Instead of being cut back quickly to a size commensurate with its remaining reserves in better seams, it was decided to maintain a large labour force for as long as possible. Face room was opened out in Middle Main, Bottom Main, Top Yard, Maudlin, Hutton, and Plessey seams. During this period there were sixty hand-filled long wall faces being operated simultaneously.

The day-to-day management of a colliery of this complexity must have been extremely difficult. Much credit goes to the management teams of that time, led by Joe Jones, Bill Riches and Isaac Smeaton, who somehow kept the output around the million tons per year level until 1965. By then considerable reorganisation had taken place. All coal-drawing at shafts had been discontinued in 1962 and the output was delivered direct to a reconstructed coal preparation plant. The Woodhorn output was gathered into the same system in 1965.

The manpower at Ashington had been reduced to 2,500 and the reserves in the upper measure were exhausted. The future of the colliery depended on its ability to work the Tilley and the Three Quarter seams. Results from the Tilley were poor, and when the Three Quarter was found to be over four feet thick at the southern section of the take, in contradiction to previous borehole information, there was a scramble to stop the Tilley and concentrate on the Three Quarter.

In 1972, manpower was cut to 1,200 and would probably have been reduced further had not social considerations, combined with a national shortage of coal, made it expedient to go into the Victoria Seam, using the difficult south access. There were misgivings when the coking market collapsed soon after the Victoria face opened.

A series of successful retreat faces in the north Three Quarter, with seam sections between 40 and 60 inches, gave the colliery a boost between 1973 and 1977. However, the future looked bleak as each successive face in the north-east Three Quarter showed a thinning down to 30 inches, with a sandstone roof.

Since it started in 1867, Ashington Colliery has produced 92 million tons of saleable coal, of which 65 million were got from the High Main, Main, Yard, Five-Quarter, and Low Main seams – the big five whose exhaustion has so often coincided with the closure of Northumbrian pits. I would like to think that the latter part of Ashington Colliery's life, whilst relatively unprofitable, has contributed, in its effort to survive in other seams, to the fund of mining engineering knowledge and technical experience which will be of value to others faced with the same inevitable problems which come to every pit. *(Extracts taken from Mr Hetherington's 1980 Presidential Address to the North of England Branch of the Institute of Mining Engineers)*

"Ashington, long and low, its one street a backbone" by Anne Chadwick

Irish by birth, Anne came from Manchester to Ashington in December 1970 to take up a position as school teacher. She gave her impression of arriving in the town:

"Our train chugged up the slope of the Pennines with its sheep, black with soot, over the top and down the other side. On and on until Newcastle and its elegant Central Station, to walk through streets festooned with Christmas cheer and shops bright with expensive goodwill.

"There was still a bus to catch and the road to Ashington to be traversed. It seemed a long way through unfamiliar places – Gosforth, Wideopen, Bedlington, and then into the country of strange rows of terraced houses and conical pit heaps, smouldering under the huge wheels of the winding gear. Choppington, the air acrid, little houses puffing smoke from each chimney, like rows of miniature dragons.

"At last, Ashington, long and low, its one street a backbone, head to the river, tail to the sea. The Grand Hotel was large with an air of having seen better days, the shops were small. It was like stepping backwards to within touching distance of Dickens and Mr Polly.

"One shop had an open fireplace, coal spluttered, brightening the merchandise with scarlet flames; in the drapers, chairs, tall-backed and brown bottomed, were set up for the convenience of the valued customer. Purchases were made in cash and transported on a magic overhead railway to a mysterious den, wherein the maiden checked and counted and from whence she dispatched the change, carefully wrapped in the receipt inside a tiny brass box.

"The indoor market (*below - had been Linton & Woodhorn Miners Hall; now Lloyds/TSB*) smelled of birdseed and leather, and stiff, cheap cotton. A sweet shop sold sweetmeats, unwrapped, sticky, and broken into small pieces, all at very favourable prices. Evidence of Christmas was meagre – little had been done to decorate the long street – it seemed that no-one was in a hurry to be lavish with hard-earned cash. The cold, hard north wind tunneled along the main street, straight off the German Ocean, sending shoppers quickly in and out of doors. They seemed drably dressed, intent on

their own affairs, pleasant, yet incurious.

"It was not a Christmas I enjoyed. This place where I had come to work owed me nothing. I had to set-to and make my own place in its society of worth and endeavour."

The 1971 Ashington Festival promised to be 'better than ever' according to the Festival newspaper it put out in May. 'Undoubtedly the most ambitious of its kind ever to be staged in Northumberland.' Among those taking part were Kenneth McKellar, Owen Brannigan, Radu Lopu, Alex Glasgow, Johnny Handel, Lindisfarne, Felling Male Voice Choir, Ewan MacColl and Peggy Seeger, Catherine Cookson, John Wain, Sid Chaplin and Jon Silkin. The 16-day event was organised by MidNAG with Festival Director George Stephenson at the helm. Events were staged at Ashington Tech College, Ashington Library, Hirst Welfare, Central Methodist Hall, Town Hall, Ashington Grammar School, North Seaton Hotel, Lampglass Cellar Club, Bothal School and Grand Hotel. Admission prices ranged from 50p for Owen Brannigan to 90p for Lindisfarne. (*This was the year decimal currency came in).*

Ashington Colliery Band (seen below) won their first Miners' Picnic under this name in 1971; in 1974 the name Wansbeck was added. Till then, Ashington, the largest colliery in the Group, did not have a brass band of their own because NUM members refused to pay a levy for the band's upkeep. These musicians in photo had mostly represented North Seaton Colliery until that pit closed in the early 1960s.

'The town's changed from the ridiculous to the sublime'

An un-named *Newcastle Journal* reporter decided to investigate Ashington in 1972. He wrote: "My first view of Ashington, by moonlight; a man leading his whippets for a walk. Second view, a fish and chip shop now called the 'Barbecue', and a Chinese Takeaway. The long main street seemed almost deserted. At one of the two remaining cinemas they were showing *'Never Give an Inch'.* There was one taxi on the rank. Driver, David Richardson, observed: 'This town is changing, but it's going to take a long time to alter its image.'

"I headed for the Conchi (strangers call it the Constitutional Club) and at the bar stood next to Ray Robinson, Club Chairman, and ex-Councillor. He told me: 'The town is changing tremendously. I would be really sorry to see the cloth-cap image go entirely. It is part of the warm and friendly side. As for removing the pit heaps, well, they were put there by blood, tears, toil and sweat. Perhaps they should remain as monuments to the miners.

"Up at the Central Club, there were only eight women crowded into a Concert Room among 250 men. The floor show that night was billed as *Scarlet O'Hara – exotic dancer.* Before the war it was unheard of for women to be members of a club. Said Dickie Jarvis, club secretary: 'The town's a hell of a lot better to live in that when I was a boy; roads weren't made up and middens ran down the street. The town's changed from the ridiculous to the sublime'." *(Note – by 1972 you can see that the Buff has been replaced by a shoe shop, on left)*

Ashington's Cloth Cap Image (Newcastle Journal – October, 1972)
In September, Ashington Council appointed Jack Ramsay, a Public Relations man who had the brief of smartening up 'cloth-cap image' of the town. Said Jack Charlton, then living in, and playing for, Leeds United: "If anyone is to blame it's me and our kid. We both had more to do with it than anybody. And Jackie Milburn. You could call it pride. We've never been afraid to be seen against a background of back-to-back houses where we grew up and played as school kids. That is where me and our kid were born and bred. And we've never been ashamed of it. Ashington is a great little town, developing along the right lines. If the Public Relations man pushes the industry, and says that the people are the best and amongst the hardest-working in the world, then he could do a good job."

Ramsay, on a salary of £2,500, replied sharply: "There is more to Ashington than the birthplace of footballers. Everyone already knows that Ashington's people are the salt of the earth – you don't have to push the people."

But Cissie Charlton, Jack's mother, wasn't convinced: "This cloth-cap image is going to take a lot of getting rid of. In the south they think we eat each other up here. They only know the bad parts of the town." (above *Bill Kell with Cissie and old Bob Charlton – not in cloth cap)*

Grand Hotel Demolished
On 18th January 1973, Ashington Council decided that the Grand Hotel was to be demolished. One of only three public houses in the area, the atmospheric Grand with its once-sawdust-strewn bar-room floor, and Rio Grand Cellar club, was to make way for a supermarket and lock-up shops. Drinkers were still to be catered for with the massive cellar below the hotel being converted into an underground trendy bar and bite. Later events were to show that the pub's distinctive clientele were driven away, their places taken by youngsters, barely above the legal drinking age.

Efforts were made to preserve some of the hotel's beautiful stained-glass windows depicting the coat of arms of Northumberland families. But one feature destined to be lost forever was a 20 foot by 12 foot painting on the staircase wall. It was the work of a pre-war sign writer who liked his Brown Ale but couldn't always afford to pay for it in cash. The hotel bore a date-stone showing 1894, but it was said that it had functioned at an earlier date as the Hirst Hotel. It also housed what was thought to be the town's oldest public clock. Said Ralph Douglas, publican at the time: 'When this place was built there were no radios or crystal sets, everyone in Ashington relied on this clock for the right time.'

In May 1973, Ashington competed against Blyth in a preliminary round of the BBC TVs It's A Knockout' competition. Organisers whittled down the 150 applications to a squad of twenty with Alan Mole, Ashington Grammar School Sports Master as the leader. Having disposed of neighbours Blyth, the team were then drawn away to Blankenberg, in Belgium. This caused great excitement in the town, especially in the Council Chambers. Ashington's appearance on Eurovision was looked upon as a wonderful chance to promote the town. There was talk of a newspaper written in French and German being distributed by the Ashington contingent when they arrived in Belgium. Said Councillor

Dick Sanderson: "When we go to Belgium in August we will have a unique opportunity to spread the word that Ashington, and our own particular area of Northumberland, is attractive and has a potential worth looking at - we don't intend to waste this chance."

Ashington Town Centre make-over

Also in 1973, final details of a half million pound project to link the two halves of Ashington town centre were announced. It was said that the town had an 'over-the-bridge' syndrome, and retailers in that area were always complaining that shoppers turned around at the railway line, ignoring the numerous shops and businesses 'over-the-bridge.'

The *Evening Chronicle* reported: 'Preliminary work (seen below) has started on an ambitious scheme to build a shopping area partly on the bridge and partly on stilts spanning the railway line. Two old buildings in Station Yard car park have already been demolished as part of the preparation work and later this month agreements will be signed by Ashington Council; London and Northern Properties Ltd, the developers; Amos Hinton and Sons Ltd., who are leasing the supermarket in the development; F P A Finnegan Ltd, the builders.

It was envisaged that the two-acre site will incorporate a supermarket, five shops, 7,500 square feet of office accommodation, and a large pedestrian-only square, with walkways to the town's library. Councillor Arthur Gallagher, Chairman of the Planning and Development Committee said: 'The new development will provide a welcome fillip to shopping amenities in Station Road which already attracts shoppers from a very wide area in Northumberland. More than that, it will eradicate for all time the psychological barrier of the old Station Yard which has resulted in the vast majority of people shopping either on the West or East ends of the road, but hardly ever on its entire length.

'Very soon, Ashington will be transformed'

The first phase of Ashington's £400,000 Marina Project was officially opened in July 1973 by Mr Geoffrey Ripon, the Environment Minister. Mr Ripon boarded a boat at Black Close to sail up the Wansbeck from Stakeford to Ashington. At the end of the cruise the minister was greeted by Councillor Dick Sanderson and cut the tape across one of the new country walks along the river bank, observing: 'Very soon, Ashington will be transformed.'

However, the town of Ashington was later voted 'The Worst for Dirty Air Pollution in Northumberland' by the same Department of the Environment. The Riverside Park scheme was one of the most ambitious every attempted by Ashington Council, and it was thought it would eventually have a boating lagoon, overnight caravan park, picnic areas, and an hotel with a ballroom built on stilts over the river.

'Ashington may become the Sports Centre of the North East'

Yet another high profile project to set sail in 1973 was Ashington's first custom-built sports centre. Newly appointed Manager, Bob Brind, reported: 'My major aim is to develop this complex for the benefit of everybody. I want to build up a sound social community here. I hope that there will be a nucleus of clubs affiliated to the complex and that major spectator events will come to Ashington. Who knows, Ashington may become the sports centre of the North East.'

The sports hall was part of a multi-million pound investment in recreational activities in the town. It was being built to incorporate Ashington Welfare Institute and the Swimming Baths which had just been renovated at a cost of £20,000, having been closed for a year due to shortage of coal during the miners' strike. The Baths were very popular, with 3,000 people using them every week. The Leisure Centre was officially opened on 26th June 1975 by Sir James Bowman.

"Miss Stimpson is doing her best"

Miss Audrey Stimpson was teaching Music at Newbiggin in 1974, but she had been attached to many Ashington schools in the same capacity, beginning at Hirst North and Hirst South in the late 1940s and early '50s. She was the subject of an article in the *Ashington Post* in January 1974 where it was reported: 'Miss Stimpson is doing her best to aid the revival of the brass band. For a few years now she has been running a small

Central Hall singers/accompanists of Handel's Messiah, Sheila Armstrong, 2nd left with Normanton Barron, Rev Gregory, Audrey Stimpson, far right Gladys Proudlock.

brass group of about twenty children. She said: "Although I was born in Ashington with brass bands virtually on the doorstep, I was not really interested in that type of music. I didn't become keen on brass bands until a few years ago when a former pupil got me to play. After that I went on a Music course at Ford Castle learning to blow brass instruments, and the whole group had tremendous fun making weird noises with their instruments." For 18 years Miss Stimpson was musical director for Ashington Operatic Society but she decided to retire from it last year (1973). She is also a member of the Ashington Central Hall Choral Society.'

Big Leisure Centre Opened

That was the headline in a local paper in 1974. It went on: 'The ambitious Ashington Leisure Centre was opened officially on Saturday when Mr Gerry White, Chief Leisure Officer for Wansbeck Council, who was treasurer of Ashington Council when the first plans of the centre were laid, unveiled a plaque. Another plaque was unveiled by Mr George Nelson, former Ashington NUM secretary. The unveiling ceremony was performed in the main sports hall, now under construction. Presiding was Cllr Dick Sanderson who said: "Ashington Council is one of the most progressive for its size of 25,000 population."

Gerry White had been one of the main people involved in negotiations with the Ashington Institute and Swimming Baths Management Committee. Said Cllr Dave Scott: "For many years the youth of the district have complained bitterly of the lack of facilities available to them. I am convinced with the completion of this building these complaints will be completely eradicated. This Centre will bring a great sense of satisfaction to the public." It was estimated that the first phase of the £650,000 complex would be ready in August. Ashington Council had planned that the final stage in the development of Ashington (*Peoples*) Park into a stadium for large-scale athletics and other events, together with football pitches, suitable for major matches.'

Riverside Scheme Goes Into Last Phase

Headline in the *Ashington Post* dated 10th January 1974. It stated: 'The ambitious Wansbeck Riverside Park scheme – the 'baby' of Ashington Council – enters its most important phase this week. A contract worth £180,000 was given the go ahead for construction of a weir, essential to the creation of two miles of waterway. Construction of the weir which is 700 ft long and is steel built, capped by concrete, started this week and it is expected that completion will be in November. The weir construction will mean a regular depth of water for sailing and boating, and the disappearance of unsightly mud flats. The timing of the weir construction is closely linked with the completion of the bridge spanning the Wansbeck being constructed as part of the Spine Road development. It is also closely liked with Northumberland County Council's reclamation scheme for the North Seaton Colliery area.'

Ashington Cinema to be Closed (News Post 9th June 1974)

The Regal, Ashington's largest cinema, is to be closed and sold because Wansbeck Council will not give the owners permission to turn it in the town's only nightspot. This shock announcement was made on Tuesday by Mr Barry Noble, head of the Noble Organisation of South Shields, which owns the cinema.

He said that his firm, which also owns Lucifer's Club in Bedlington, had definite plans to convert the cinema into a nightspot and turn the Wallaw – the only other cinema in town – into a twin cinema. But these plans have now been cancelled due to Wansbeck Council's refusal to accept the Regal conversion and the firm is to sell the property.

'You try and do something for the good of the town,' said Mr Noble, 'and they throw the plans out. The Council have been informed that his organisation was prepared to twin the Wallaw to replace the cinema lost by the plans for a club, but this did not seem to make any difference.' Plans for the Wallaw have also been scrapped. Would Mr Noble be considering modernizing the remaining Ashington cinema? "I don't think so."

Mr Jim Stewart, the sixty-four year old manager of the Regal, was in the dark about the closure of the cinema. "This is the first I have head about it," he told a *News Post* reporter. "I know the owners were meeting the Council on Monday to discuss the plans, but they must have fallen through." Mr Stewart, who lives in Arundel Square, Ashington, has been the manager of the Regal for the past nine years. He has worked in cinemas in the Ashington area all his life. He said he would be sad to see the cinema close, but added that he could understand why the decision had been taken as the cinema was too big for present day needs.

The Regal was taken over by the Noble Organisation two years ago, and twelve months later they were refused permission to turn it into a bingo hall. An official statement issued by Wansbeck Council this week said: "The Wansbeck Land and Development Committee decided at its meeting on 9th April to refuse planning permission for the change of use of the Regal Cinema (seen below) to a ballroom on the recommendation of the County Planning Officer.

"In his opinion the proposed use of the premises as a dance hall would have had a serious adverse effect on a residential area because of the noise and disturbances. There was also no provision made for extra car parking facilities at the site, which it was felt could cause road safety difficulties and lead to a serious nuisance of noise to residents from vehicles parking in their streets, especially during the evening."

News of the demise of the Regal was given in the above article which appeared in the *Ashington Post* in May 1974, although strength of public opinion kept it going for another five years. The Regal had originally been called the Miners' Theatre, built in 1894, as a meeting place for the local miners, and later turned into the town's premier theatre catering for dozens of variety acts as well as the local operatic society. Queues to get into the Regal stretched around St Aidan's School for those who patronised the stalls, whereas the queue of 'posh folks' going upstairs meandered up Station Road as far as the Portland Hotel. Near the entrance was the Miners' Temperance Bar, once owned by Peter Mazzolini and later the Badiali brothers. Conrad 'Porky' Ehrmann's butcher shop was also ideally placed, offering succulent pork sandwiches dipped in gravy for those waiting in the queue.

Gardeners Facing Tough Contest

One of the outcomes of an all-embracing Wansbeck Council in 1974 was that Ashington gardeners would now face stiff opposition from horticulturists from Bedlington and Newbiggin in the annual gardening competition, once run by Ashington Council, and adopted by Wansbeck Council. Chairman of the Recreation and Amenities Committee, Cllr Dave Scott, told his members: "I hope with Bedlington and Newbiggin residents taking part, the competition will be that much keener. We have eight trophies with classes for private and NCB houses and, in addition, we have a tidiest street class." Sub committees were set up comprising the following councillors: Dave Scott, John Oliver, Charlie McGuigan (Ashington); Ken Roach, W Fitzsimmons and T O'Neil (Bedlington); and George Loggie, Bob Storey and Geoff Spain (Newbiggin).

Bin Scheme can save £40,000

If it was all sweetness and light between the three authorities on the gardening front, a controversial scheme put forward by Ashington councillors had the *Ashington Post* in January 1974 reporting: 'Differences of opinion still remain within the Wansbeck Environmental Committee as to whether the new authority should have a once or twice a week refuse collection. A scheme of once a week, with twice a week where necessary, had previously been approved by the Committee but rejected by the Council who asked for a full report. Cllr Jack Thompson (Newbiggin) declared: "The bone of contention for everyone is exactly which areas will be once a week and which twice a week. I am concerned that some areas in Newbiggin will have their dustbins emptied once a week when I believe they need a more frequent service."

'Wansbeck Link with College will become much closer'

That was a newspaper heading March 1974 brought on by a speech from Cllr Ken Roach, chairman of Wansbeck Council, when presenting awards at Ashington Technical College. He said: "Discussions are taking place now over a wide area in which we can assist each other and I know the Principal, Mr Brian Hardcastle, is as optimistic as I am over the outcome of these talks. One major joint venture is the possibility of an Arts centre covering a theatre, rehearsal studios, educational activity rooms, and now the probable inclusion of a branch library in the scheme.

"I am pleased that, as a person employed in the mining industry, the college developed from the original Mining School in Ashington.. The building of the present college began in 1952 and in 1956 there were 1,380 students. And now in 1974 there are almost 5,000 students getting the benefit of further education from this college." Award winners included:

- Department of Building: Stephen Wright, Alan Dalby, Alan C Thompson, David Curry, John Lonsdale, Alan Stewart, Arthur Kennedy, Ian Baird, George Straughan, Alan Kerr, George Peart, Thomas Oxnard, David Dawson, Edward Weallans, Thomas Brown and Cuthbert Moat.
- Business Studies: Evelyn Shears, Valerie Gibson, Lilian Halliday, Anne E Brown, Winnie Simpson, Irene Taylor, Hazel Stephenson, Robert Critchlow, Neil S Brown and Sandra Baston.
- Department of Catering, Health and Fashion: Kathleen Blair, Allan B Dixon, Barbara Selby, Mary Dunn, Pamela Grimwood, Kenneth Newman, Kathleen Blackhall, Linda Purves and Jenny Davison.
  Department of Engineering: Brian Richardson, Paul Fenwick, John Fletcher, Alexander Weddell, John D Tate, Trevor Collins, Andrew Tait, Ian Straker, John W Cain, Herbert Tipple, Leslie Jaggs, Robert J Bell, Ronald Brown, David Nevens, Thomas Harvey, Matthew Stephenson, Michael Ferguson, Andrew Leitch, John S Dodds, Frederick Hepburn, James R Scott, James Luke and Chris Smith.
- Department of General Studies: Marianne Taylor, Kenneth Shippen, Christine Leitch, Maureen Price, Geoffrey Fisher, William C Potts, Hugh Brookbanks, George Waters and Patrick Brannigan.
- Department of Mining: Brian White, John Summers, Leslie McMorn, John N Riddell, Cyril Beddard, Alan Dodds, Raymond Richardson, William Turner, Henry Critchlow, James Beadle, Colin Dawson, James Sissons and Michael Swinhoe.

If I had been asked in 1954 when filling coal on to a 100-yard conveyor at New Moor what I would be doing in 1974, I could not have predicted that in twenty years I would be standing in front of a class of burly teenagers, attempting to convey to them the rudiments of Business Studies. When I gave my father that exciting news, standing in the greenhouse of his allotment at Green Lane, his response was: "What the Hell dee ye knaa about Business?" Not much given to praise or encouragement was Jack Kirkup.

I had been working at Duke Street Coal Depot for almost ten years when Billy Mason, who was in charge, said one day: "Michael, do you never fancy going into teaching? There are a couple of chaps – Stuart Miles and Joe Grieve - from Ashington Colliery who are now teaching at local schools. It would be better than wasting your life in a pokey little office like this. It's too late for me, but you're still a young chap." Billy was then in his fifties, I was thirty-five.

I had worked at this 'pokey little office' all that time and never once thought of doing anything else. It is so easy to get into a rut. Workmates who had come to the Depot included Tommy Tinkler, who looked after concessionary coal deliveries by NCB wagons; John Foster who had been there since he was fifteen and kept Dave Moody's bag coal drivers happy with their delivery cards, and a mixture of Stu Sinclair, Geordie Cowell, Geordie Charlton, Cecil Wood, Tom Brown and a few others who came and went over the years, including Eric Imrie.

I took heed of Billy's wise words, and so it was that in 1969, I began a three-year teacher training course at Newcastle College of Education; it was for 'mature' students, and, even at thirty-five, I wasn't the oldest by any means. But even before that I had to get the minimum five 'O' levels in order to get on the course. These I obtained by studying at night using text books borrowed from Peggy Kilbourne at Ashington library. In fact, I enrolled at Ashington Tech for *six* 'O' levels, reasoning that if I failed one then I could still have the obligatory five. In the event, I passed all six with grades of 'C' or above. As I had had experience of clerical work, but little in the way of academic study, I was allowed on the course on the condition that I become a teacher of Business Studies, which had just been added to the curriculum of most comprehensive high schools because of the imminent (ROSLA) raising of the school-leaving age to sixteen.

I had a marvellous time at college, and could easily have become a perennial student, but in 1973, upon graduation, I had to seek a job, which again proved relatively simple. The Newcastle College of Education, with its large intake of mature students, was extremely popular with local schools, making their students much sought after. I was even offered a job as an English teacher at one Newcastle high school

After spending my probationary teaching year at Heaton High, near Newcastle, I found myself with a position at Ashington High School in the Business Studies Department in August 1974. '*What the Hell dee ye knaa about Business?*' The school on Green Lane had held its grammar-school status for only 14 years when a change of educational thinking brought about comprehensive education – one size fits all. It was radical and I was naïve enough to believe that it would work. Like all new teachers I was determined to change the world ... at a stroke. As if. What had been a perfectly good school of academic excellence with first-class teachers and facilities, catering for 300 eager-to-learn pupils, was turned overnight into a 1,200-pupil school taught by a staff swelled from thirty to ninety.

And there was another drawback to the comprehensive system: good teachers who were perfectly happy at their secondary modern schools suddenly found themselves uprooted and crammed into a school that was ill-prepared to cope in almost every department. Teachers like Doris Holland had to pack her Needlework bag and leave the happy atmosphere of Hirst East School; George Templey was forced to bring his woodwork tools from Newbiggin County Modern; and the ever-smiling Jimmy Jacques, like me another former miner, transferred his Mathematic skills from Hirst Park, which was then turned into a Middle School. Worse was to follow when the new intake of teachers found that all the increment points that guaranteed promotion and a pay rise had been grabbed by the 'sitting tenants'.

It was a closed shop. The old grammar school staff did not mix with either the new pupils or, indeed, the new staff. Some teachers of the old school still wore their university gowns and floated around the cramped corridors as though nothing had changed. In my opinion (*that phrase again*) they neither wanted nor taught any of the burly fifteen-year-olds that had invaded their inner sanctum from the Bothal and Park schools. Even the classes were named 5 Hirst and 5 Bothal in order to differentiate them from what was obviously thought of as an elite group of children. Far from being comprehensive, it was segregation on a massive scale. What a beginning! Headteacher Gordon Lister, a former Army officer, epitomized the whole sorry situation by turning a blind eye to the chaos around him. What an example to set the young incomers whose only crime was to fail their eleven-plus exam. But in Ashington, and right across the county, comprehensive education (with its *three-tier* system) was being embraced with open arms.

Wansbeck Welcome for Big Schools' Reform

Parents and teachers of thousands of Wansbeck children this week (16-5-74) welcomed the massive shake-up in school education. The changeover – the biggest this century – will go ahead in September when pupils return from their summer break.

Instead of the Junior and Senior school there will be a three-tier system. Children going to school for the first time at five years old will go to First Schools and will leave at nine to go to Middle Schools. The eleven-plus exam to determine which secondary school a child will go to has been abolished and instead all children will go on to a High School when they are thirteen years old. There are to be three High Schools in the Wansbeck area. These are: Ashington High School, which is based on the present Ashington Grammar School; Hirst High School and Bedlington High School, which is based on Bedlington Grammar and the Bedlington Station School that was partly destroyed by fire.

The Headmistress-to-be of Seaton Hirst Middle, a purpose-built school, is Mrs M P Gilbert, the present Headteacher of the Hirst East Secondary School. How did she view her role as Head of the new 9-13 age group school? "I do not think eleven has been a successful breaking point between primary and secondary education – children are more ready to move at 13. The staff too is satisfied with the new arrangements and is looking forward to the change-over."

Mr William Nicholson, retiring Headmaster of the Hirst Park Secondary School said "Everything is going very smoothly. The preparations have been going on for this for over a year and everything seems to be well organized." The present Secondary School becomes the Hirst Park County Middle School and will take 500 pupils. First schools in Ashington are: Milburn and Cavendish, now the Hirst North schools, and Hawthorn and Welbeck First, at present the Hirst South schools; Alexandra First, at present Hirst East Primary, Wansbeck First and Coulson Park First.

Mr Normanton Barron (left) brought hundreds of celebrities to the Central Hall from all over the world. But he often gave a platform to local talent, such as when Janice Cairns sang there in the 1970s. Ashington's Mr Music passed away in 1977.

Tombstone Terror - Underground Blaze Causes Havoc in Ashington Graveyard

An underground fire is devastating an Ashington graveyard, and burials at the Church of the Holy Sepulchre have been suspended indefinitely (28-5-74). The fire has been caused by spontaneous combustion in a buried rubbish tip that was once on the site.

It has caused serious subsidence and headstones have toppled over. Stonework surrounds have been displaced and grass is scorched. Trees have been burnt and are dead and dying. All over the graveyard there are dry gaping holes belching grey wisps of smoke. The whole area is shrouded in foul-smelling mist.

A meeting of the Parochial Church Council, attended by the new Vicar of Ashington, the Rev John Bunker, and by Mr Bill Curtis, Chief Engineer to Wansbeck District Council, discussed the problem this week. Full investigations are being launched to try and find a solution.

Jobs Jackpot - Factories Must 'Do Battle' For School Leavers

A jobs jackpot awaits 750 young people who are leaving East Northumberland schools next month (July 1974). In the past, school leavers have often had to wait months for their first job, but now firms are preparing to do battle. The number of vacancies has been rising sharply since last summer with the raising of the school leaving age to 16.

VACANT	More than 100 jobs for machinists at Hepworth's Tailoring Factory in Ashington.
VACANT	90 jobs for boys in the Northumberland Coalfield, the majority of which are in the Blyth, Ashington area.
VACANT	More than 40 jobs for school leavers and students at Welwyn Electric at Bedlington.
VACANT	'As many machinists as we can get' at the John Temple tailoring firm at the Kitty Brewster Trading Estate in Blyth.

A spokesman for Ashington Career's Office said more than 300 young people would be leaving school in the town, plus some from Ashington Technical College and Grammar School. "We are not having any difficulties really. The only trouble is that while the young people are getting more qualifications by staying on at school until they are 16, the types of jobs available has not changed.

'Ashington dialect seemed brutal, guttural, clotted with glottelstops'
John Earl joined us at Ashington High School as an English teacher in 1974. Always interested in local dialects, he remembers: "It was my second job as teacher of English; my first was at an independent day school on Tyneside, where I was earnestly asked by a parent whether I would stop his son and heir speaking Geordie. If I had been able, as a newly arrived Southerner, to work out the difference between Geordie and the usual strange argot spoken by all teenagers, then I might have tried to comply with this strange request.

"No such problem confronted me in Ashington. Here was an adventure into language as well as a completely different community, even though only a few miles up the coast. Particularly noticeable from the start to a school teacher reading through the registers was the large number of old Border names: Bells, Cessfords, Kerrs and Armstrongs. Ashington folk seemed a world apart.

"The language did, too. I had only just got an 'ear' for Tyneside dialect – I did not realise there was more than one kind of Geordie to adjust to. Ashington dialect seemed brutal, guttural, clotted with glottelstops and full of strange ejaculations like 'How!' 'Yee!' shouted at full volume, or muttered references to 'That wifey', referring to a woman.

"I remember a class of slow learners who entertained me considerably with their skills in dialect, an area where they were anything but slow. I learnt what 'hotching' was, a particularly expressive word for to smell, and 'hockling', as in 'How, sir, he's hockled on me book.' Hockling was a word to avoid if possible, meaning spitting, but somehow conjuring up a whole new sense image that left the ordinary 'spit' far behind. The verb 'to knack' amused me considerably, being used on every possible occasion as also was 'wick', as in 'Ee, sor, this is wick' meaning everything from difficult to mind-bendingly boring.

"One character sticks in my mind. He was from Linton, built like a barn door, and like many of the pupils who had been forced to stay on an extra year with ROSLA, resented every minute of it. His speciality was sitting behind some miserable weed (in relative terms, since most brick walls were less well-built than this lad) and persecuting the life out of him. One day I got fed up with this and told him to go and see the Deputy Headmaster (or Heedmaster as he was called in Ashington). I will never forget the sight of him standing furious, filling the door frame and yelling 'I'll knack ye for this.' I did not need a translation.

"I later met Fred Reed, the pitman poet, who was one of the last to understand the linguistic possibilities of this dialect that was fast disappearing even as he was shaping and caring for it in his poems. Some of the old words like 'lowse' that even teachers used meaning 'leaving work' come direct from the pit, and whereas they will probably survive even now that all the pits have gone, I cannot help feeling that the language will lose a great deal of its vigour. Whatever does happen, I am proud to have known something of the Old Ashington when the words, like the coal, came up from the pit and burnt in the fires of experience."

Happy Ending for ex-MP's Life Story

A three-year wait by former Morpeth MP, Mr Will Owen, ended this week with the announcement that the proceeds of his published life story are finally to reach charities he named to benefit. Mr Owen, who lives in Carshalton, Surrey, where he retired after being acquitted of eight charges brought under the Official Secrets Act, is now a happy man.

"I am glad it is over and that the charities I named to benefit from my life story, published in the *Sunday Express*, are to get their money" he said. The story, in fact, started when Mr Owen faced charges under the Official Secrets Act and, until his acquittal, he had spent five months in Brixton Prison, an experience he says he will never forget.

The *Sunday Express* (4-4-74) wanted his life story and Mr Owen agreed. He was to receive £6,000 but there was a condition that the money be dispersed to charities named by Mr Owen. This total was less £1,000 for the ghost-writer and the solicitor. Mr Owen named Moorfield Eye Hospital, London, where he underwent serious operations on both eyes to save his sight and the League of Friends of Ashington Hospital, Morpeth Northgate Hospital, Morpeth St George's Hospital, Morpeth Cottage Hospital, and Stannington Hospital, all within his old constituency.

Mr Owen said: "All the money which was paid for my story, and my wishes for it to be paid to the named charities, have been legally carried out. I am only sorry it has taken so long and is not more."

'Pit Ponies Will Die'

An article in the *Ashington Post* of 7th February 1974 warned of the consequences of a miners' strike that was imminent. It reported: 'It's All Out tomorrow night for 15,000 East Northumberland miners. And the burning question is: Will they have the pits to come back to?'

'In the last strike (1972) deputies and overmen stopped pits flooding by manning the pumps; but this time they say they will do only vital inspection work. And if a pump breaks down they will just inform the colliery manager, said Mr Michael McCormack, Northumberland secretary of the National Association of Colliery Overmen and Deputies (NACODS). He continued: 'We will not undertake any work normally done by NUM men.'

'A senior NCB official at their Ashington H/Q said: "If the pumps fail, the pits will flood, the ventilation shafts will be blocked and rock-falls will choke up roadways. It could take a long time to rehabilitate the pits. Millions of pounds are being spent on the pits in this area. The management side of the industry are sacrificing themselves to try and keep the pits open for the men to come back to. If it wasn't for them the pits would be in a very serious state. They are under a considerable strain. Pit ponies will die underground during the strike if the pickets refuse to allow management staff into the pits." It was understood that 42 ponies at Ellington Colliery would have to stay underground. During the 1972 strike there had been angry scenes when NACOD's members had to run the gauntlet of pickets at Woodhorn, Ellington and Lynemouth. Police were called in.'

Wansbeck Takes Charge

That was the *Ashington Post* headline on 4th April 1974 when it reported "Wansbeck District Council, largest of the five making up Northumberland, was launched on Monday with the slogan 'Forward with Wansbeck'. Chairman of the new authority is a mineworker and Justice of the Peace, Cllr Ken Roach, of Wembley Terrace, Cambois, who has been chairman of the steering council for nine months. His deputy is an ex-miner and trade union official, Cllr Dick Sanderson of 16 Myrtle Street, Ashington, who was chairman of Ashington Council last year.

The appointments were made at Wansbeck Council's annual meeting when Cllr Roach, on election, said: 'This is an historical occasion and one we have looked forward to for the past two years. The transition from three separate authorities into Wansbeck has been achieved by close co-operation between councillors, officers, staff and workmen. I confidently predict that we can serve the public well in the field of housing, health, renovation and the attraction of more industry. Together, we can make the slogan 'Forward with Wansbeck' mean exactly that.'

At a ceremony to unveil a road sign marking the new authorities boundary at Hartford Bridge, Cllr Roach said: 'This is a very significant day in the history of local government ... perhaps some people will mourn the passing of old councils, but I am confident that reorganisation will open up new opportunities to develop our district even further, and ensure the brightest possible future for the area and its people.'

New Council will spend £2 Million on Homes

There was good news immediately for the Wansbeck authority when it was announced by Cllr Jim Freathy, chairman of the new council's Finance Committee, that a good proportion of the housing allocation would be spent on general improvement of council houses. He said: 'It is no good putting up leisure centres if people have to go back to damp homes. But we are in a much better position than other district councils, in that we are getting our houses up to a high standard. Some of the money will be spent on building new houses and even starting new estates. We have got plans for the area of Woodhorn Pit leading down to Woodhorn Bridge to be used for houses, and the site on the left of Green Lane leading down to Jubilee Estate. Wansbeck will certainly be concentrating on its housing for many years to come.'

'Houses Must Come Down' says Council

Flexing their muscles late in 1974, Wansbeck Council said that houses in 10th and 11th rows, Ashington, would come down because they were unfit to live in. Some residents refused to go because the council houses they were offered were miles from their friends. Some said houses they had seen are more unfit to live in than the ones they are leaving, others needed more specialised houses and won't move until they get it. One man who had lived in the same house for 30 years said that he would not go at all – he said that the Council should leave his home till last and then pull it down with him still inside it.

According to *Ashington Post* reporter Tom Chape: 'The whole area is derelict. Gardens once tended by enthusiastic miners have been left to grow wild as tenants are re-housed. Rubbish from modernisation schemes in the Ninth Row has been dumped at the bottom of these gardens and there are some reports of rats.' A spokesman for the Council said: 'We are re-housing the people because the houses are unfit. The houses will *not* be improved because they are on the line of a road which will be built in the future.'

Wansbeck Councillors plan trip to Germany

'Eight councillors and two council officials will represent Wansbeck on a visit to the area's twin towns in Germany later this year (1974).' An *Ashington Post* article went on: 'The trip, designated as "An approved duty for all purposes" will be attended by the following: Mr Roy Nuttall, Chief Executive Officer, Mr Gerry White, Chief Leisure and Publicity Officer, and councillors John Birch, Charles McGuigan, Jim Haig, Dave Scott, Geoff Spain, Jack Thompson, Billy Wright and the new Chairman.'

'Ashington was nothing like I expected it to be' from Bill Bryson's Notes from a Small Island, (published 1993 - an extract)

'I took an Inter-city train to Newcastle and then a local to Pegswood, eighteen miles to the north, where I emerged into splendid, unseasonable sunshine and hiked a mile or two along an arrow-straight road to Ashington.

'Ashington has long called itself the 'Biggest Mining Village in the World', but there is no mining any more and, with a population of 23,000, it is scarcely a village. It is famous as the birthplace of a slew of footballers – Jackie and Bobby Charlton, Jackie Milburn and some forty others skilled enough to play in the first division, a remarkable outpouring from a modest mining community – but I was drawn by something else, the once famous and now largely forgotten Pitmen Painters.

'Ashington was nothing like I expected it to be. In a photograph from a book it appeared to be a straggly, overgrown village surrounded by filthy waste heaps and layered with smoke from the three local pits, a place of muddy lanes, hunched under the perpetual wash of sooty drizzle. But what I found instead, was a modern, busy community, swimming in clean, clear air. There was even a new business park with fluttering pennants, spindly new trees and an impressive brick gateway on what was clearly reclaimed ground.

'The main street, Station Road, had been smartly pedestrianised and its many shops appeared to be doing a good trade. It was obvious there was not a great deal of money in Ashington – most of the shops were of the Pricebuster/Superdrug/Wotta Loada Crap variety, their windows papered with strident promises of special offers within.

'The Ashington Painters represented only a small fragment of greater hunger for betterment in places like Ashington, where most people were lucky to come away with more than a few years of Primary education. It is quite astonishing, seeing it now, to realise just how rich life was, and how enthusiastically opportunities were seized in Ashington in years before the war.

'At one time the town boasted a Philosophical Society with a busy year-round programme of lectures, concerts and evening classes; an operatic society; a dramatic society; a worker's education association; a miner's welfare institute with workshops and yet more lecture rooms; and gardening clubs, cycling clubs, athletic clubs and others in a similar vein, almost beyond counting. Even the Working Men's Clubs, of which Ashington boasted 22 at its peak, offered libraries and reading rooms for those who craved more than a pint or two of Federation Ale.

'The town had a thriving theatre, a ballroom, five cinemas and a concert chamber called the Harmonic Hall. When in the 1920s the Bach Choir from Newcastle performed on a Sunday afternoon at the Harmonic Hall, it drew an audience of 2,000. Can you imagine anything remotely like that now? And then one by one, they faded away – the thespians, the operatic society, the reading rooms and lecture halls. Even the five cinemas all quietly closed their doors. Today the liveliest diversion in Ashington is Noble's Amusement Arcade.'

1970s NEWS IN BRIEF

1970 – When the Cosmopolitan Social Club closed, it became the first to call 'Time' in Ashington – one down 19 more to go; George Grant, miner, takes over as MP from Will Owen who is involved in a 'leaked secrets' scandal.

1971 – Ashington Colliery Band win first ever prize under their new name at that year's Miners' Picnic; Ashington FC grandstand burned down; Derek Ezra takes over as NCB Chairman; new Presto supermarket opens up at 'top end' of Ashington.

1972 – Alcan Aluminium smelter commenced; NUM call their first national strike; Jack Charlton testimonial match takes place at Portland Park.

1973 – United Bus Company premises enlarged; Grand Hotel demolished on 2nd April; new Leisure Centre opens in Ashington; and so does

Riverside Park; clearance begins on unsightly pit heaps at Woodhorn and Ashington.

1974 - Death of Andy McLaughlin, Pitmen's Boxing Champion; St Aidan's Parish centre opens in old school building; a £45 minimum pay for face-workers puts Ashington's miners at the top of the pay league once more; Ashington finally merges with Newbiggin and Bedlington to form a new alliance to be called Wansbeck Council.

...e Best of wishes

Keith Swallow

ASHINGTON CENTRAL HALL

Minister: Rev. Leslie D. Gregory

Musical Director: Normanton Barron

SUNDAY

MARCH

14th

1971

7-45 p.m.

★

Programme

3p

150th

Celebrity Concert

The Central Hall Celebrity Concerts were founded in 1944 by Normanton Barron during the ministry of the late Rev. Norman Glanville.

JANICE CAIRNS, Soprano
Student Royal Scottish Academy of Music

JAMES SHEPHERD, Solo Cornet
Black Dyke Mills Band

KEITH SWALLOW
Solo Pianist and Accompanist

The Central Hall Choral Union
Organ: ADA M. DAVIDSON
Piano: AUDREY STIMPSON
Conductor:
NORMANTON BARRON

Programmes kindly donated by
Dr. J. J. HOBBS
Ashington

Above, Central Hall Celebrity Concert programme for 1971, featuring some well-known names; autographed by one of the performers, Keith Swallow, in a concert starring Ashington home-grown opera singer, Janice Cairns and that fine Newbiggin musician, Jimmy Shepherd.

To end this five-decade back-tracking exercise, I am including a 1970's poem found in the scrapbook of Miss Florence Buck, popular Head at Hirst North Girls. It is not possible to say who wrote the piece, but I think it sums up quite admirably the feelings of the canny folk of yesterday.

WOR TOWN

Some towns can boast a history
made long ago to last,
with castles, knights and manors
reaching far into the past.
But wor town has no such claim
to history, it would seem,
except the fact that long ago,
its name was Essendene.

Black diamonds, far beneath the earth
from ancient forest born,
have made the town of Ashington
a town whose breast is torn
by shafts and pulleys, heaps and smoke,
and chimneys rising high;
their blackened shapes in silhouette
against the evening sky.

Around the shaft at *Fell'em Doon*
wor town began to grow,
homes for the men were built, and soon
the streets grew, row on row.
Of generous length and spacious breadth,
with shops and buildings tall,
and peopled by the *canny* folk
who work for black *King Coal*.

This place, where people matter more
than buildings ever can,
where kindness, tolerance and friendship,
are the rights of every man.
It's the birthplace of bright soccer stars,
of art and education,
of humble men, who, striving hard,
won national acclamation.

Some say *King Coal* has had its day,
that mines may cease to be,
and Ashington will have to seek
new fields of industry.
No matter what the future holds,
nor where their fate should fall,
the good folk of wor town shall stand
upright, forever tall.

Ashington Co-op — believe it or not!

Ashington Arcade as it was in the old days. But will it ever be the same again?